Planning a Wedding

A Wiley Brand

Planning a Wedding

by Sarah Lizabeth Barker

A Wiley Brand

Planning a Wedding For Dummies®

Published by: **John Wiley & Sons, Inc.,** 111 River Street, Hoboken, NJ 07030-5774, www.wiley.com

Copyright © 2022 by John Wiley & Sons, Inc., Hoboken, New Jersey

Published simultaneously in Canada

No part of this publication may be reproduced, stored in a retrieval system or transmitted in any form or by any means, electronic, mechanical, photocopying, recording, scanning or otherwise, except as permitted under Sections 107 or 108 of the 1976 United States Copyright Act, without the prior written permission of the Publisher. Requests to the Publisher for permission should be addressed to the Permissions Department, John Wiley & Sons, Inc., 111 River Street, Hoboken, NJ 07030, (201) 748-6011, fax (201) 748-6008, or online at http://www.wiley.com/go/permissions.

Trademarks: Wiley, For Dummies, the Dummies Man logo, Dummies.com, Making Everything Easier, and related trade dress are trademarks or registered trademarks of John Wiley & Sons, Inc., and may not be used without written permission. All other trademarks are the property of their respective owners. John Wiley & Sons, Inc., is not associated with any product or vendor mentioned in this book.

Planning a Wedding For Dummies **is not based on or derived from** *Wedding Planning For Dummies,* **3rd Edition.**

LIMIT OF LIABILITY/DISCLAIMER OF WARRANTY: WHILE THE PUBLISHER AND AUTHORS HAVE USED THEIR BEST EFFORTS IN PREPARING THIS WORK, THEY MAKE NO REPRESENTATIONS OR WARRANTIES WITH RESPECT TO THE ACCURACY OR COMPLETENESS OF THE CONTENTS OF THIS WORK AND SPECIFICALLY DISCLAIM ALL WARRANTIES, INCLUDING WITHOUT LIMITATION ANY IMPLIED WARRANTIES OF MERCHANTABILITY OR FITNESS FOR A PARTICULAR PURPOSE. NO WARRANTY MAY BE CREATED OR EXTENDED BY SALES REPRESENTATIVES, WRITTEN SALES MATERIALS OR PROMOTIONAL STATEMENTS FOR THIS WORK. THE FACT THAT AN ORGANIZATION, WEBSITE, OR PRODUCT IS REFERRED TO IN THIS WORK AS A CITATION AND/OR POTENTIAL SOURCE OF FURTHER INFORMATION DOES NOT MEAN THAT THE PUBLISHER AND AUTHORS ENDORSE THE INFORMATION OR SERVICES THE ORGANIZATION, WEBSITE, OR PRODUCT MAY PROVIDE OR RECOMMENDATIONS IT MAY MAKE. THIS WORK IS SOLD WITH THE UNDERSTANDING THAT THE PUBLISHER IS NOT ENGAGED IN RENDERING PROFESSIONAL SERVICES. THE ADVICE AND STRATEGIES CONTAINED HEREIN MAY NOT BE SUITABLE FOR YOUR SITUATION. YOU SHOULD CONSULT WITH A SPECIALIST WHERE APPROPRIATE. FURTHER, READERS SHOULD BE AWARE THAT WEBSITES LISTED IN THIS WORK MAY HAVE CHANGED OR DISAPPEARED BETWEEN WHEN THIS WORK WAS WRITTEN AND WHEN IT IS READ. NEITHER THE PUBLISHER NOR AUTHORS SHALL BE LIABLE FOR ANY LOSS OF PROFIT OR ANY OTHER COMMERCIAL DAMAGES, INCLUDING BUT NOT LIMITED TO SPECIAL, INCIDENTAL, CONSEQUENTIAL, OR OTHER DAMAGES.

For general information on our other products and services, please contact our Customer Care Department within the U.S. at 877-762-2974, outside the U.S. at 317-572-3993, or fax 317-572-4002. For technical support, please visit https://hub.wiley.com/community/support/dummies.

Wiley publishes in a variety of print and electronic formats and by print-on-demand. Some material included with standard print versions of this book may not be included in e-books or in print-on-demand. If this book refers to media such as a CD or DVD that is not included in the version you purchased, you may download this material at http://booksupport.wiley.com. For more information about Wiley products, visit www.wiley.com.

Library of Congress Control Number: 2022938380

ISBN 978-1-119-88320-3 (pbk); ISBN 978-1-119-88325-8 (ebk); ISBN 978-1-119-88324-1 (ebk)

SKY10034604_052622

Contents at a Glance

Table of Contents

Introduction

Wedding planning isn't stressful. I'm certain you have been told that it is, but that's a lie. Planning a wedding should be one of the most memorable experiences in your life. It's the beginning of something that will last a lifetime. The hard part was finding the person that you will begin a life journey with as partners. The wedding day is the first day of the rest of that life together.

The mission of *Planning a Wedding For Dummies* is to simplify the wedding planning process, break the myth that wedding planning is stressful, and give you the tools you need to plan and execute a perfect day. This is a day that you will remember for the rest of your life as the best day ever — if you're willing to use the tools you will learn in this book. Oh, and in the meantime, enjoy the wedding planning process! I'm aware that's a concept that many who plan a wedding don't experience, but maybe they never read this book, so we'll cut them some slack.

About This Book

Planning a Wedding For Dummies contains over two decades of knowledge, experience, and lessons learned through my career as a wedding planner. It is a process, and I have set it up in a way that will walk you through the process to planning a perfect wedding day. From choosing a venue to hiring your vendors to the dress, decor, and reception, this book has you covered!

This book was created with you in mind and designed to be a team-building experience with your partner. As you navigate the details, there will be times when one or the other of you will feel very passionate about something. When I say "passionate," that really means it might end up in a knock-down-drag-out. And guess what: that's okay. For some reason — which you probably won't understand— it's important to the other person. Embrace those opportunities to love each other more, and consider it an opportunity to problem-solve together. Try to understand the "why" behind the passion.

Foolish Assumptions

Generally, I know it's not a good idea to make assumptions. But for this book, I've made a few to better serve your needs:

>> Your work duties and/or social calendar don't allow you much free time to plan your wedding.

>> The thought of planning your wedding seems overwhelming and stressful.

>> You don't know the first place to start when planning a wedding.

>> You want to make sure you're maximizing your budget to be able to get as many items on your must-have list as possible.

>> You're stuck on how many guests you should invite to your wedding and who should be in your bridal party.

>> Picking your wedding vendors seems like a daunting task with more options than you can manage.

>> You want to create the most amazing wedding day and enjoy the planning process.

Icons Used in This Book

Sometimes when reading a book, you need a little picture in the margin to get your attention because you really need to consider what I am about to say to you.

REMEMBER

If you see a remember icon, it means that I want you to remember to do whatever I'm telling you to do. This way you won't miss a step of the process to planning your perfect day. These icons are important to take note of and put on special list of things to remember.

TIP

This book is packed full of all kinds of tips, so if you see a tip icon, it is a very special tip! While writing the book, I thought, my new friend really needs to know this because it can save them money or help them avoid a problem or maybe even allow them to enjoy the wedding planning process!

WARNING

In wedding planning and in life, if you see a warning — pay attention. If I put a warning in the book, it is to give you advice so bad things don't happen. That is based on bad things happening to me through the years. Since we're on this journey together, I don't want them happening to you!

Beyond the Book

This book is packed with information, but sometimes, you just need more. If that is the case, there is an online Cheat Sheet available that points out the most important things to do when planning a perfect day. To access this informative Cheat Sheet, go to www.dummies.com and type **Planning a Wedding For Dummies Cheat Sheet** in the search box.

Additionally, I've added a sample detailed schedule of events on my website for you to use and customize. Just go to www.sarahlizabeth.com/planningawedding fordummies

This schedule of events document is a vital part of planning a perfect day. Use it as a tool to create your own schedule of events.

Where to Go from Here

It's time for your journey to begin. You may be wondering how to even start. Trust me, you are normal. When I created this book, I wanted it to be in a certain order. It is set up in the order that I would suggest you reading from cover to cover. Just as I would walk my clients through the process of planning their wedding, I have done the same for you in the layout.

However, you're probably excited about your big day, and you want to skip to a chapter that's on your mind. It's okay to do that as well. Every part of your wedding planning process is only yours. You get to customize the experience. If you are someone who loves the process, start at the beginning and read to the end. If you don't like structure, divide and conquer as you wish!

I want to thank you for coming along with me on this journey of planning your perfect day. Perfect is defined as "having all the required or desirable elements, qualities, or characteristics; as good as it is possible to be." Through our journey together, my vow to you is to give you all the required elements, qualities, and characteristics to plan your wedding day. If you use them, you will have a day that's as good as it can possibly be. Happy planning!

1

It's YOUR Day!

IN THIS CHAPTER

» You're getting married

» How you can enjoy planning your wedding

» Figuring out when to get married

Chapter **1**

You Said Yes!

W hy hello there, my engaged friend. I want you to stop and take a minute to think about all the steps you have taken in your life. Think about all the paths that went right and you went left. Think about the perfect little plan you had for your life and what your life looks like today. Think about your fiancé and all the steps they took in their life to get to this point. It's amazing to think about how all those steps led you to pick up this book, and now you're planning your big day.

My job is to help you get to the steps when you're walking down the aisle. Those steps right there are going to be fun! Yes, there will be bends, bumps, and road-blocks along the way but together we will plan day one of the many steps you will take together. In this chapter, we will celebrate that you're engaged and break the myth that wedding planning is stressful. We will also work through picking your perfect wedding date. You know, the number that will be embroidered on a blanket one day? Yes, that one!

Congratulations, It's Time to Celebrate

It's official — you're engaged and that's something to celebrate! One of the biggest decisions you'll ever make is who you'll spend the rest of your life with. It's the greatest partnership that you'll have in life. So yes, it's time to celebrate!

Get dressed up and go to dinner. Wear your nicest clothes and drink the expensive wine. If that isn't your style, make a homecooked meal and light some candles. Regardless, take a minute to celebrate as a couple that you have decided to journey through this life together.

You already did the hard work; you picked the person who will be with you until the end, until death do you part. Before we jump into the wedding planning, which we will soon, take a few moments to be grateful that you're about to go on an amazing journey of planning your big day. More than the day itself, you're going to have an amazing marriage. That is really what we're planning for.

We will talk about referrals and how valuable they are in picking your vendors later in the book. Just like referrals, start the celebration by hanging out with married friends. The knowledge you'll gain for what comes after the wedding planning will be of value. Celebrate with those who know all about marriage. You will laugh and maybe cry but they'll be able to give you all the intel on being and staying married.

Living by the Three Ps of Wedding Planning

I've been serving couples and their families from across the United States for almost two decades. Whenever there is a "passionate" moment, it isn't because the linens are white instead of ivory. There is always a "why" behind the client's reaction. When your partner is "passionate" about having hot chicken bites over bruschetta for an appetizer, maybe it's because their grandmother always made the best hot chicken bites when they were a child. Or maybe that first dance song that you love and they hate takes them back to memories of an ex-partner who also loved that song. Whatever the reason, take my advice: no one will remember those small details. If you follow my simple steps to planning a perfect day, they'll walk away from your wedding day knowing who you are as a couple.

Through the years, I've worked with my clients on the three Ps to wedding planning: **perspective, process,** and **pause.**

Perspective

If you don't hear anything else I tell you, hear this. You must have perspective while planning your wedding day. Yes, it is a big day, and yes, you may have dreamed of this day since you were a little kid. However, it is the first day of what we hope is a lifetime together. Now, if I was dismissive about planning an amazing day, I'd be out of business. The point isn't to negate the fact that you're getting married, or that you want an amazing wedding day. The point in having perspective is that the real beauty is in the fact that you will be married. Let me say that again. You will be married at the end of the day, regardless of whether you have strawberry cake or chocolate cake, whether you serve your food on real china or disposable plates, or whether you have a band or a DJ. The real joy comes after day one, when you start living life together.

TIP

As you go through this journey of planning your wedding, I want you to always go back to that. When you find yourself stressing over whether you'll offer fried chicken or baked chicken, remember that at the end of the day, you will be married. When your bridesmaids start bothering you with a million questions about things that you don't feel they need to know, remember that you will be married. When you and your fiancé get in a fight over the seating chart, remember that you will be married. When it rains on your wedding day, remember that you will be married.

REMEMBER

Yes, we can plan an amazing day together and we will; I have no doubt about that. But very often clients lose that perspective and never truly enjoy the process of the wedding day itself. You can get so caught up in the details that ultimately don't matter that you lose focus on what's most important. It's an easy thing to do and happens to a lot of people, but as your friend, I encourage you to stay focused on the big picture — your marriage.

I once had a client who got so caught up in the details that when her wedding day finally arrived, she didn't enjoy a single moment. When we first met, I could see this was going to happen to her and I started very early talking to her about perspective. She was being pulled in a million directions by everyone around her. She would call me when she got upset about the smallest things, all things that were completely out of her control.

When her wedding day arrived, it rained, and I lost her. Typically, when it rains on someone's wedding day, I let them have their "moment." I tell them that is it okay to be sad. No one wants rain on their wedding day, and the person who said it was good luck had a perfect beautiful day. They deserve to have a moment and if situations come up on your wedding day that are out of your control, you can have a moment. But after that, move on.

I watched her start to go downhill with each passing minute. Every time I checked on her, she got sadder and sadder. In the end, she was never able to get past the point that something was happening on her wedding day that she couldn't control or change. So the rain won, stealing all her joy on the wedding day.

Another one of my clients experienced a power outage at the church due to a storm. We didn't plan on what to do if the church lost power. I went in and spoke to this bride when the power went out. I was honestly expecting to see her sitting in a pile of tears. Instead, she looked up at me and said, "I'm just ready to marry my best friend." I said to her, "Let's do this!" and left the bridal suite to figure out logistically how we were going to pull off her wedding without power.

The church was full of guests sitting in a dark sanctuary. I walked up to the front of the church and said, "Hello, I'm Sarah the wedding planner. Normally, you don't see me, but today we are going to work together to give this couple the best day ever. As you know, we don't have any power, so as the bridal party enters the church, I want you to imagine the most beautiful music playing in the background. We aren't going to delay and wait for the power to come back on; we are going to get these two amazing people married."

The crowd cheered and I went back to line everyone up. As I sent the bridal party down the aisle, the guests started to hum, providing the music that we couldn't play due to the power outage. It was one of the most beautiful moments I've seen in my career. It was time for the bride to enter the church.

My favorite moment at every wedding is one that few get to see: the moment when the bride is waiting to enter the ceremony. There is so much raw emotion and love in that moment. No matter whether she's by herself or with her father or other family member, I always tell her to stop and take it all in. It's the moment we have been planning for, and now it's time.

As we stood there in that moment, her faced was filled with joy. She was about to marry her very best friend and it didn't matter if the power was off. Yes, the songs we worked so hard to pick out wouldn't be heard. Yes, the vows wouldn't be heard because it was a big church, and we didn't have any working microphones. But in that moment, she didn't care because she was about to be married.

As I opened the doors and sent her down the aisle, I was sad for her. I was sad because she had the most amazing perspective and she deserved to have the power on. Well, wouldn't you know, all of a sudden, the power came back on! I still get emotional even writing her story because to her, it didn't matter. I wish everyone who's planning a wedding could have that perspective. If you can keep that as your number one priority while planning your wedding, I can assure you, good things will happen.

A LESSON IN PERSPECTIVE

My grandparents were married September 13, 1949. On the day of their wedding, their photographer never showed up. They didn't have a single picture from their wedding day. We don't know how beautiful my grandmother was or even what her dress looked like. I'm certain my grandfather was very dapper in his suit, but we'll never know.

What they did have was perspective. Their love story was unlike any I've seen in my lifetime. They loved, valued, and respected the other the way you read about but wonder if that kind of love actually exists. Well, it did exist for them, and together they had three sons, three daughters-in-law, nine grandchildren, and eighteen great-grandchildren. They lived a wonderful life honoring the other until they were separated by death.

My grandfather was an artist. I will never forget the Christmas morning we were all sitting around, and he shared with us the story of how their wedding photographer never showed up to their wedding. They were sad that they only had their memories, which were fading, to remember their day. My grandfather gave us all this picture he had drawn as a gift and a reminder that life is always about perspective. For us, as grandchildren, it was our picture, one we would remember forever. The important lesson that my grandfather wanted us to know was that it wasn't about having beautiful photos of their wedding. The beautiful was in their love story.

Wiley Miller

Process

When I make flower arrangements for my clients, I have a process. I set out all the vases I need, and I start adding one type of flower to all the arrangements before I start on the next variation. There are amazing florists out there and they may or may not do the same thing, but in the end we both have beautiful floral arrangements. The same thing goes for wedding planning. What you are about to read is my process for planning a perfect day. It took me years to perfect my process but I own it. I challenge you to take the tools you will learn in this book and create your own process to plan a perfect day. Own that and you will have a successful wedding day.

Pause

I want you to stop right now and think about how this book ended up in your hands. Are you newly engaged, feeling overwhelmed, or just trying to make sure you are doing the right steps for a perfect day? Whatever the case, take a minute to stop and think about all the things that had to align in your life for you to be reading this book. Now go (I'll wait).

Here is what I know. You will remember this moment when an author asked you to stop and think about why you were reading this book. Now, apply that to your wedding planning process, wedding weekend, wedding day, and honeymoon. If you take the time to stop in the middle of everything going on around you and mentally record the people around you, the flowers, the decor, the sounds, the laughter, the tears, you *will* remember your wedding day and all the events around and leading up to the big day. So often, I have seen couples walking through the day like a deer in headlights. Those clients never remember anything about the day. The ones who have been able to truly take in everything around them remember all the details. So, in the middle of the crazy, remember to pause and take it all in. You will thank me for that gift later.

Enjoying the Planning Process

So many books, blogs, and online resources tell you that planning a wedding is the most stressful thing you'll ever do. But as I said in the introduction, planning a wedding should not be stressful. Planning a wedding should be an enjoyable experience, but often we get in our own way and complicate the process — we are the ones that make it stressful.

I once read that being a wedding planner was one of the top five most stressful jobs. Well, it *is* stressful, but only because I take on the stress so that my clients don't have to. Through this book, I share my process of planning clients' weddings so that you don't have to stress while planning yours.

In this section we talk about setting boundaries with your family and friends as well as the importance of checking in with your fiancé and the value of premarital counseling. To eliminate the stress for you, I'm going to give you my wedding planning checklist that I use for every single client's wedding. It's my roadmap and will soon be yours!

Setting boundaries with family and friends

You're so excited to get married and you're sitting with your family one afternoon chatting about how the wedding planning is going. You start talking about the beautiful white flowers you've picked, because white flowers are your favorite, and someone in your family says, "I hate white flowers. Why would you pick white flowers?" All of a sudden, you're second-guessing every decision you made. In this section we'll talk about how it's important to set boundaries with the ones you love the most while planning your wedding.

REMEMBER

You're planning your wedding. You are not planning the wedding of your parents, your bridal party, or your friends. This is *your* wedding, and it should reflect you as a couple. If you love white flowers, then you need to have white flowers. I cannot tell you how many clients have allowed outside influences to impact their big day — not just impact but completely ruin their wedding. You wedding day isn't about anyone else other than the two of you. I know that is a very hard concept to understand when your outside influences are so strong, but please remember that this is about you, no one else.

I once watched a mother of the bride walk down the aisle while screaming profanities about the groom and how she didn't like him. I couldn't fathom what was happening right in front of my face. How could someone do this? How could anyone possibly think that this was the time to let everyone know what she thought about the person her daughter was about to marry? I stood there not knowing what to do. Was I supposed to tackle her, or just stand there and cry with the bride? How dare she do this to my friend!

That was a traumatic experience, but the fact is that people around you may often insert their thoughts and feelings about something you're planning for the wedding. There is a reason for this. There is always a "why," and I challenge you to find that out. It will open communication and help avoid problems down the road or aisle.

Why did this mom do this to her daughter? My guess is that from the time her daughter got engaged until the wedding, they never once spoke about the fact that mom didn't like the groom. It was brewing inside and when she hit the aisle, everything came to the surface, and it was not good.

REMEMBER

If your parents are paying for your wedding, it's important to sit down with them and talk about whatever is important to them regarding your wedding. Ask them if they have any needs or expectations for the wedding. It's an unbelievable gift that they're paying for your wedding, so you need to have a conversation about their expectations. Ask them some of the following questions:

>> How many guests do you plan on inviting?

>> Do have a particular menu in mind?

>> Do you have an idea of what kind of entertainment you want to provide?

>> Is there anything that you want to see at the wedding?

>> Are you excited about the big day?

>> Do you have any reservations about the wedding day?

Having conversations with your parents will help you avoid any problems down the road. As the mother of three girls, I'm certain that I will be feeling all kinds of emotions when they get married. I hope that those emotions come out in a positive way. If they don't, it's most likely because I felt as though my opinion or voice didn't matter. That is my "why." I want my voice to matter.

TIP

Find out the "why" behind your parents' opinion. Trust me, they have a reason why they hate white flowers. Acknowledge that and then explain to them how much you love white flowers and as much as you appreciate everything they're doing for you, it's important to you to have white flowers. Setting those boundaries early in the wedding planning process will help you plan the perfect day that reflects you and your fiancé.

In Chapter 2 we'll talk about picking the perfect bridal party. They are your people. Some you have picked, and some are picked for you because they're family. Regardless, you have them and everything that comes with them. My hope for you is that they behave, but what if they don't? Too often, clients tell me stories about something one of their bridesmaids is doing or a groomsman who isn't holding up to his job duties. Regardless of what the situation may be, it only stresses out the couple, leaving them frustrated and wishing they had picked a better squad.

Just as in marriage, communication is key to setting boundaries with your bridal party. Logistical details are all they need to know during the wedding planning process. Give them the specific information they'll need, such as what to wear, when to arrive at the rehearsal, the time and location of the rehearsal dinner, and what time to be at the venue on the wedding day.

I know you're excited about the details and you may want to share those. But please know that your bridal party will have opinions, so if you're comfortable with listening to their opinions, then share away. It would be amazing if when you share details with them, they are excited and think your choices are the best possible choices. However, the frustration comes in when they offer their opinion and it upsets you. I don't want that happening for you.

TIP

The main point I want you to hear is that there are so many special people in your life and that is amazing! All those people have opinions. Keep those boundaries up between your dreams and their opinions. This day is about the two of you and no one else, period. Respectfully listen and then filter out what isn't of value to your wedding or doesn't reflect who you are as a couple. Stay focused on your fiancé's opinion and build a day for the two of you to enjoy because white flowers are your favorite!

Continuing to date your fiancé

Remember that time you and your fiancé used to date? You had butterflies just thinking about going out on the town together or cooking dinner at home. Now you're in wedding planning mode and all you do is talk about the wedding. Your conversations may even end in a big fight because you can't possibly understand why it's important to your fiancé to play a certain song at the reception. You hate that song and don't understand why they like it and there is no way you are playing that song, so you argue. In this section we'll discuss the importance of dating the person you are going to marry and maintaining the relationship through the wedding planning process.

TIP

Wedding planning can cause stress in a relationship. It can be frustrating to disagree on the details or upsetting that they don't seem to care about those details. You feel as though this should be the most important thing on their list of things to do, but maybe it isn't. Wherever you fall on the spectrum, take a break from constantly talking about the wedding and go on a date. When you're on that date, you are not allowed to talk about the wedding.

You're planning an event and problem-solving together. This can bring up unexpected emotions because, let's face it, planning a wedding is a big deal. But you're both different people. One of you may be so excited about the details while the other feels stressed and overwhelmed. In your marriage, there will be decisions that you have to make together — big decisions like buying a house or car or starting a family.

REMEMBER

The most important thing to do is to take care of your relationship through the wedding planning process. Like I've said, there is life after wedding planning, and you will be married. Take the time to continue to build your relationship outside of the wedding planning box. Think back to before you were engaged, and you spent time together. What did you do for fun? Make every effort possible to continue to do those things and focus on building your relationship.

In case you forgot what it's like to go on a date with your fiancé, I put together a list of some fun team-building date night ideas. And remember, no wedding talk!

>> Camp out under the stars.

>> Build a bonfire together.

>> Recreate your first date.

>> Make something from scratch.

>> Plan a scavenger hunt.

>> Attend a paint or pottery class.

>> Make homemade pizza.

>> Do something that your fiancé loves to do and you don't.

>> Build a fort in the living room, like when you were a kid.

>> Take a dance class together.

Considering premarital counseling

If I could gift every client something, it would be premarital counseling, because I believe it's extremely valuable in preparing for your marriage. I understand that this may not be your cup of tea and that's okay. In this section, we'll talk about what it is, offer some advice, and see if it's something you want to be a part of your wedding planning journey.

What is premarital counseling? Premarital counseling is a therapy with your fiancé prior to getting married. The main focuses are on defining marriage, dealing with past relationships, roles inside the marriage, money management, planning for a family, and communication in your marriage. Let's talk a little more about each of those.

>> **Defining marriage:** It's important to discuss your expectations of marriage. If you're going into the marriage with one expectation and your fiancé has a different expectation, this will cause tenson inside your marriage. Your

expectations are formed by your past. What did you witness in your parents' relationship? What do you see in your married friends' relationships? You both have different influences, and it's important to determine what your marriage definition is as a couple.

» **Dealing with past relationships:** We all have past relationships. Some have been very painful, and we continue to deal with that pain. You may carry emotions from the past into your marriage without even knowing you're doing that. It's important to understand what has worked and not worked for you in your past relationships to help your marriage thrive in a healthy environment.

» **Roles inside the marriage:** Our influences, good or bad, have defined what we feel are the roles inside of marriage. If you're good at something such as accounting, then take care of the finances. If you're a good cook, then take care of making dinner. Talk through the roles that each of you will play in your marriage. We all bring different strengths to the table and if you can figure those out and implement them, you both will feel valued.

» **Money management:** As you may already know, a lot of marriages end in divorce due to money problems. This can be due to a variety of reasons, such as poor money management or hiding money from your spouse. Money is a subject that few enjoy talking about, but it's important to determine what your plan will be to handle your money as a couple.

» **Planning for a family:** You just got engaged and there's a chance someone has already asked if you're going to start a family. Well, what does your fiancé think of that? It does take two to tango, so make sure you're both on the same page when it comes to planning for a family. The last thing you want is to think your fiancé wants to have children and then find out when you get married that they don't.

» **Communication in your marriage:** I personally believe communication is the key ingredient to having an amazing marriage. So much can be lost in poor communication, and working with a therapist can help define your communication skills in a marriage. We all communicate in different ways, so understanding your partner's way of communicating will benefit your marriage. It may not be like yours, and that's okay. Remember, you are two different people with different influences.

TIP

If you do decide to do premarital counseling, I would suggest you do it with the person who is officiating your ceremony. There are multiple reasons why I would suggest this. First, you will be able to build a relationship with the person who is marrying you. You may need this relationship later down the road and they'll have history with you from the beginning. They will also be able to speak about your relationship during your ceremony. I love when the officiants know the couple because they have seen them on good days and bad. They can personalize the ceremony in a way that someone who doesn't know you as a couple can't. (See the section "Selecting Your Officiant" in Chapter 11 for more about this.)

Make sure to check with your officiant prior to booking them to find out if they offer premarital counseling. If they do, ask them how many sessions you will have and what their availability is to make sure it aligns with your schedule. If they do not offer premarital counseling, reach out to your church or local community to connect with a trained and licensed premarital counselor. Remember, you are building the foundation for a lasting marriage. It's important to ensure that when the storms of life come, your marriage can stand strong.

REMEMBER

In most states, if you do premarital counseling with the person who is performing your ceremony, you can receive a discount on your marriage license fees. In Chapter 11 we will discuss in detail how to obtain a marriage license, but make a note that this could save you money. They will fill out a form stating that you did premarital counseling and then you will take that form with you when you get a marriage license.

I understand that some people just don't like the idea of going to see a counselor. It shows weakness, right? Well, I think the complete opposite. I believe that seeking counseling means that you care about being your very best and dealing with the past that has influenced your future. Take care of your relationship in preparation for marriage. I highly recommend you consider premarital counseling.

Sample wedding planning checklist

Well, here it is, friend! My sample wedding planning checklist. This is the checklist I use with all my clients. Remember what I said in the introduction about process. Others have different processes, but this one is my process. In Table 1-1, I share with you my wedding planning checklist. Remember, this is just a sample. Don't let it stress you out. If you're behind, you can catch up! Adapt it to fit your needs and dreams for a seamless wedding planning process.

Picking the Perfect Date

Oh, the perfect date, the one you will remember forever. You celebrate it on every anniversary, and you embroider it on a pillow. But how do you pick the perfect date? In this section we'll discuss some topics that might determine that for you and how you'll have a date that you'll remember for the rest of your life.

TABLE 1-1   ## Sample Wedding Planning Checklist

Timeline	Task
12+ months	Choose your date
	Determine your guest size and guest list
	Determine your budget
	Book your venue
	Hire a wedding planner, if needed
	Book your photographer, caterer, and band or DJ
	Pick your bridal party
9–11 months	Order your Save-the-Dates
	Book your officiant and videographer
	Pick the couple's and bridal party attire
	Mail your Save-the-Dates
6–8 months	Reserve hotel room blocks
	Book your transportation
	Hire your baker, bartender, rental company, and florist
	Confirm your guest list
	Create your wedding website
	Create your registry
	Order your invitations
	Plan your honeymoon (and consider whether you want to ask for contributions to a honeymoon fund)
	Purchase wedding bands
4–5 months	Order thank-you cards
	Select your songs for prelude, cocktail hour, dinner, and dancing.
	Book your honeymoon
	Book your rehearsal dinner venue
2–3 months	Order your wedding favors
	Book the honeymoon suite

(continued)

TABLE 1-1 *(continued)*

Timeline	Task
	Schedule your dress fittings
	Schedule your trial hair and makeup
	Purchase guestbook, cake cutter, champagne flutes, flower girl basket, and ring bearer pillow
	Order menus and programs
	Send out wedding invitations (2 months)
	Send out rehearsal dinner invitations
1 month	Collect RSVPs
	Write vows
	Meet with officiant to go over the ceremony
	Send the details to your vendors
	Finalize seating arrangements
	Print place cards
	Put together welcome baskets
	Get your marriage license
	Purchase gifts for bridal party and parents
	Schedule your final dress fitting
2 weeks	Give the final guest count to your vendors, especially the caterer
	Make final payments to your vendors
	Update your registry
	Get a final cut or color
	Check in with your bridal party to make sure they know the details
1 week	Pack for your honeymoon
	Book a spa day
After the wedding	Send in marriage license
	Make sure all the tuxes are returned
	Start writing thank-you notes

Timeline	Task
	Change your name
	Take your dress to the cleaners or preservationist
	Design a wedding album when you get your pictures
	Think about the best day ever repeatedly
	Enjoy being MARRIED!

Picking a date is typically one of the first things you'll do, which is very exciting. You would think picking a day would be simple, but for some it's quite complicated because there's a lot to consider. Just remember, it's supposed to be fun! Think about those who have had to reschedule or postpone their weddings — they had to go through the process all over again.

Here are some things to consider when determining your perfect date:

>> **Time of year:** If you're someone who knows without a doubt that the summer is out because you sweat so much, then maybe the fall is more your style. What time of year is your favorite? Do you love the spring when everything is in bloom? Do you love how the leaves change colors in the fall? Remember, everything you do reflects on you as a couple, so if fall is your favorite, pick a fall date! Focus on your favorite time of year and start there.

Another thing to consider when thinking about the time of year is the likely weather. Yes, the spring is beautiful, but it rains a lot. The saying is true: April showers bring May flowers. Depending on where you're getting married, picking the perfect date may involve considering if there is a rainy season, or you don't like snow and want to avoid a blizzard on your wedding day. Here in the south July is crazy hot, so we don't do a lot of weddings during that month because you can hardly walk outside.

>> **Life:** What do you do for a living? Are you a teacher who has the summer off? Maybe that's a good time to get married. Did you start a new job and don't have any time off for a certain period of time? Consider what your life looks like when you're picking the perfect date. Your life might determine the time you have to put into planning a wedding and taking time off to get married.

>> **Venue availability:** We will talk in detail in Chapter 6 about picking the very best venue for your big day. Often your perfect date will be determined by the venue's availability. You can't have a wedding if the venue isn't available. When you do tour venues and fall in love with one, make sure to have several perfect dates in mind so that you don't have your heart set on a date that isn't available. I've seen it happen repeatedly. The client wants a very specific date but the venue they love isn't available. They never seen to get past that, and I don't want that happening to you.

>> **Different rates:** Venues often charge less for a weekday or Sunday wedding. If you're looking to save money, consider a day other than Saturday. Saturdays tend to have the highest rate because that's the most popular day. If you do pick an alternative day to save money, don't forget to check in with your bridal party. They may not be able to travel for a Friday wedding because they would have to take off two days for work. It may be a good way to save money, but if your best friend who you can't imagine not being at your wedding can't make it, then it's not worth the savings.

>> **Cool numbers:** Finding a date that's easy to remember within that calendar year (such as 02-12-22 or 11-11-11) is a popular approach. These are so much fun, but you should know that everyone else is thinking the exact same thing. Those are typically the first dates booked. If you're set on a cool number, be aware that someone else may have the same idea and it might prove difficult to book a venue for that date. The additional vendors that you need may already be booked as well.

>> **Holidays:** Holidays are always a fun time to get married. New Year's Eve and the Fourth of July are the most popular — probably because of the fireworks. Clients typically have the mindset that if it's a holiday, everyone will be off work, which means they can attend the wedding. If you do plan a holiday wedding, make sure to notify your guests as soon as possible. Your guests may have booked their holiday weekends far in advance because it may be the only time they get off work. When booking a holiday wedding, be thoughtful of religious holidays and Mother's and Father's Day. The people you're inviting may love you like family, but they may want to be with their family on those days.

REMEMBER

Regardless of what your date may be, I am here to help you make it a perfect day. Don't forget to celebrate your engagement, enjoy the planning process, and date your fiancé. It's the foundation of a perfect day.

Chapter **2**

Sharing the Exciting News

I t's time to start spreading the news! You've celebrated, you understand the importance of enjoying the planning process, you and your fiancé have continued to date, you've picked the perfect wedding date, and now you get to let everyone know! Well, you'll let those you want to know and save the rest for later.

When I buy a gift for someone, I typically can't wait for them to receive it, so the minute I buy it, I give it to them. "Here's your Christmas gift in October!" It's confusing to them, but I'm just so excited that I can't stand it and I want them to have it. This is obviously not what you're supposed to do. The same thing is true for announcing your engagement and inviting your guests to the wedding. There is a process and a time when you should let everyone know.

In this chapter, we'll discuss the timing of spreading the good news, work though how to inform your people, learn about picking your bridal party, and explore all the fun parties we get to throw along the way. Let the fun begin!

Spreading the Word

Even though you're so excited to share the good news, there's a process to whom you tell first and when you let everyone else know. I know you want to shout it to the world, and you will soon. Surely your fiancé had a ring before the proposal. If they had given it to you the day they purchased it, that moment wouldn't have been as special as the one you had. There is beauty in the waiting because you and your fiancé have a little secret between the two of you that no one knows.

In this section we'll discuss how to announce your engagement, throwing your engagement party, and the social media announcement.

Announcing your engagement

Being engaged is an exciting time. You finally found the one you'll spend the rest of your life with, and that person asked you to marry them. That's a big-deal life moment to be celebrated and shared with the world. But how do you do that? When can you finally change your relationship status? Here are some tips on how to announce your engagement, listed in the order that I suggest you follow when it's time to let everyone know that great news!

>> **It's between the two of you.** Before you share the news of your engagement with anyone else, take time to celebrate with just the two of you. Because we live in an instant society, many people don't do this. Everyone wants things immediately, but when you wait and take a minute just to celebrate together, it makes the sharing with everyone else even more special. You stopped and took a minute to look each other in the eye and be grateful that all the steps you have taken in life led you to each other. You are about to get bombarded with congratulation texts, likes on social media, and phone calls. Before the chaos begins, pause and be grateful that you have each other.

>> **Put family first.** It's important to make sure your family knows first. As a mother, if I saw on social media that one of my daughters was engaged and they didn't tell me first, they would be in trouble. When letting family know, reach out to them via phone or video chat if you're unable to see them in person. Do not send them a text. This is big news and deserves to be shared with your family in person or over the phone. There are so many fun ways you can let them know. Maybe plan a visit with them and ask them what they're doing in the fall. Then say, "Well Dad, I was wondering if you would walk me down the aisle!" Make it special for those you love, the most important people in your life.

>> **Share on social media.** I'm certain you have seen your friends post about their engagement. You want to be happy for them, but you wish it was you. Well, now it's your time to share with the world! Later in this section we'll discuss some fun ways to share the news on social media. For now, it's time to let everyone know on social media and change your relationship status. Post on social media first so that everyone can see that you got engaged. Your friends will comment and like and celebrate with you. A few days later, change your relationship status. This will allow time between both posts for your friends to see the original post that you got engaged. Additionally, keep the details of your wedding to yourself. You won't be inviting all of your social media friends, so those who aren't invited to your wedding won't be hurt by seeing the details and never getting an invite.

>> **Consider the mail.** I know, no one mails anything anymore. That's what makes mailing an engagement announcement so special! I would suggest a postcard announcement to save on postage, and it's something that can go on your friends' fridges. This will also allow you the chance to lock in your guest list. This is not the a Save-the-Date; that will come later. How special would it be for someone to receive an announcement in the mail? I don't know about you, but I love getting mail, especially if it isn't a bill. If you got engaged around the holidays, design a cute holiday card announcing your engagement. Holiday cards are perfect for Save-the-Dates as well.

Planning the engagement party

Who doesn't love a good party? This girl does! An engagement party is a wonderful way to bring those you love together to celebrate. In this section, we'll discuss who's throwing the party, the timing of the party, who to invite, location, how to invite your guests, the ambiance, food, and what to wear.

>> **Who's throwing the party?** Traditionally the brides' parents would host the engagement party. However, today anyone can throw the party. Often, the couple hosts their own party to celebrate with friends and family. It's also acceptable to have multiple engagement parties. Let's say your parents live in another state. It's your hometown and a lot of your close friends still live near where your parents live. Most likely, those people will be invited to your wedding. Have your parents host an engagement party in your hometown. You may also have a group of friends who live where you and your fiancé currently live. You as a couple can throw your own engagement party where you live with your close friends.

» **Timing of the party**. It's best to host a party as close to your engagement as possible. If you've been engaged for over six months, the excitement of your engagement has probably dwindled because you're now in full wedding planning mode. Celebrate your engagement when everyone is excited about the news and before you have dived face first into planning your wedding. Be prepared for the questions to begin. When is the wedding? Where are you having the wedding? Do you have a dress? If you host the engagement party as close to the engagement as possible you can reply, "We don't know any details yet, we are just excited to celebrate our engagement first. We will start planning soon and will let you know all the details as soon as possible."

» **Who to invite**. An engagement party is usually an intimate event with immediate family and your closest friends. If you already have your bridal party in mind, consider inviting just your bridal party and their dates and ask them at the engagement party to be in your wedding. If you have other friends who are invited, consider telling your bridal party at a different time to avoid hurt feelings. Invite the people in your life who do life with you. Invite mutual friends and your individual close friends. This is the first time that you'll have all the people you love at the same event. It's an exciting time to see your lives and the people who have influenced you individually come together to celebrate your life as a couple.

» **Location**. An intimate engagement party at either the host's home or your home is always a special night. There is something about having your closest friends and family with you in your home that makes the party so meaningful. If you're inviting a large group of people, consider renting out a room at your favorite local restaurant. They'll be able to handle all the food and beverages so you don't have to worry about that. This will be more expensive than a home party but if you have the budget to do it, then plan away. A local restaurant is a great place to celebrate, and you won't have to worry about cleaning your home — either beforehand in preparation or after the party is over.

» **How to invite**. Once your guest list is established, it's time to invite your guests. Engagement party invitations can be sent in the mail or electronically. They don't have to be as formal as your wedding invitations. They can also be any style or design that you like. At this point you most likely don't have your wedding invitations picked out, so these don't have to match. Send them out a month before your engagement party and set the RSVP date for two weeks before your party. This will allow plenty of time for your guests to respond so that you know how many people will attend.

» **The ambiance**. Simple flowers and decor are all you need for your engagement party. There will come a time later in the planning process where you can go all out on the flowers. The engagement party needs only simple flower arrangements or decorate with just candles. Candles are my best friend to give a romantic feel to any event. You'll want to create an intimate atmosphere at this special event with your special people. They'll appreciate just being invited, so save your money by designing a simple ambiance that everyone will enjoy.

» **The food**. There's no need to provide a four-course meal at an engagement party. Appetizers are perfect for this, such as a charcuterie board, sliders, and dips. This will create a casual environment where your guests can eat as they like while talking with you about how excited they are that you're getting married. If you're hosting a home party, these are items that you can make on your own. If you're hosting a party at a local restaurant, pick some of your favorite appetizers for your guests to enjoy.

» **What to wear**. Momma needs a new dress! Buy yourself something fun to wear for your engagement party. Treat yourself, because this is a special occasion. If you really want to spice things up, coordinate your outfit with your fiancé. This might be the first time that you get to wear white. Or maybe a vibrant dress because you want your joy to shine bright. Either way, have fun planning your outfit and pamper yourself a little bit with something new to wear. A cocktail dress or summer dress for the women and a sports jacket or button-up with slacks for the men would be the perfect attire to celebrate with.

Making the social media announcement

You have seen all the fun social media posts when someone gets engaged. You have also seen all the hashtags. Announcing your engagement on social media should be fun — the first thing you send out to show the world a reflection of who you are as a couple. When thinking about what you're going to say, have fun with this! Don't stress about making your post perfect. Honestly, it doesn't really matter what anyone thinks. This is about the two of you, so enjoy thinking through options for how you'll tell the world. In this section, I share some of my favorite social media posts. Customize them to fit the two of you as a couple and share away!

Social media is likely the most popular way that couples all over the world spread the news of their engagement. Here are some ways to share the good news:

» **The location.** If the location of your proposal is special to you or just a neat spot, use it in your post. Share a picture of the actual proposal. If you didn't catch it on camera, recreate it after the proposal is over with your phone camera.

>> **Do it together.** Take a photo together and make it unique. You can buy fun novelty items such as T-shirts, hats, or cups and take a picture with those items. For example, one person wears a shirt that says, "He [or She] asked!" and the other wears a shirt that says, "I said yes!"

>> **Use a prop.** On a chalkboard or poster, write, "I said yes!" Then take a photo with the prop and share the news. Or make a sign that says, "It's time to celebrate! I'm changing my last name."

>> **Take a selfie.** A selfie is most likely the most popular way to share the news. Take a selfie together with big smiles and say, "We're getting married!" This is the simplest and fastest way to share the news, and who doesn't love a good selfie?

>> **Show off the bling.** You have a ring on your finger; now show it off! Whatever way you choose to share, make sure that ring is in the photo. Everyone wants to see the ring, so including it in your social media post is always a good thing — the classic symbol that you're engaged.

>> **Use a pet.** Let's face it, pets are just cute. Everyone loves them, so use them in your social media post. They're part of your family and are just as excited as you are that you're getting married. Well, I like to think they're excited — I haven't been able to get any of my pets to talk to me but I'm going to guess they're excited too!

Whatever way you share the news, have fun with this! It's the first thing you do in the wedding planning process. Now that it's official, it's time to share your excitement and joy with the world in a playful and creative way. Everyone will be excited for you and love your creativity. Congratulations, the world officially knows it's official!

Selecting Your Squad

The bridal party you pick are your people. They are the ones who have seen you on your best and your worst day. They know your deepest secrets; they have seen your heartbreaks and are on your side no matter what. Picking your squad is an important task when planning your wedding. Who will make the cut? Who will be standing next to you on your wedding day?

I have seen the good bridesmaids and the bad. I have also seen the good groomsmen and the bad. I have stories for days about bridal parties. Some are funny but some are heartbreaking, like the time a best man professed his love for the bride during his speech at the reception. That was a moment in my career that I will never forget.

My hope is that after you read this section, you'll be able to pick the very best team to love and support you beyond the wedding and into your marriage. In this section we'll discuss the job requirements of your bridal party, what it means for them to stand by your side, and the logistics of the order and how you're going to ask them.

Understanding the job requirements

We all know that the bridesmaids and groomsmen stand by your side during the ceremony. But, what else to they do? Do they have job responsibilities? Yes they do! It's an honor to be chosen as part of a bridal party, and it's important to understand the bridal party's job so you can pick the perfect squad.

First, let's start with the fact that you don't need a bridal party if it's not important to you to have one. Maybe you're blending families with your fiancé, and you want only your children to be with you. Or maybe you have too many friends to pick just a few to be in your bridal party. Whatever the case, know that you do not have to have a bridal party if that doesn't fit your life.

>> **Maid of honor, matron of honor, and best man**. If you do decide to have a bridal party, picking your maid of honor (a single person) or your matron of honor (a married person) and the best man or men is first on the list of creating the perfect team. If you are female and have a best friend who is a male, he would be your man of honor. If you are a male whose best friend is female, she would be your best woman.

Traditionally, these people are either relatives or your very best friend. Prior to the wedding, the job responsibilities of these people are to help with any planning, throw showers or parties in your honor, help with selecting the attire for the bridal party, and anything else that you need during the planning process. On the wedding day they are by your side to troubleshoot any problems, hold the rings during the ceremony and give a speech at the reception. They have your back no matter what. If you need anything, they should be there to help.

On many occasions, I've seen parents of the couple serving as the matron of honor or best man. This is a special way to acknowledge parents who have been your number one fan. If that is the case for you, I say do it. They know you the best and will support you like no one else.

>> **Bridesmaids and groomsmen**. The bridesmaids and groomsmen are additional siblings, siblings of your fiancé, or very close friends. They too have responsibilities, which include helping with any planning needs, attending dress fittings, assisting with showers and parties, and standing next to you on the wedding day. They attend the rehearsal, rehearsal dinner, and the wedding day.

>> **Flower girl**. The flower girl is typically a relative, such as a young cousin, sibling, niece, or a family friend, between one and ten years old. Some of my clients who are teachers use their students as the flower girl. You can have one or multiple flower girls. They will throw rose petals down the aisle — if permitted by your venue — or may wear a flower crown.

>> **Ring bearer**. The ring bearer is typically a relative, such as a young cousin, sibling, nephew, or a family friend, between one and ten years old. Traditionally, the ring bearer carries a pillow down the aisle, but I have had clients who took the very cute approach of having the ring bearer carry a box that says, "Ring Police."

WARNING

It's popular to think that ring bearers actually hold the rings, but they do not. Those rings cost a lot of money and the last thing you need is for them to get lost on the way down the aisle. Give the ring bearer a fake ring, which can be purchased online or a local craft store. The real rings need to be given to the best man or maid or matron of honor prior to the start of the ceremony.

TIP

If you don't have a little potential ring bearer in your life, consider incorporating your pet on your wedding day (make sure your venue allows animals!). Assign someone in your squad to take care of the pet for the remainder of the evening or have someone pick them up and take them to where you will be at the end of the night. I can't tell you how many times clients don't think about this, and our team is left to watch their animal for the night. While we are all animal lovers, it needs to be assigned to someone in your circle.

>> **Junior bridesmaids and groomsmen**. If you have someone special in your life whom you want in the wedding but they're too old to be a flower girl or ring bearer and too young to be a bridesmaid or groomsman, they can be your junior bridesmaid or junior groomsman. Their responsibilities are not as extensive at the bridesmaids and groomsmen but you can include them based on age-appropriate activities. (I'm certain they would love to attend the bachelorette or bachelor party, but they may be too young.) They will stand with you on your wedding day with the rest of your bridal party.

>> **Mother of the bride**. The mother of the bride is a very important person on the wedding day. She will typically be with the bride all day and help her get ready. She will make sure she is dressed and ready to go for her big moment. The mother of the bride is most often the one who hosts showers and parties for the bride. She will also be the one who stands first when the bride enters the ceremony. Sometimes at the rehearsal dinner or the reception, she will give a speech.

>> **Father of the bride**. The father of the bride is traditionally the parent with the most responsibilities. He is the one who walks the bride down the aisle. If the bride chooses, he also gives her away to be married to the groom. At the reception, he gives the welcome and the toast to the bride and groom. He also dances with the bride during the father-daughter dance.

TIP

Not everyone's story is the same, so if you don't have a father figure, an uncle, cousin, brother, or close friend can fill this role. I have also seen couples who have children take on these responsibilities. If you can't pick just one parent, consider both of your parents walking you down the aisle.

>> **Mother of the groom**. The mother of the groom gives all her love and support to the groom on the wedding day. She serves as a support if he needs her in anyway. She will co-host the rehearsal dinner with the father of the groom, and she will be a part of the speeches at that dinner. She also dances with the groom at the reception during the mother-son dance, a special moment between the groom and his mother.

>> **Father of the groom**. The father of the groom also supports his son on the wedding day. I have often seen the father of the groom hanging out with the groom and his groomsmen to offer support as needed. He will also co-host the rehearsal dinner and give a speech to honor his son and fiancée.

>> **Ushers**. The ushers are typically males who are close to the couple or related to the couple but are not bridesmaids or groomsmen.

TIP

If you don't want to select additional men, you can utilize the groomsmen as ushers. Their job responsibility is to escort the female guests into the venue for the ceremony. They let guests know which side to sit on based on whether they know the bride or the groom. You should have two ushers per one hundred guests.

>> **Guestbook/program attendants**. Typically, these are female relatives or friends who are close to you but not bridesmaids. Their job is to make sure the guests sign the guestbook at the ceremony and pass out the programs as guests enter the venue for the ceremony.

That is your bridal party and their responsibilities. When you ask your bridal party to be a part of your wedding, it's important to discuss their responsibilities with them. Make sure they're comfortable and willing to help you prior to and on your big day.

In Table 2-1, write in the names of the people in your bridal party. Down the road when we plan your ceremony, it will be helpful to have all the names in one spot.

TABLE 2-1 ## Your Bridal Party

Title	Name
Maid of Honor/Matron of Honor	
Best Man/Men	
Bridesmaids	
Groomsmen	
Flower Girl(s)	
Ring Bearer(s)	
Mother of the Bride	
Father of the Bride	
Mother of the Groom	

Title	Name
Father of the Groom	
Ushers	
Guestbook/Program Attendant(s)	

Standing by your side

Now that you have picked your bridal party, it's time to figure out where everyone is going to stand and sit during your ceremony. In Chapter 12, when we create your ceremony, we'll talk about how your bridal party processes or enters and recesses or exits the ceremony. For now, we're going to work through the order of your bridesmaids and groomsmen and discuss where the parents sit during the ceremony.

I have a fun assignment for you to do together. Actually, because it's fun, let's call it a team-building opportunity. In Table 2-2, write the name of your bridesmaids and groomsmen in order, and then parents and grandparents. A few things to note when you do this:

>> Where you see "Bride" and "Groom," that's you.

>> Make it your own. The chart can say "Bride" and "Bride" or "Groom" and "Groom." But the "bride" is always on the left.

>> Imagine standing at the front of the church. As you go down the chart, write in the names closest to you. The maid/matron of honor will be first, followed by the bridesmaids. Same thing for the groom's side; the best man will be first followed by the groomsmen.

>> Fill in the names of your parents and grandparents. They will not be standing at the altar with you, but this will help you visualize which side of the ceremony seating they will be on.

TIP

Now for the fun part. As you fill in the chart, figure out together who would make the perfect pair. If you have married couples in your bridal party, keep them together. If you have couples who used to date, keep them apart. No one wants that drama!

TABLE 2-2   ## Your Bridal Party Order

Bride's Side	Groom's Side
Maid of Honor/Matron of Honor	Best Man/Men
Bridesmaids	Groomsmen
Bride's Parents	Groom's Parents
Bride's Grandparents	Groom's Grandparents

Having an uneven number of bridesmaids and groomsmen is okay. Depending on where the numbers fall, if you have more groomsmen than bridesmaids, two groomsmen will walk with one bridesmaid. If you have more bridesmaids than groomsmen, two bridesmaids will walk with one groomsman. Do not stress about that! You both have different family and friends. It's fine if they don't line up perfectly.

If you are not doing "sides," I still want you to fill in this chart because these are the people who get assigned seats at the ceremony. Additional family and guests can sit on whichever side they'd like. The reason we do this with the specific people in the chart is so that your immediate family will be seated on your side.

Proposing to your bridal party

I love to see how my clients propose to their bridal party. Asking your bridal party to be in your wedding is a long-standing tradition, but now we "propose" to our bridal party. When I started my career as a wedding planner, clients would just ask their bridal party, "Hey, want to be in my wedding?" Now we have elaborate ways to ask them and if you're into it, let's explore some fun ideas. I'll also discuss the good old-fashioned way to ask them to be a part of your big day.

These are special people to you and whether you want to go all out or keep it simple, they deserve to feel special. They have obviously influenced your life in a positive way, so in this section, we're going to talk about some ways you can honor them and ask them to be on your squad. Most importantly, you need to make sure they are available on the big day!

» **Special dinner**. If all of your bridal party is in one location, plan a special night out where all of you — including spouses or dates — go out to dinner at a local hot spot. Thank them for being so special to you and ask them at dinner to be in your wedding. Of course, it's unlikely that everyone lives in the city where you live, so individual dinners held as you can are fun too!

» **Phone a friend**. There's a good chance that your bridal party all live in different locations. If you can't see your bridal party in person, at minimum call them rather than texting them. You need to speak to them directly and tell them how much it would mean to you if they were in your wedding. Make sure that they are comfortable with the financial obligations and commitment of supporting you during the process.

» **Write a letter**. A handwritten letter is a special way to ask your bridal party to be in your wedding. We don't often receive letters in the mail anymore, so this is very meaningful. A personal letter to each member of your bridal party isn't elaborate but would mean so much to the recipients. Explain in the letter why you want them to be in your wedding. Include the date and location to make sure that when they respond to your letter, they can make it to your wedding.

» **Gift or gift basket**. Many resources online have cute premade gifts to help pop the question. Who doesn't love a good gift? A themed gift asking them to be on your squad is even better. If you make your own, include bridal party items such a tumbler with "Maid of Honor," "Best Man," "Bridesmaid," or "Groomsman" imprinted on it. You could send a robe or cufflinks, and a mini bottle of champagne. Send a puzzle that they must put together that says, "Will you be my bridesmaid?" or "Will you be my groomsman?" The options are endless, so be creative and have fun designing the perfect gift for your crew. Whatever you choose, make sure to include a card asking them to be in your wedding.

Showers, Bashes, and Parties

One of my favorite parts of the wedding planning process are all the parties that are thrown in your honor leading up to the big day. They bring people together who may or may not be able to attend your wedding but want to celebrate with you.

The problem is that few people know how many parties to have. How many is too little? How many is too much? We expect that if someone is getting married for the first time, they will have lots of showers and parties, but what if this isn't your first marriage — do you still get to celebrate? I believe all good things should be celebrated, and you should be celebrated no matter your life story.

You are probably wondering, if you do have parties, who throws them? What do you do if no one has offered to throw you a party? How many guests do you invite to your parties? What do you wear? These are all questions we'll address in this section. Additionally, we'll discuss gift registries, the bachelorette bash, bachelor party, couples' shower, and bridal shower. It's time to sit back and be pampered a bit. It will go by fast, and this is one of the moments I want you to enjoy.

Gift registries

Registering for gifts is a fun task to do together. First, you must determine your need. Wherever you are in life, you both bring different items into your marriage. You may have a lot of stuff while your fiancé has just the basics. It's important to consolidate your items and determine what you need. If you register in a store, they'll give you a scanner. Trust me, it's so much fun scanning everything on display and listening to the beep-beep of the scanner. You may want to scan every item you see but in reality, you do not need everything in aisle 44 or maybe you do?

TIP

Before you start registering for gifts, sit down with your fiancé and come up with a list of items that you need. Do you need new pots and pans, towels, lamps, decorative items, coffee mugs, or a new coffee machine? Think about when you make a list before you go to the grocery store so you spend less money and avoid thinking that you need all those snacks. It prevents you from getting home to make dinner, realizing you really didn't buy any actual food, and now you're trying to create a meal out of popcorn and doughnuts. The same thing is true for your gift registries. Come up with a plan before you search online or in a store. It will help you avoid getting a cute lamp but no shade, or ten throw blankets.

This is your next team-building experience. You are designing the home in which you will start your life together. How exciting is that? You'll learn a lot about your fiancé that you might not have known. I'm not exactly sure why picking out home items changes people. You look over at your fiancé and all of a sudden they are so excited to choose silverware. Maybe you realize they have horrible taste when it comes to interior design. Whichever way, it gives you an opportunity to learn about each other and grow closer together.

TIP

Once you have a plan in place on what you need, it's time to go to the store or start a registry online. If you choose to go to a store, stay away from the local mom-and-pops that guests who don't live in that area can't resource. I love to shop local, and I encourage you to do that if there is a store that you love. Use that store for a bridal shower or couples' shower in your area where everyone invited is local. Pick national chains where all your guests can access your registry in-store or online for your wedding.

TIP

When the gifts are picked out, include your registry links on a wedding website or with your invitation on a registry card. (Head to Chapter 7 for more information on sharing your registry on your wedding website.) Some of your guests may not be tech savvy and would prefer to have a card with the information over an online link. It's important to share this information with your guests so that you don't end up with ten silver platters that you don't want.

You and your fiancé may find that you have everything you need. If that's the case, consider a cash or honeymoon fund. Those can be easily created online and again linked on your wedding website or shared with your guests on a registry card in your invitation. If you choose to go this route, please know that many guests like to purchase tangible items. Most of your guests will likely do what you ask but some will want to get you a physical gift.

>> **Cash Fund**. A cash fund is where you ask your guests to give you cash rather than a conventual wedding gift. Several online services can help you set this up. You'll link your cash registry to your financial institution and the company you pick will send the money your guests give you straight to your bank account. They will take a percentage of the gift to cover the fees associated with the transaction. So, for example, if your guests give you $100, you may receive only $97.00. You can also apply the cash funds towards a larger item such as a new refrigerator or washer and dryer. Your guests will see how much has been contributed to that item and can add to that fund as they like.

Designating items that you would like the money to go to will help those guests who don't want to just give you cash on your wedding day. They may feel it's too impersonal or they don't have a lot of cash to contribute to your fund and don't want their name on a website saying they gave you $25 when they really want to be able to give you $100. Picking out items that they can contribute to will help them feel like their gift is of value and is going towards a specific item.

>> **Honeymoon Fund**. A honeymoon fund is a way to ask your guests to contribute towards your honeymoon. There are several online resources that can help you set this up. Again, you'll link your honeymoon fund to your wedding website or send it with your invitations on a registry card. Your guests can pay toward your flights or hotel rooms for your honeymoon.

A downside to this is that you'll typically plan your honeymoon before the guests receive your registry. Having a honeymoon fund can cause stress late in the process because you must wait to book your travel. You may also be limited on the nights you can travel based on how much has been contributed.

The only time not to register for gifts is if you are planning a destination wedding hosted at an all-inclusive resort or overseas. A destination wedding is where all your guests travel to a location other than their home for your wedding. They all pay for their travel, hotel, and food. They are spending a lot of money to be a part of your day; this is their gift to you. Don't worry; some people will still bring a gift or give you cash. Just as for traditional guests, send a thank-you note to those who traveled to be a part of your big day. Even if they didn't send you a tangible gift, they deserve to be thanked for taking time off work and covering their travel expenses.

TIP

When planning your parties that we'll discuss in the following sections, there are two important pieces that I want you to remember. For each party, if your guests bring gifts, make sure you have someone taking notes with the guest's name and the gift they gave you. That way you won't lose track and can send a thank-you note that matches the guest with their gift. Additionally, give the party host a gift for holding a party in your honor. I'm certain the host is not expecting it, but it's important to thank them for all the time and effort they put into making your party so special.

Bachelorette bash

The bachelorette party is all about celebrating the bride with her bridesmaids and possibly close friends and family. I'm certain you have heard it's the bride's "last weekend of freedom." Although some do still see it this way, the bachelorette party is a special weekend spent with your closest friends to celebrate your upcoming marriage.

The party or weekend is typically planned by your maid/matron of honor or bridesmaids. However, if they are not available to help in the planning, plan your own! Figure out something that you love to do. This party is all about you and what you love. If you love the spa, plan a spa getaway. If you love to hike, go to the mountains and trails.

The season may determine when you plan your bachelorette party, but it's best to plan the event one to two months prior to your wedding day. If bridesmaids are traveling to your wedding, space the timing a little further out to give financial space between the cost of the bachelorette party and the wedding.

Speaking of cost, who pays for the bachelorette party? Traditionally, each bridesmaid will pay for their own expenses. Then you'll find a price per person and the bridesmaids will split your cost. If the price per person is $200.00 and you have five bridesmaids, each bridesmaid will pay an additional $40.00 over their own cost to cover your costs. This is very generous but by no means expected.

Bachelorette trips are always packed full of custom items such as T-shirts, mugs, robes, and tumblers. This is the perfect time to embrace all the bride-to-be swag. A weekend away can be filled with fun activities touring the location. Make sure to book those excursions before your trip since you'll typically have a higher number of people.

TIP

If a trip is not something that you can manage financially or maybe your work schedule is preventing you from planning a getaway, consider a home-cooked meal with your bridesmaids. Another option is to do something special with just your bridesmaids on the wedding weekend. Go to the spa, plan a brunch, or get your nails done. Whatever your plan, enjoy a little time off with your friends to celebrate your upcoming marriage.

When you are planning the perfect get-a-way location, consider the financial expense that your bridal party will endure to be able to attend your weekend away. Remember that they will be taking on most of the financial responsibility. Make sure they are financially comfortable with taking on that expense when you consider the perfect trip.

Bachelor party

The bachelor party is all about celebrating the groom with his groomsmen and possibly close friends and family. Again, this is often referred to as the last "free" weekend prior to getting married. I am personally grateful that in recent years bachelor trips have evolved into more of a male bonding trip than the groom's last chance to go crazy on the town. After all, you are engaged. One of the best man's jobs is to make sure the groom doesn't get too crazy on the bachelor trip.

Like the bachelorette party, the best man or group of groomsmen typically plan the getaway, but it's fine if the groom wants to plan his own weekend away. It's also nice to make sure that the groom's trip costs are covered by the groomsmen. If the price per person is $200 and you have five groomsmen, then each groomsman will pay an additional $40 to cover the cost for the groom.

The groom should pick activities that he enjoys, such as a golf weekend, time on the lake, or a fishing trip. This is meant to be a weekend away spent with your groomsmen to get a little guy time. Plan activities that everyone can participate in and enjoy the company of your friends. Be thoughtful of minors if you do want to bar crawl.

Regarding timing, the bachelor party should take place one to two months prior to the wedding. There is no need to send formal invitations. Create the guest list and make sure to share that with your best man if he is planning the bachelor party. It's common to invite friends who aren't in the wedding. Reach out to your friends and get a sense of how many people will attend the bachelor party so that you can plan appropriately.

I would suggest renting a home share or resourcing a family or friend's lake or beach house. If you do rent a home share, be sure that the host allows their space to be rented to a bachelor trip group. That has caused problems in the past for clients who didn't disclose this when they booked and arrived to find that the host would not allow them to stay there.

The bachelor trip is a wonderful time for the groom to spend a little time away with his guy friends. Remember to have fun and enjoy your weekend but respect your bride-to-be. Although this may be referred to as your last night of freedom, when you put that ring on her finger, you already committed to be faithful to her. Whatever decisions you make, have fun!

Couple's shower

A couple's shower is a party where both people who are getting married attend. This is a wonderful way to bring people together on both sides to celebrate your marriage. The guest list is co-ed and more inclusive than just one of you hosting a shower. It also takes the pressure off one or the other because you attend the party together and the attention is on the happy couple.

This shower is often planned by the bridal party, parents, or close friends, but a couple can opt to plan their own. A couple's shower can be a dinner party like the engagement party, or it could be held in a brunch setting. You may also consider a group activity. The great news is that there are lots of options and everything is fair game!

A couple's shower should occur one to two months prior to your wedding. The host can be a person in your bridal party, parents, or a close family friend. The guest list is limitless regarding who you can invite, but the location of your shower might determine who can attend. If a relative or family friend is hosting your shower, consider a backyard BBQ. You can also rent an intimate event space or a location that offers a group activity, such as duckpin bowling; golf is also a favorite option.

TIP

A good theme will enhance your couple's shower. Consider incorporating where you met or where you got engaged. Include your favorite food or cater in your favorite local restaurant. The important piece is that this shower reflects you and your better half. Consider coordinating your outfits for this party. After all, you're doing this together. Have fun planning what to wear with your fiancé.

Paper invitations are appropriate for your couple's shower and should incorporate each of you. The invitation should include the title of the event, your names, date, time, location, RSVP information, and your registry. The RSVP date should be two weeks before the event and your host should collect the responses via phone or email.

Games are a shower tradition, and at a couple's shower they can be themed to incorporate both of you, such as having your guests fill out a premade card that includes a list of items: Who is better at cooking? Who is better with their money? Who sleeps in? Your guest will answer each question and you'll share the correct answer. Whoever gets the most answers correct wins a prize. This game always keeps the guests laughing as they wonder which one of you hits the snooze button fifteen times and which one wakes up as soon as you hear the alarm.

Bridal shower

A bridal shower is a party that honors the bride-to-be. To me, they are the "catch-all" showers. You may have one or multiple showers based on what your life looks like. For example, if you live in city A, your parents live in city B, and your partner's parents live in city C, it's appropriate to have three showers, with three different hosts, to include each group of people. Whether this is your first marriage or second, a shower is a wonderful time to bring your closest friends together to celebrate your future marriage.

TIP

Having multiple showers is common practice, so it's important to speak to each host to avoid overlapping on the timing of the events. The bridal shower is typically held one to two months before your wedding day. I would suggest that all parties and showers are wrapped up by a month out from your big day. As we go through the planning process, you'll see that there are a lot of last-minute i's to dot and t's to cross. If your parties are scheduled too close to your wedding day, you may be overwhelmed with your busy party schedule and the already long list of thank-you notes to send.

The bridal shower host can be someone from your bridal party, a close friend, or a relative. The host will take care of sending the invitations, cover the costs of the party, and make sure the party is a success. Be sure to discuss with each host how many people they feel comfortable having at the event. They are covering the financial costs of the shower, so check in with them first before you start planning the guest list.

A paper invitation or digital invitation is appropriate for your shower. When your host designs the invitation, make sure to include the title, your name, date, time, location, RSVP information, and your registry. They will also collect the responses from your guests. Feel free to check in with them to see who will be attending your shower. The wedding day is so busy that your bridal showers are the perfect time to catch up with old friends — another opportunity to see those you love prior to the big day.

Bridal showers are typically packed with games for your guests to enjoy. Those games are intended be fun and give your guests a little insight into who you and your partner are as a couple. To avoid being completely embarrassed in front of some friends who have known you your entire life, reach out to the host and see what games they're planning so that you're prepared.

REMEMBER

Enjoy a little time off from planning the wedding, wear your favorite sundress, and enjoy being pampered and celebrated. Being the bride is so much fun! Take time to stop and take it all in. It will go by fast, and each party is another piece of the pie in your wedding planning. Have several pieces!

IN THIS CHAPTER

» **Understanding what's important to you and your budget**

» **Determining what's included in your budget**

» **Navigating additional fees, tips, and gratuities**

Chapter **3**

Everyone Has a Budget

Before you start researching your vendors, you need to determine what you have to spend. Let's face it — weddings are expensive. That doesn't mean you can't have everything you want; it just means you need to be intentional with what you have to spend. Before you fall in love with an expensive photographer or design elaborate flower arrangements, it's important to determine your budget.

You've probably already checked the resources to determine a percentage of what each item should be in your overall budget. This is my biggest pet peeve in the wedding industry; those percentages were created to be a guide, but they are not yours. One thing that was forgotten when those standard percentages were created is *you*!

That's right — you decide what your budget will be. In this chapter, we'll determine what's most important to you, figure out who's paying and what you have to spend, work out what your budget should include, and look at something often overlooked in the overall budget: additional fees and tips and gratuities.

REMEMBER

Planning your budget doesn't need to be stressful. Together we're going to customize your plan and maximize your money. There's no need to go into debt over your wedding. We'll be smart in planning where your money needs to go, where you can save and where to splurge.

Knowing What's Most Important to You

I'm sure you have attended your friends' weddings. What did you love? What did you dislike? Did you notice the fancy china? Do you remember what you ate? What color were the flowers? What did the linens look like? Did they have paper napkins or cloth napkins?

In Table 3-1, write in some of the things you loved about your friends' weddings and some of the things you disliked. This will help you see how much you remember about other weddings you have attended. Focus on the details to help you determine your own loves and dislikes.

TABLE 3-1
Loves/Dislikes from Your Friends' Weddings

Your Loves	Your Dislikes

Looking over this list, are you surprised by how much you didn't remember? I'm not. Now, if you just attended a wedding last week, chances are you remember a lot. But if it's been over six months, you may have struggled to recall any of the details.

The point in doing this is to remind yourself that, when you design your budget, no one will remember what they had to eat; they'll only remember if it was good. No one will remember who your DJ is; they'll only remember if they were entertaining. No one will remember if you had white polyester tablecloths or designer linens; they'll only remember if the tables were covered.

Now it's your turn. In Chapter 4, we'll pick your top five vendor categories, but for now focus on what's most important and least important to you on your wedding day. In Table 3-2, fill in the pieces that are most important to you when you think about your wedding day.

TABLE 3-2 **Your Most Important/Least Important Parts of Your Wedding Day**

Most Important	Least Important

For example, you're a lover of food so the food must be top notch; you don't really care if you have a video so a videographer is low on your list; you want an amazing dress that makes you feel incredibly beautiful; you're not a fan of stationery and want simple invitations; you want your guests to dance all night long so an amazing DJ or band is a must-have. We'll customize your budget soon to fit your needs and desires for the big day.

TIP

Determining what's most important and least important to you is a key factor in determining your budget. Our focus now is to put most of your money on the pieces that are most important to you and save on those that are least important. There's no need to spend a ton of money on something you don't care about. That's what's wrong with the standard formulas. If something isn't important to you, why spend the money they tell you to spend on it? Why not apply that money to something that really matters to you?

I had a client who wanted simple flowers and must have told me that a thousand times during our planning meetings. She didn't even like flowers and would often break out because she was allergic. Somewhere along the way, someone in her life told her she needed extravagant florals. But why would she need elaborate flower arrangements if she didn't want elaborate flower arrangements? Was it to impress the guests? Why do we do that?

WARNING

Of course we'll keep your guests in mind when planning your big day, but if you're planning something to simply impress your guests, remove that as a motivation right now. If I've learned anything in life, it is that you cannot and will not make everyone happy. Additionally, your friendship shouldn't be about who's impressing whom. This is a special day in your life and those who are invited should love you no matter if you serve filet mignon or chicken.

How did it end up for my client? She overspent on flowers and ended up with a lovely case of hives on her wedding day. All to make someone else in her life happy.

REMEMBER

Focus on who you are as a couple, and budget together. In your marriage, you will have to budget. You'll also have to have conversations about what you'll spend your money on. Use budgeting for your wedding as practice for money management in your marriage.

Figuring Out Who's Paying

If I was a gambler, I would bet on the fact that talking about or asking for money isn't your favorite thing to do. Most people don't want to ask for financial help, which makes you normal. When planning a wedding and determining your budget, it's important to have those sometimes uncomfortable conversations so you know exactly what you have to work with.

The first step in determining your budget is to consider all your options regarding financial contributions. Traditionally, the bride's parents pay for the wedding, but that may not be your situation for any number of reasons. In this section we'll explore a few options for who pays the bill.

» **Parents of the bride:** If the parents of the bride are financially able to pay for the wedding, sit down with them and determine how much is too much. They may or may not be able to tell you an actual number because there are moving pieces to any wedding budget, but they should be able to let you know the max they can financially commit to. When you receive that number, you can determine how many guests you'll need to fit into that budget. The total amount they're willing to pay should include everything that we'll discuss in the next section.

» **Stepparents:** If you're part of a blended family, it's appropriate to discuss with all parties involved and seek financial contributions for your wedding. Each set of parents will be able to tell you what they can financially commit to and that will give you your total budget. If this is your situation, consider opening a wedding checking account where you can deposit all the funds into one account. This way you won't have to keep track of which parent contributed what and you'll have all your wedding funds in one place.

» **Parents of the groom:** I have worked with several clients who resource the groom's parents to pay for the wedding expenses. Whatever the situation, it's perfectly appropriate for the groom's parents to cover the cost of the wedding if that's what works best.

>> **Close relatives:** If you have a close relative who wants to contribute to the wedding, consider factoring this into the total wedding budget. Often there's a bonus mom or dad who wants to contribute as a mother or father would, and using those contributions toward your wedding or honeymoon can absolutely maximize your budget.

>> **The couple:** Nowadays, it's very common for the couple to cover the cost of their wedding themselves. The typical age where someone gets married for the first time is later in life, when they have already established their careers and have a nest egg in place.

WARNING

If you're planning to pay for your wedding yourselves, please do not go into debt over your wedding. Stay within your means and accept any contributions from family or friends. Save your money for future projects when you're married.

What Does Your Budget Include?

Now for the fun part well, talking about money isn't always fun, but I'm going to try and make it fun. After you have determined what's most important to you, it's time to create your custom budget. Don't worry — everyone has one. In this section, we'll discuss what items should be included in a wedding budget, what percentages they should have, adjusting the percentages to fit your needs and forming your own budget.

Let's start with what's included. The right column of Table 3-3 lists items typically part of a wedding budget. In the left column, put an X, a check mark, or a smiley face (whichever you prefer) if you need that to be included in your overall budget.

There are several pieces to the pie that someone may pay for, so you don't have to include that in your total budget. For example, maybe your parents have given you money for your wedding, but they want to also pay for your dress and aren't considering that as an item you need to include in your budget. Or maybe you have a relative who hasn't given you money for your wedding but wants to pay for your cake.

TABLE 3-3

What's Included in Your Wedding Budget?

Do You Need This In Your Budget?	Budget Items
	Wedding dress & accessories
	Tux
	Bridesmaids attire
	Groomsmen attire
	Flower Girl attire
	Ring bearer attire
	Ceremony venue fee
	Ceremony musicians
	Officiant
	Guest book
	Florist: Flowers for the ceremony
	Aisle runner, candles, accessories for the ceremony
	Marriage license
	Reception venue fee
	Caterer
	Baker
	Alcohol
	Bartender
	Reception entertainment
	Rental items: Tables, chairs, linens, silverware, china
	Specialty rental items: Soft seating, stage, dance floor, tent
	Catering rental items: Serving platters, drink dispensers, chaffing dishes
	Cake knife, toasting flutes, garter
	Florist: Reception flowers
	Specialty lighting or draping

Do You Need This In Your Budget?	Budget Items
	Parking
	Valet
	Transportation: Bridal party
	Transportation: Couple
	Tips & gratuities
	Photographer
	Videographer
	Wedding bands
	Gifts for your bridal party
	Hair & makeup
	Wedding party hair & makeup
	Rehearsal dinner
	Save-the-Dates
	Invitations
	Programs
	Menus
	Escort cards
	Favors: Cups, koozies, napkins
	Thank-you cards
	Photobooth
	Honeymoon suite
	Honeymoon
	Wedding planner

Use Table 3-4 as a guide to help you set up an Excel file that will include all your wedding budget needs, how much each vendor costs, payments made, the date of those payments, the remaining balance due, and your total budget. The reason to do this in an electronic form is so that you can adjust the budget as needed based on your specific requirements.

TABLE 3-4 **Sample Budget in Excel**

Item	Cost	Paid	Date Paid	Balance	Due Date	Total	$40,000
Planner	$5,000	$2,500	M-D-Y	$2,500	M-D-Y		
Venue	$8,000	$4,000	M-D-Y	$4,000	M-D-Y		
Florist	$2,500	$1,250	M-D-Y	$1,250	M-D-Y		
Photographer	$5,000	$2,500	M-D-Y	$2,500	M-D-Y		
Videographer	$3,000	$1,500	M-D-Y	$1,500	M-D-Y		
Baker	$1,200	$600	M-D-Y	$600	M-D-Y		
Entertainment	$2,300	$1,150	M-D-Y	$1,150	M-D-Y		
Transportation	$1,000	$500	M-D-Y	$500	M-D-Y		
Caterer	$6,000	$3,000	M-D-Y	$3,000	M-D-Y		
Rentals	$3,500	$1,750	M-D-Y	$1,750	M-D-Y		
						Over/Under	
Total	$37,500	$18,750		$18,750		$2,500	

Percentages of how much you should spend per item do not hold as much clout as they did in the past. Remember, the key is to consider what is most important to you and your fiancé. Table 3-5 is designed to serve as a guide, to give you a general idea of how much you should spend on each category. It's not going to fit you exactly, so if you don't need an item, allocate that percentage to something important to you. The categories are set up to be very vague so that everything under that category fits within the percentage.

TABLE 3-5 **Budget Percentages**

Item	Percentage of Budget
Wedding planner	10%
Attire: Dress, tuxes	5%
Ceremony: Officiant, flowers, decor, guest book, etc.	10%
Reception: Venue, catering, bar, entertainment, baker, flowers, decor, rentals	60%
Photo & video	15%

Resourcing your connections

Let's talk about who you know. Is there anyone in your life who provides a service that you need for your wedding? Resourcing your connections can help you save money on your budget. If someone provides a service you need (not a product), you may even eliminate the financial obligation if they donate the service to you for your wedding day.

In the next chapter, we'll discuss picking your perfect team. Using your connections can be very valuable in saving money for your wedding. However, sometimes, you get what you pay for. We'll spend time discussing that soon, but for now, if it's an important item on your list, make sure you're using a pro. For an item that isn't as important, this is an area where you can save.

TIP

Once you have determined how much you have to spend, if you find yourself over budget, reach out to people you know and see if there is a resource you could use to save some money. Your friends will hopefully be the most honest resource you have in picking good vendors and saving you some money. Social media is also a great resource to see who your friends have booked for their events or if you have any friends who provide a service you need. Additionally, there are several local forums where other couples post what they're looking for and their budget. If you need to save money in a certain vendor category, resource those forums and ask for referrals.

Regarding flowers and decor, hit up the local buy-sell trade. After a wedding, couples often sell the items they don't need anymore. It's a resource to purchase linens, candles, and table decor. My only caution about this is that you need to make sure it's worth the savings. If all the candles are already almost burned fully, there's no need to purchase those. If the linens are stained and in bad shape, then try renting those through your rental company.

Mostly, be resourceful if you need to save money on your budget. It's easy to fall in love with a vendor online and then find out there's no way you can possibly afford them. I don't want that for you, so determine your budget, figure out what's most important to you, start plugging in those numbers, and then get resourceful!

Setting limits

The biggest budget buster is not setting limits on your guest list and budget. It's important to make sure you have determined how much you can spend so that you avoid scrambling in the end, trying to come up with money you simply don't have.

Your budget is often determined by how many guests you're having at your wedding. Whether you have 50 guests or 200 guests, your budget will have to include everything you need to put on the size of a wedding that you planned. When you tell a vendor you'll have 100 guests and you end up with 150 guests, that will be a big budget buster.

When I'm discussing a guest list with a client, I often say to them, "Can you hand each person on this list $200, and say, I want you to come to my wedding?" It's easy to get caught up in who should and should not be invited. It's a train that you can't stop. You invite one person, then you must invite another person, then another, and another, and all of a sudden, you have 50 people on the invite list who really shouldn't be.

I know, we've all been there and it's easy to fall into this never-ending cycle. Therefore, it's very important to put limits on how many people you invite. The more people you invite, the more budget you'll need. It's just that simple. In a wedding there are variable costs and fixed costs. The variable costs are anything that has to do with goods such as your food, bar, or rentals. If you have more people, you need more food, alcohol, or chairs. A variable cost is a service such as a DJ, photographer, or videographer. Those costs will not change based on how many people you invite.

I always encourage my clients to divide the list between their parents' friends and their friends. It can be frustrating to feel like you need to invite someone because they're friends of the family. You don't really know them but now you must pay for them to come to your wedding. Set those limits early in the planning process. Consider your friends being 50% of the list and then divide the remaining 50% between both sets of parents. Make sure those limits are set and stick to it to avoid additional costs that weren't originally factored into your budget.

Another train easy to get on is the "add-on" train. Here's how this one goes. You met with a vendor; you locked in what you want included and what you don't want included. Then here come the add-ons! "Why yes, we would love an extra floral arrangement that we don't need." "Yes, let's do another signature drink." "Yes, let's add another band member. I just love a good trumpet player." This train will never stop, and you'll add what seems to be a simple thing every time. Before you know it, you have increased your budget by 5% in things you didn't know were important to you. Stick to the plan. After you have everything in place and know that you have additional money in your budget, then add away!

Setting your limits, and sticking to them, will help avoid the dreaded scramble for more money. You have only what is in your budget. It isn't magic money, so stay within what you have, and your planning process will be much more enjoyable.

Buyer beware: Service fees

There is a very important fee you should be aware of. Often, this fee goes unnoticed until the final bill. When you're aware of it, the vendor may have whispered it or maybe said it in the middle of a cough. It's what I call the "Service ++ Fee." Often, you won't know what the "++" is. Is it 5% or 50%? Because we don't know, it's very important to talk with your vendors about it. Each state has different rules and regulations on food and alcohol tax. It's important to find out what yours is in the location where you're hosting your wedding.

WARNING

These fees will sneak up so fast you won't know what hit you. I once had a client who received an initial quote from her caterer with a teeny, tiny line at the very bottom that said, "Service Fees," but that line was empty. Later, when she submitted her final guest count and received her final invoice, the bill went from $25,000 to almost $40,000. I don't know about you, but that's what I call a big difference!

I also had a client who had a friend read a scripture at their wedding. The friend saw a podium sitting over in the corner of the room and pulled the podium over so that she could place her reading in front of her. Well, after the wedding, the client got a final bill with a $250 service fee. When she inquired about this mysterious charge, the ceremony location said it was for the use of the podium. You know, the one that her friend moved over by herself? Now the client had to pay for a podium she didn't even want.

TIP

Service fees are the "catchalls." Often vendors don't know how to categorize something, so they call it a service fee. Be aware of these fees so that you don't get caught off guard and again wind up searching for magic money to appear. When you meet with your vendors, make sure to discuss these mystery fees. Request an *invoice*, not an estimate. An estimate is always changing, but an invoice is locked in.

Tips and gratuities

Tips and gratuities are often forgotten when determining your budget. If you want to tip your amazing team of vendors, don't forget to include them in your total budget. In this section, we'll discuss whom to tip, what to tip, and how to deliver your tips.

Tips are never expected but always appreciated. Most of the people who receive tips on your wedding day are being paid by the hour and tips help offset the costs that occurred for them to be at your wedding. If you feel like a vendor has done an amazing job for you, then give them a tip. If you feel like they have not measured up to your expectations, don't tip them.

Table 3-6 is a cheat sheet to help you figure out how much to tip each vendor. This is only a guide. Anyone you tip will appreciate the additional cash in their pockets, no matter how much you tip.

TABLE 3-6

Vendor Tip Percentages

Item	Percentage of Budget
Wedding planner	10–15% or a nice gift
Caterer	Check to make sure there isn't already a service fee built in; if not, 20% of the staff fee
Photo & video	$100+ per person
DJ	$50–$100 per person
Band	$25+ per band member
Bartender	Check to make sure the tip isn't already included in the bill; if not, 20% of staff fee
Officiant	$100–$300
Ceremony musicians	$25+ per musician
Hair & makeup	$15–20% of service
Transportation	$20 of bill
Deliverers (for example, baker, florist, rental company)	$25+ per person

TIP

Delivering your tips to the appropriate person is a great task for your parents, best man, maid/matron of honor, or wedding planner if you hire one. This is something that you need to prepare before the day of the wedding. Determine your tips per vendor and get out those envelopes. On the envelope, write the name of vendor receiving the tip. Then include the cash and seal the envelope. (Your tips should be cash only.) Make sure to tell the person you've asked to distribute the tips to check in with you first to see if you're happy with the service prior to giving the tips to the vendors. The last thing you want is to distribute the tips and not be happy with the service and have to try and get that cash back.

REMEMBER

Tipping your vendors is a wonderful way to thank them for all their hard work and being a part of your wedding day. You may not believe me when I say this, but there's a chance you'll remember your vendors more than you'll remember some of the guests who attend your wedding. Show them how much you appreciate them. Happy tipping!

2

Taking Care of Logistics

IN THIS PART . . .

Finding the perfect vendors and understanding contracts

Determining if all-inclusive wedding planning is right for you

Picking the perfect venue

Getting the word out to family and friends, including figuring out who to invite

Adding special touches with flowers for the bridal party, ceremony and reception

Chapter **4**

Your Day Is Only as Good as Your Team

Couples run the gamut of wanting to do everything themselves to letting everyone else handle everything about their wedding. Where do you fall on the spectrum? Are you good at letting go? Does that statement alone scare you?

The truth is, you have to trust others when it comes to your wedding. Yes, you can plan your own wedding, but there will come a point when you just need to be the couple getting married. At the very least, you'll have someone officiate your wedding, even if you handle every other detail yourself. But most likely, you'll depend on several vendors to make your day everything you've dreamed of.

I always tell my clients, "Your day is only as good as your team." In this chapter, I help you pick the perfect team for your perfect day. Everyone has different expectations, budgets, and dreams for their wedding. As we discover those together, you'll be able to make the best decision to set everyone up to succeed, and at the end of the day you'll be the rock stars! I also give you some pointers about what to keep in mind when signing contracts with vendors because you want to be sure your interests are protected.

Putting Your Plans in the Hands of Others

Even though you're hiring vendors for a one-day event, you're hiring them for one of the most important days of your life. So you want to make sure you can trust them to carry out your wishes to the best of their abilities. In the following sections, I explain how to make sure you select the best people who will help make your day memorable — in a good way!

Developing the all-important trust factor

When I meet with a new client, the first thing I do is ask them several questions about themselves. How did the two of you meet? How did you get engaged? What do you like to do together? What do you love most about your fiancé? The point in doing this is to build a relationship with them. I want to know as much as I can about them so that I can make good decisions on their behalf. My goal in getting to know my clients is that they will trust me to do my job.

TIP

In order to let go and trust that the vendors you have hired are going to do their job, you need to get to know your vendors. Reach out to them for coffee, lunch, or happy hour. At the end of the day, you'll remember the people who were working for you on the day of the wedding. Although it's hard to imagine, you will most likely remember them more than even the guests who attended your wedding.

Here are some tips for putting trust in your vendors so you can enjoy your wedding day:

>> **Build a relationship with your vendors**. On the day of your event, you should feel as though your vendors are your advocates. No matter how well you planned your wedding, there are so many things that can happen on a wedding day that are out of your control. If you don't know your vendors, it will be harder to let go and enjoy your wedding day.

>> **Trust the vendors you have hired to do their job.** This might be the hardest point to remember, but it's the most important. After all the vendor meetings, phone calls, and planning tasks are over, you must be able to trust that the team you have built is going to do their job. I understand that there could be some bad apples in the bunch, but through the years, I have witnessed other vendors stepping up to the plate to help if another vendor isn't doing what they should be doing. If you have built an amazing team, let them do their job. Situations that occur can be addressed after the event is over.

Remembering that quality is worth the cost

If something is important to you, splurge on that and save in other areas that aren't as important to you. The saying is correct that you do get what you pay for. When choosing where to cut costs, please make certain you're not trying to save money on your list of the top five most important pieces of your big day. If you don't like cake, don't spend a lot of your budget on an elaborate cake that you aren't even going to enjoy. If you want the dance floor packed and your guests entertained, hire an amazing DJ who will keep the party going all night long!

When a client told me she had a friend who was an amazing DJ who was giving her an amazing deal to DJ the reception, I was thrilled for her. My client was on a tight budget and resourcing a friend's services would save money on the overall budget. The ceremony was held at another location so when I arrived at the reception, I met with Mr. DJ Friend. I introduced myself and started going through the reception order. He seemed fine with the schedule of events, almost as if it really didn't matter to him what the schedule was.

Our conversation was going great until I said, "This is when you will announce the bridal party intros." At that moment, Mr. DJ Friend let me know that he does not speak on the microphone. Wait, you aren't going to do announcements? For a moment, I had a minor panic attack. I couldn't comprehend how a DJ didn't feel comfortable speaking. Every DJ I have ever worked with served as the emcee for the event. Why was Mr. DJ Friend different? I immediately went into fix-it mode and thought of all the ways I could convince him that he was actually comfortable with speaking on the microphone, and he was going to be the most amazing emcee anyone has ever seen at a wedding.

No matter how much I tried to convince him, Mr. DJ Friend was not going to speak. So what were my options? Maybe a close friend who was good at entertaining? Maybe the best man? Maybe Grandpa? Honestly, I didn't care as long as the bridal party was introduced, the dinner was called, and the cake cutting was announced. After searching anyone in the room who remotely looked as if they could speak on a microphone, the only option was me.

I am willing to do just about anything that a client needs me to do to make their day perfect. However, speaking in front of total strangers was not part of my Plan A, or even Plan B or C. I knew the couple were about to arrive at the reception, so I quickly met with the wedding party to make sure I was announcing their names correctly. It was bad enough that I had to speak on the microphone, but it would have been worse if I pronounced a name wrong.

The couple arrived at the reception, and I greeted them out front to make sure that they weren't alarmed when they saw me on a microphone introducing the bridal party and the newly married couple for the very first time.

My plan was to look down, focused only on the paper that was shaking in my hand. It was time and I wanted to crawl into a hole. Mr. DJ Friend started the upbeat intro music and I said, "Ladies and Gentlemen, welcome the bridal party!" For a moment, I imagined, I was introducing a basketball team. The fans were screaming, and the lights were flashing. I drew out each person's name much longer than I should have.

The moral of this story is that there are places where you can save money on your wedding day without affecting the overall event. My client resourced her connections and was able to hire someone she knew. However, the quality was less than someone who would have been paid to DJ the event. A DJ who doesn't speak on the microphone is like hiring a photographer who doesn't bring a camera to the event.

In Chapter 3, I ask you to write down your top five most important vendor categories and your five least important vendor categories. This is where I want you to apply the highest quality to your top five. Table 4-1 shows an example based on my top five. Fill in the empty Table 4-2 to include your top five.

TABLE 4-1   **Top Five Most Important Vendor Categories**

Vendors	Why They Are Important to You
Officiant	I want a religious ceremony where the pastor talks about the love that we have for each other and gives us guidance on our life as husband and wife.
Wedding Planner	I want to be able to relax and enjoy my day knowing that everything is going to be taken care of, so I don't have to worry about anything.
Photographer	I want a photographer who will be able to capture candid photos and our love for each other. It's important that they also have a great personality so that we can relax and have a good time during the photos.
Band	I want a band who will play music that my friends and my parents' friends will be able to dance to together all night.
Photobooth	I want a photobooth so that my guests can take a picture home from the event and remember our wedding forever.

Now, fill out Table 4-2 with your Top Five Most Important Vendors from Chapter 3 and why they are important to you and your fiancé.

REMEMBER

Do not budge on the vendor categories that are the most important to you. Those are the categories where quality is the most important. If you stay focused on picking quality vendors in your top five, you'll have an amazing wedding.

TABLE 4-2

Top Five Most Important Vendor Categories

Vendors	Why They Are Important to You

Getting referrals

I cannot stress enough the importance of getting referrals for your big day. When you ask for referrals, you talk to friends and family who have hired the type of vendors you need to hire. You ask them how the vendor handled good and not-so-good situations that came up. Are they able to control your crazy aunt who wants to be in every photo? Can they manage a bridal party of 30 people? Are they able to stay on schedule? How is their personality?

WARNING

Navigating the web and picking a vendor based on whether they have a pretty website can backfire. Most photographers, for example, are going to have beautiful websites. Vendors only put on their websites or social media what they want you to see. That's another reason to ask your network of friends and family for referrals.

Referrals are a valuable tool in picking your vendors because your friends and family can honestly tell you how their experience was with that vendor. Although reviews can be helpful, it's very easy for a vendor to remove a review that they don't want you to see. The best form of information gathering is going straight to someone else who has used them in the past.

If you hire a wedding planner, one of the main benefits is the referrals they can give you based on working with vendors at past weddings. They'll know how the vendor is to work with leading up to your wedding, during the event, and afterward. Wedding planners will be able to tell you actual experiences where they went to a food tasting and the food was wonderful for four people but on the wedding day, the caterer didn't bring the same food that was at the tasting. Wedding planners will know that if a certain photographer promises the images in 4 to 6 weeks, they actually mean 10 to 12 weeks. They'll be able to guide you with your vendor selection, but remember one very important thing. This is *your* wedding, and ultimately you need to be the one who picks your vendors.

My assumption is that, in picking up this book, you're going to try to plan your own wedding. If that is the case, please reach out to your trusted squad for help with gathering important intel on vendors that you need for your big day. I can assure you, they'll give you all the dirt!

Deciding how much outsourcing you're comfortable with

There is no need for you to be a superhero while planning your wedding. When you're choosing your team, think about the parts that you want to do and those you can let go of. If I were to put my house on the market, I wouldn't list it as "For Sale by Owner" because I have no idea how to sell a house. I would hire an agent who knows how to list, market, show, sell, and close on my house. Let's compare that to you. What are you good at when it comes to planning your wedding?

Are you good with flowers and plan on making your own bouquet or floral arrangements? Are you a talented graphic designer and can design all your stationery? Are you a great baker who wants to bake cookies or cupcakes for your guests to take as their favors? What are your talents and abilities when it comes to planning your wedding? Now, some of you may be reading this and saying, "Absolutely nothing." Others may think that you're good at everything you need for the wedding. Let me encourage you to find what you're good at (if anything) and then stop there!

I will never forget when a client of mine thought she was able to handle all her stationery, signage, and personalized items for the wedding. During one of our planning meetings, she sat down and told me all the items she was going to design and produce: the invitation, RSVP card, information card, wedding website, programs, menus, place cards, welcome sign, bar sign, thank-you cards, and personalized notes for each guest.

Well, life sometimes has a way of defining our limits. Although the intentions were good, she was way over her head in paper products. She was late with every print deadline and was extremely stressed and consumed by the task at hand. And for what? Did she save a lot of money? No, she didn't. Did she open her own wedding stationery company? No, she didn't. She was overworked, stressed, and staying up until three in the morning on her wedding day trying to get everything done.

Find your limits and stick to those. There are amazing vendors who can give you everything you want, within budget and with less stress on you. Find what you're comfortable with and let the professionals take care of the rest so that you can enjoy your wedding planning experience.

Researching on social media

When I started my wedding planning business, the only way to find me was in the yellow pages, at a bridal show, or through a referral. We didn't have the social media outlets that we do today. Social media has allowed small businesses to promote and grow their business more than in the past. But there are both good and bad aspects to social media marketing.

When vendors create their social media marketing, they want to paint the picture of perfection and make you feel like you can't possibly get married without them on your team. It's almost as if you're made to feel like you're making a big mistake for not booking them, no matter the price.

But just because these businesses put a spin on their social media posts doesn't mean you should ignore what they have to say. Social media is an amazing outlet to vet vendors, and I believe you should do that. However, I wouldn't judge a book by its cover, meaning don't base your decision on social media alone. (I explain what else to consider later in the section "Selecting the Very Best Vendors."). The bottom line is that all your vendors are human. They make mistakes in their career, and they all have personal lives.

Here are some tips about what to look for and look out for when you research vendors on social media:

>> **How often do they post?** Trust me, I understand that there is a balance between managing your social media posts and taking care of your clients for your vendors. However, if there is a large time gap between social media posts, that vendor may not be working as much anymore. There is probably a reason why they haven't posted in months.

>> **Check the comments**. The comments on social media posts can tell you a lot about a vendor. It can also be a great source for you to get referrals. For example, a past client could post, "You are the best! Our day was perfect thanks to you and your team!" That would be a good indication that they do great work for their clients. The same is true for negative comments. If someone had a bad experience, they'll use these outlets to share with the world.

>> **Following or followers?** It's always a good idea to see how many followers a potential vendor has and how many people they're following. If the number of people they're following is substantially higher than the number of people who are following them, there may be a discrepancy. You want to look for vendors who have a following on their own because people just can't wait for their next post!

>> **Content over quantity.** Take a look at what the vendor is posting. Do you notice a theme to their posts? Be on the lookout for authenticity in content over quantity of posts. Hiring a vendor who posts about real weddings and past clients will give you an idea of their clientele and their relationship with their clients.

MAKING THE BEST OF THE WORST OF MOTHER NATURE

It was a beautiful day. Everything was going just as we had planned for months and months. The setup was complete, the vendors were checking in, the guests were arriving, it was go time. The client was having her dream outdoor wedding. As I went to line up the bridal party for the ceremony, everything was perfect.

Fifteen minutes later, when I opened the door to send the bridal party out to the ceremony, I looked up to see the darkest sky I have ever seen. I immediately pulled out my weather app and there was nothing on the radar. I was confused because all I saw was a dark scary sky that was about to ruin this wedding. The groom, family, and groomsmen had already gone down the aisle. I honestly didn't know what to do. I was about to send out the bridesmaids when I looked at the bride, who was now seeing what I was seeing. Where did this storm come from? No one knew.

We were able to get everyone down the aisle and about ten minutes into the ceremony, it started to drizzle. It was a very light rain that didn't seem to bother anyone, so the ceremony continued. A few seconds later, the bottom fell out, the arch fell over, and all the bridal party and guests ran as fast as they could for cover. My worst nightmare had finally come true. We were all drenched but we able to collect ourselves under cover and proceed with the rest of the ceremony.

The easy thing for me to do is never ever to show anyone those pictures of a fallen arch and a drenched bride standing at the altar. But that was the opposite of what I did. I posted those pictures for the world to see, because sometimes things happen that are out of our control. I also posted them because the beauty was not in the horrible-looking moment. The beauty was in the couple, standing together completely drenched, vowing to each other that they were going to love each other through the good times and bad. Through the storms, they would always choose the other.

Selecting the Very Best Vendors

In this section, I share with you all my secrets for booking your vendors. Remember, this is your day and it's important when you're booking your vendors that they'll be able to fit into your vision. I have spent over two decades walking each of my clients through the vendor selection process. I share with you my tips in each vendor category so that you have the tools to select your perfect team on your own. I created Table 4-3 to give you a timeframe of when you need to book your vendors.

TABLE 4-3

When to Hire Your Vendors

Vendor	When to Hire
Wedding Planner	1–14+ months prior to your wedding
Florist & Decorator	6 months prior to your wedding
Rental Company	6 months prior to your wedding
Photographer	10–12+ months prior to your wedding
Videographer	8–9 months prior to your wedding
Caterer	6–12 months prior to your wedding
Alcohol & Bartender	6 months prior to your wedding
Baker	6–8 months prior to your wedding
Entertainment (DJ & Band)	10–12+ months prior to your wedding
Transportation	8 months prior to your wedding
Hotel Room Blocks	4–8 months prior to your wedding

Wedding planner

As I said earlier, I'm assuming you're reading this book because you want to plan and execute your wedding on your own. Or maybe you want as much information as possible about planning your wedding so that you understand the process. If you aren't hiring a wedding planner, you're likely not going to read this section. But before you go, I want to let you in on a big tip!

TIP

At the very least, have someone serve as your go-to person on your wedding day. Thank you for reading that; now read it again! As someone who cares about your wedding day even though we may never meet, trust me on this one. There are so many moving pieces on the wedding day that I highly recommend you ask one of your detail-oriented friends or maybe a family member to be "the person" all the vendors will go to for any questions. My wish on your wedding day is that you can just be the bride or the groom or the mom or the dad. That is all you need to be on the day of the wedding. Leave the constant questions and running around to someone else.

Okay, now if you aren't going to hire someone to coordinate your wedding then you can skip to the flowers and decor section. Or keep reading so that you know what the responsibilities of that person will be.

First, let me just say, the responsibilities of a wedding planner are not as clear as some of the other vendors that you'll hire. A photographer will take your pictures, we know that or at least we hope they will! But what will a wedding planner do for you? When I meet with a new client, one of the first things I ask is what their expectations of a wedding planner are. I can tell you it's all over the board! I ask this because there is a wide variety of reasons why people hire a wedding planner. There is also a big difference between a wedding planner, a day-of coordinator, and a venue manager. I would love to share with you what makes each of them different!

>> **Full or partial wedding planner:** Wedding planners often have two levels of service that you can book. The difference between the two is the amount of time they work with you prior to the wedding day and how involved they are in helping you select your vendors. Regardless of which package you select, the work they do on the day of your event should not vary. A full-service wedding planner is going to be with you from day one, giving you referrals for your vendors, helping you book them, and keeping you on track with your budget. They will create a timeline for the day and distribute that to your vendors. A partial wedding planner may give you referrals, but you'll be the one communicating with your vendors until the designated start date of your wedding planner's contract. Most partial wedding planners begin their work for you one to two months prior to your wedding. At that point, they'll take over all the logistics and finalize all of the details leading up to your big day.

Regarding the day of the event, both levels should greet all of the vendors upon arrival and make sure they are setting up to your standards and are comfortable with the logistics of the day. A wedding planner should make sure the family and bridal party know where to go and when to be there. They assist with making sure the candles are lit and the ambiance is exactly how you dreamed it to be. They are also the last ones to leave, ensuring that everything is picked up by your vendors based on the venue's rules and that all the personal items are removed from the venue.

>> **Day-of coordinator:** A day-of coordinator will only be involved in the rehearsal if needed and the day of your event. They do not help you with the planning of the wedding. Their job is to take your plan and implement it on the day of the wedding. They should, however, meet with you prior to your wedding to get the schedule of events, offer any logistic suggestions, and communicate with your vendors just prior to the big day to make sure they have all the information they need to succeed. On the day of your wedding, they will greet all your vendors and make sure that they know the plan and set up correctly.

If you hire a day-of coordinator, I highly recommend that there is a main coordinator and an assistant. The coordinators are pulled in so many directions on the day of the wedding that it's important to have someone with them to troubleshoot where needed. They can't be in two places at once, so the assistant is there to run and grab Dad for the photos or make sure the DJ has the right song ready to go for the bridal party entrance while the coordinator stands with the bridal party and makes sure they are in the correct order for their big moment.

WARNING

>> **Venue manager.** If only I had a quarter for all the times I've heard, "The venue has a coordinator, so I don't need your services," I would be a very wealthy woman. If the venue tells you they have an in-house coordinator, it's important that you know for sure what they're going to do for you regarding the planning and execution of the plan. Will they meet with you before the event to get all the details? Are they going to be the person who lines the bridal party up for the ceremony? Will they make sure the timeline is followed for the night? Will they light your candles and make sure the decor is set up to your standards? Will they be the point person for the vendors? A venue manager's main job is to make sure the venue is clean and taken care of, the lights are on, and there are toilet paper and paper towels in the restroom. I think it's wonderful if there's an in-house team, especially if you're doing everything on your own to take over on the day of the wedding. However, make sure the expectations are discussed so that you aren't caught off-guard when they are only there to take care of the venue itself.

Flowers and decor

This might be where you started reading this book because everyone loves all the pretty things! If it is, it's nice to meet you! I have been a florist for over two decades and I am excited to share with you some of my tips and tricks for flowers and decor. This is an area where you can save money or blow the budget! In Chapter 8, we will discuss in detail how you can create a look that would be featured on a blog. In this section, I want us to focus on determining your style, how to save money, and what questions to ask a florist if you choose to book one for your wedding.

Table 4-4 is designed to get you to start thinking about your design style. Feel free to jot in the margins the answers to these questions so that when you do pick your flowers, you can come back and reference your selections.

TABLE 4-4   ## Your Flower and Decor Style

Spring–Summer Flowers	Anemone, sweet pea, tulip, rose, ranunculus, lisianthus, spray rose, peony, lilies, freesia, magnolia
Fall–Winter Flowers	Garden rose, calla lily, mums, delphinium, dahlia, freesia, orchid, alstroemeria, amaryllis, gardenia
Colors	What are your colors? Bridesmaids' dresses, groomsmen suites, table linens
Favorite Flowers	What are your favorite flowers?
Flower No-no's	What are flowers you dislike?
Your Style	Are you modern, classic, romantic, bohemian, country chic, or whimsical?
Size	Do you want small, medium, or large centerpieces?
Inspiration	Start researching flowers and decor online and create an inspiration board. You may be surprised as you continue to save the same style repeatedly. And just like that you found your style!

There are several ways you can save money on your flowers and decor. Let's face it, flowers are expensive and hiring a florist isn't always an option. If you're looking to save some money on your budget, here a few tips on how to save money but also have beautiful flower arrangements on your big day.

>> **DIY:** As a florist, I teach flower classes to those who want to learn how to make centerpieces or bouquets. It's a fun evening filled with information on how to design and build your centerpieces, plus tips and tricks. Research florists in your area who also give classes where you can learn how to make your centerpieces. A few days before your wedding, plan a fun night with your wedding party, friends, and family to enjoy some snacks and beverages and make your own centerpieces together. Buy inexpensive floral containers and at the end of your reception, give away your flowers to someone at the table to take home and enjoy.

>> **Wholesale over retail:** Buying wholesale flowers in your area can save you about 40 to 60 percent off retail floral costs. Research your area first to find a wholesale florist who sells to the public. If you don't have anyone in your area, there are several online resources that will ship you your flowers. Always place your order at least two weeks before the arrival date and schedule the pickup or delivery for two days prior to your event.

>> **Candles are your new best friend:** Candles can transform a table center-piece! Fill your tables with a lot of candles and you'll be in awe of how amazing your reception looks. They can be purchased online in bulk cost-effectively. If your venue doesn't allow real candles, LED candles can still do the trick and then you can sell them after your wedding is over.

>> **Reuse and repurpose:** If you have a large bridal party, consider reusing their bouquets as centerpieces on the tables. To do this successfully, whenever the bridesmaids are not using their bouquets, place them back into their water containers. This will allow the flowers to remain alive and fresh through the entire day and make it to your reception tables. If you're using flowers at the church, arrange for someone to transport them to your reception as well. Those are great accents for the check-in table, the bar, or flanking the cake table.

Hiring a florist can be a daunting task, and there are many options to choose from. I will help you navigate them so you pick the perfect person for the job! If you don't have a green thumb or you need to save money, a florist can help turn your vision into reality. One of my favorite moments on a client's wedding day is when I get to reveal to them the flowers and decor. It's the moment their dreams become a reality and they see the whole picture.

When I first started designing flowers for my clients, I'd pull out books and books of flower samples. The problem is that if you don't have a sense of floral design — which most people don't — it's hard to visualize exactly what you're going to get. You may see a bouquet that you like but it isn't the right color or the exact flowers that you like. Today we have many online resources for you to explore. The main thing I want you to focus on is what keeps coming up over and over again that you like. With those images, a florist will be able to make suggestions based on your style and budget to fit your vision.

TIP

There's no reason to research florists who can't deliver to your wedding location, so explore florists in the area where you're getting married. Look at their past work and see if there is a certain style that they do all the time or if you see a variety of styles. Read their reviews to see past client experiences. Set up an appointment with the ones you like to discuss your wedding vision. Prepare for this meeting with your style choices from Table 4-4. You'll also want to know how many bouquets, boutonnieres, corsages, and centerpieces you're going to need. (We discuss who gets those in Chapter 8.) The best way to estimate how many tables you'll need is to plan one arrangement per ten guests. If you have 100 guests, you'll need ten table centerpieces. Here are some questions to ask potential florists during those meetings:

>> **Do you have the date available?** First and foremost, are they available? When you set up a meeting, check this first with all your vendors. There is no need to meet with a vendor who is not available for your wedding day.

» **How many weddings do you do a day?** It's very possible for a vendor such as a florist or a caterer to manage multiple events on a single day. I wouldn't let this bother you if they have a team who can manage all the moving parts. Chances are your setup and another customer's setup will be close to the same timeframe so they can't be in two places at once and will need to have a staff who can manage the delivery and setup within your designated time-frame.

» **How long have you been a florist?** I understand that everyone had to start somewhere to end up where they are now. I have a confession for you, friend. When I first started in the floral business, I would meet with a client, and I had no idea what I was doing. I'd watch videos online to figure out how to make what the client wanted. Experience is a good thing in the floral industry! An experienced florist will know when to order and prep the flowers, how many to order so you aren't buying more than you need, and offer suggestions of flower substitutes that will fit your vision and budget.

» **Are there additional fees for a sample arrangement?** Sometimes it's hard to completely visualize what your floral arrangement will look like. Florists often offer a sample arrangement, but it will be at a higher price because flowers arrive in bunches. Your arrangement might call for 5 of a certain type of flower, but the florist must order 12 to make your sample.

» **How close to the wedding can we change our order?** This is very important to find out and when you do, mark the date on your calendar! Flowers must be preordered, so it's important that all your final changes are given to your florist before their order cutoff date to ensure that you'll have the flowers you ordered.

» **Are there any flowers we can substitute to maximize our budget?** If you love peonies but you don't have the budget, there are flowers that can be substituted to give you the same visual feel at a fraction of the cost. Splurge on your bouquet and substitute where you can on the guest centerpieces.

Rentals

Rental items are often confused with your decor items. Decor items are candles, arches, custom signs, lighting, draping, and so on. Rental items are tables, chairs, china, linens, glassware, dance floors, stages, lounge furniture, tents, and the like. Booking your rental company needs will be determined by the venue you book. If you book a venue that is a blank slate, then you'll need to bring in all your rental items, such as table and chairs. If you book a venue that already has tables and chairs, then you won't need as many rental items.

REMEMBER

When researching rental companies, it's very important to check in with your venue on their policies. Some venues allow only certain rental companies to work at their venue, for many reasons. It's also important to confirm the load-in and load-out times with your venue. If you rent a venue for 12 hours, you must confirm whether, within those hours, that includes the rental companies' setup and tear-down. If the venue is flexible on the delivery and pickup of rental items, then this is a way you can save a little money on your delivery fees. For example, for a Saturday wedding, if a rental company can deliver on Thursday or Friday and pick up on Monday, this will save you money because if they must deliver and pick up on the same day the rental company will charge a "same day" fee.

Most rental companies have the same or similar inventory and pricing. As you determine your flowers and decor, schedule a time to go to the rental company's showroom to see the items in person. If possible, resource all your rental item needs from one company. This will save you a lot of money on delivery and pickup fees, damage deposits, and labor. If you need a tent, find a company that can provide both the tent and the tables and chairs rather than using two separate companies.

If you're a visual person, reach out to your venue for a digital copy of their venue floor plan. When you have your final selections and you know your final guest count, send that floor plan to your rental company sales representative, who can upload the floor plan into their system and put your rental items into a digital floor plan for you to see prior to your big day. This floor plan will allow you to number your guest tables if you want to assign seats to your guests. (In Chapter 7, I help you set up your table assignments and place cards.) Having a floor plan will make this process simpler to manage.

Figure 4-1 shows a sample floor plan. When designing your floor plan, it's important to note the guest tables, cake table, head table (if you have one), DJ or band location setup, dance floor, bar, and check-in/gift table. You'll add this into your event details document that you'll send to all your vendors so they'll know where to set up. This will eliminate a lot of questions from them on the day of your wedding so that you can just sit back and enjoy the day.

TIP

Your rental company will charge an additional fee to set up and tear down all your rental items. If your budget allows, pay them to set up and tear down the tables and chairs so that your family and friends don't have to do that. It's a minimal cost with maximum benefit! Additionally, ask your wedding planner, caterer, or friends to put linens on the table, and set the napkins, china, silverware, and glassware. A fully set table makes a big difference for your guest experience and your photos.

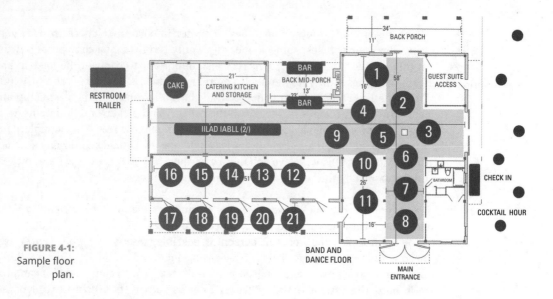

FIGURE 4-1:
Sample floor plan.

Finally, check in with your caterer to see if they need additional items from your rental company such as trash cans, catering equipment, chafing dishes, serving platters, serving utensils, drink dispensers, trays, and tray jacks. Catering companies often have those supplies, but it's not a guarantee. Confirm with them prior to finalizing your rental order to ensure a smooth wedding day!

Photography

At the end of the wedding day, what will you have to remember your day? Earlier, I explain the importance of stopping to take mental pictures of the day so you'll remember it. Memories may fade, but your photos will last a lifetime! In a time of high technology, there are so many photography options that it can be overwhelming, so I'm here to help you filter out the weeds and pick the perfect person.

When there isn't a wedding planner, often the photographer steps into the role of planning the day's schedule and keeping everyone on track on the day of the wedding. They are great with scheduling based on their understanding of how the day should flow and how long it will take to capture all your pictures. Whether or not you have a wedding planner, it's important to hire a photographer who can manage the bridal party and family during the photos. As discussed earlier, a wedding planner or coordinator is often pulled in a million directions, so an organized, assertive (but not rude) photographer will make a big difference in the overall flow of the day.

Nowadays it seems like anyone and everyone can be a photographer. Technology has advanced so much that you may believe you can just put a nice camera in someone's hand and voilà, they're a photographer! Let me share a little information as your friend. If the budget allows, hire a professional photographer to capture all your special moments. I understand that this will be a big expense, but someone who understands lighting, has an eye for imagery, and can work miracles in postproduction will be worth the expense. If your budget doesn't allow you to hire a professional photographer, reach out to universities in your area and hire a student photographer. They are studying to perfect their art and would most likely love to build their portfolio.

When you research a photographer online, pay attention to both the mood and the location of the photos on their website:

>> **Mood:** Do you prefer a darker appearance or a bright and airy look in your photos? You'll notice a theme to their photos, and if you don't like the overall look, they may not be the photographer for you.

>> **Location:** This is key in picking a photographer. Are all their photos outside on a perfectly sunny day? What if your wedding is inside? Can they photograph inside or adjust that perfect sunny day feeling to your day, which may be overcast and rainy? I know it won't be, but what if it is?

TIP

Once you find a photographer online you like, it's very important to meet with them in person. With some vendors, there's no need to meet before you book them, but it's very important to schedule a meeting with the photographer so you can get a sense of their personality. If you don't like their personality it will be very hard to "fake it" in your photos. I want you to like them so that when there is a camera in your face, you'll feel comfortable and able to enjoy your experience. I can assure you that if you're uncomfortable in anyway, your photos will capture it. Additionally, we want to book an assertive but not rude photographer. It's important for them to be able to manage everyone in your bridal party but not yell at them. Trust me, I have seen this happen often.

When you meet with a potential photographer, here are some things to discuss to determine if they are a good fit for you:

>> **Availability:** Some photographers have multiple people who photograph under their company name. It's important to meet with the person who is actually photographing your wedding day. Ask them how many weddings they do in a day.

>> **Experience:** There are several questions to consider when determining their experience. Ask them how long they have been photographing weddings. Have they photographed both large and small bridal parties? Have they photographed a wedding at your venue? Can they send you the full portfolio of a past client's wedding?

» **Style:** Every photographer has a style preference. We want to make sure it aligns with yours. Ask them if they photograph both inside and outside. Do they use film or just digital? Do they have a particular style that they prefer? Do they shoot candid photos or structured portrait shots?

» **Pricing and delivery:** It's important to know what you're getting for the price. If you don't fit into one of their packages, can they adjust for your needs? Does the package include an engagement session or rehearsal dinner coverage? How many hours are included? Will you have the rights to your images? How are the images delivered to you? How long will it take to receive your images?

TIP

Cut down the hours you book a photographer or videographer by having them arrive one hour before you're dressed and ready to go. No one wants to be photographed or videoed without makeup on. Having them arrive at this time will still allow for them to capture the "getting ready" photos and avoid standing around repeatedly taking the same photos of your bridal party getting ready. This will also allow them enough time to get pictures of your tables, flowers, and decor because those pieces will be ready to go closer to the time that you're supposed to be ready to go.

TIP

Even if you don't need an engagement session, book one with your photographer. Often, they're already included. The reason to do this is to get a sense of how your photographer is behind the camera. What is their personality like? How do they get you to show your own personality in front of the camera? It's a wonderful ice breaker that will only benefit you on the day of your wedding.

WARNING

One very important detail to make sure you clearly understand is if you have the rights to your photos. This means that you can reprint the photos or turn them into an album without the photographer's watermark. Most photographers do offer albums that can be purchased after your wedding. If your budget doesn't allow for that, you want to make sure you have the rights to be able to make your own album after the wedding. It also means you can post on social media outlets. When you post on social media, are you required to tag or credit the photographer? Make sure you understand the photographer's social media rules.

Videography

Pictures do last a lifetime, but your video will capture the emotions, moments, and words that a photo can't capture. A lot of clients through the years save booking a videographer as one of the last things they arrange, and only if they have the money for it in the end. A lot of my clients have also said that not booking a videographer was their greatest regret.

THE FIRST LOOK

The *first look* is a moment shared between the couple prior to the guests' arrival and before the ceremony. The purpose of the first look is to be able to capture all your photos before the ceremony begins so that after the ceremony, you can get to the reception quickly.

Photographers often encourage a first look rather than upholding the tradition of not seeing each other before the wedding. There are several reasons for this. If you're getting married in the late fall or winter, the sun sets earlier and after the ceremony may not allow for enough time to capture those beautiful sunset couple photos. Another reason is that if all the photos are done before the wedding, then there's no need to run around trying to find family members who should be in a photo after the wedding. Finally, if you must hire a photographer for a shorter timeframe, then a first look is encouraged so that the reception can start immediately following the ceremony.

Yes, there are a lot of good reasons to do a first look. But as your friend, I want you to know that if you do not want to see each other before the wedding, please don't do a first look. Although first look moments can be special, you won't have that one moment of seeing each other for the first time when you're walking down the aisle. If you determine that is important to you, stand your ground. There are ways that you can wait and take pictures after the wedding without taking a long time and having your guests wait around at the reception. One suggestion is taking as many of the individual photos as possible before the ceremony and leaving the combined family, bridal party, and couple photos until after the ceremony.

When I speak with a client years after their wedding day, they always tell me that they pull out their wedding video every anniversary and watch their highlight video rather than pulling out their pictures. There is something about seeing the video on a screen that takes you back to that moment every single year.

A photographer and videographer will work together on the day of your wedding almost as if they have choreographed their movements. The same rules are true for your video team regarding personality, because if you can't fake not liking the person in a photo you surely won't be able to do it in a video. It's important to make sure that you like the person behind the camera so that you feel comfortable.

I understand that some items we discuss are just not going to be in the budget, and that's okay. If you can't hire a videographer, I encourage you to assign one person you know to videoing the ceremony and big moments of the reception. You'll thank me later that you have at least those moments on video.

If you can hire a videographer, please research their work online. There are several different approaches to how a videographer edits the highlight video, which is a four- to six-minute video of the day from start to finish. The entire ceremony or speeches are not included in this video. Typically, there is a voiceover, such as the officiant's message or your vows or maybe the best man's speech.

TIP

When you book a videographer, it's important to book them for as long as you booked the photographer. Make sure they will produce a highlight video and give you all the raw footage. This is a copy of every moment they captured during the day. It won't be edited but should at minimum include getting ready footage, the ceremony, and reception moments such as the entrance of the bridal party, cake cutting, toasts, and special dances.

Catering

What's for dinner? First, think about what you like to eat. When you go on a date, what do you typically order? None of your guests will remember what they had to eat; they'll only remember is if it was good or not. In Chapter 14, I cover every option in selecting the perfect dinner menu based on your answer above, but in this section I want to hit the highlights of picking a good caterer and what their responsibilities will be on the wedding day.

Regardless of whether you're hiring a local restaurant or a catering company, make sure they're licensed and insured. They last thing you want is for a guest to get sick at your event because the food wasn't properly prepared. Yes, if you need to save on your budget, a potluck is always an option, but I've never been to a potluck yet and not left with an upset tummy.

The most expensive option will be a catering company — a company that specializes in custom dinner menus and brings the staff to set up, maintain the food, and tear it down. The least expensive option will be a food truck or your favorite local restaurant. For both options, it's very important that you discuss their responsibilities beyond making the food and setting it up. A caterer's job responsibilities should include delivery of the food, setting up the food, filling the water glasses if they are preset on the tables, setting the china and silverware if you want them on the table, restocking the food if it's set up as a buffet or stations, tearing down the food, and clearing the tables.

TIP

One of my client's favorite parts of the planning process is the food tasting. I mean, who doesn't love to try food? Prior to setting up a food tasting, get a copy of the caterer's food selections. Send your favorites to the caterer and have them send you an estimate based on your selections and your guest count. Make sure the estimate is within your budget before you set up a food tasting. Confirm how many guests you can have at the tasting and if there is a fee to do a tasting. Often, a caterer will charge a fee to cover their food costs and then if you book them, they'll take that fee off your final bill. Once those items are complete, its time to try some yummy food!

A food tasting with a caterer is a perfect time to try your menu selections and adjust the menu. It's also the perfect time to discuss vegetarian options or dietary restriction options. During the tasting, remember this: "Your guests won't remember what they had; they will only remember if it's good." Have fun picking out good food and don't sweat having to have the best cut of beef. There are many delicious options that won't break your budget! Stick with those and you'll have an amazing menu selection and happy guests in no time.

Bar and bartending

Deciding if you want to serve alcohol at your wedding may be either the easiest decision or the hardest decision you make. Do you want a cash bar where your guests pay for their drinks or a host bar where you pay for their drinks? Do you want to offer just beer and wine or have a full bar with liquor and mixers? If you decide to serve alcohol at your wedding, you'll find everything you need to know in Chapter 14. In this section, I want us to focus on what you're serving and the importance of hiring a bartender.

I can tell you a million and one stories about guests who have had too much to drink. I could write a book on just that subject! When guests are given free alcohol, the outcome is usually the same. When you offer liquor, the odds increase that someone will have too much to drink. The best chance of controlling those odds is hiring a bartender for your wedding reception.

WARNING

You might be thinking right now that you're just going to have a backyard party and put your drinks in a cooler or container for all to enjoy. As simple as that sounds, you could find yourself with a big problem. Who is responsible if someone leaves your backyard party and gets in a serious accident? You are.

A bartender or bartending service holds the liability of how much a guest is served at your wedding. It is their responsibility to cut someone off if they have had too much. Even if you don't think it will happen to you, having a licensed and insured bartender serve your alcohol can eliminate a lot of stress and headache for the big day.

Not only do they hold the liability insurance, but they can also supply the alcohol or serve the alcohol you provide. They'll take care of making sure it's iced properly and ready to go. Bartenders can also provide the cups, napkins, drink dispensers, mixers, ice, and other supplies needed to keep your bar flowing all night long.

Some venues offer in-house bartending and alcohol, while others allow you to bring in the alcohol and bartender. Think through what type of alcohol you will serve at your wedding. Beer and wine are the most popular, but often clients want a signature drink or a full bar with liquor. Which do you prefer? Do you want to offer a signature drink? This is a specialty drink often named after the couple that includes some form of liquor. If you're struggling about whether to offer liquor, adding a signature drink could be a good solution. Either way, hiring a bartender can ensure a safe and enjoyable evening for all.

Baker

A baker is the person making your cake or desserts — your sweet tooth's new best friend! Cakes come in all shapes and sizes. Do you want buttercream or fondant? Fondant is that gummy-textured coating on the outside of the cake that gives the smooth finish. Do you want fresh flowers or artificial flowers? Do you want a large cake or a small cake with additional desserts? In Chapter 14 we will discuss all the options for the bride's cake, groom's cake, and other desserts. In this section, I'm going to share some tips on booking your baker and trying some cake!

Some of my clients save money by having a friend make their cake. One of my brides told me that a lady from her church had made her birthday cake ever since she was a baby, so of course she wanted her to make the wedding cake. If that works for you, then I say do it! However, if you're excited about having an elaborate cake to display at your wedding, then I suggest hiring a professional baker to bring your dreams to reality.

Research bakers local to where you're having your reception and set up some tastings. Make sure to confirm how many people you can bring because, let's face it, everyone wants to attend the cake tasting! Even though it's an exciting part of the planning process, this is a fun thing to do with just your fiancé. See if you can schedule your food tasting and your cake tasting on the same day and make it a date! Even better, if they don't charge for the tasting, you've just saved some money, and you had a date together. Win-win!

When you set up the tasting, ask your potential baker a few questions. First, bring inspiration photos with you and compare them to their portfolio. Ask them if they have done a cake design like yours before. Sample the different flavors they offer. Do they do specialty cake flavors, or standard cake flavors such as vanilla or chocolate with specialty fillings? How big a cake do you need, based on your guest list size? Do they include a cake stand or do you need to rent one from your rental company? If you pick real flowers over artificial flowers, do they put them on the cake, or do you need your florist to do that? What time will they deliver the cake? If your reception is outside in the middle of summer, they may suggest putting the cake inside until it's time to cut the cake, so it doesn't melt.

TIP

Are you going to follow the tradition of keeping the top tier of your cake to enjoy on your first anniversary? If so, don't factor that portion into the size of servings. The baker should leave a small box for your cake topper, and there are steps you can take to preserve it so it doesn't spoil. After your wedding, remove any flowers or decorations that were placed on your cake and put the cake in the freezer for a few hours so it hardens. This will allow you to wrap the cake without messing up the frosting. Then wrap the cake in multiple layers of plastic wrap. When you think you've wrapped it enough, wrap it some more! Next, place the cake back in the cake box. Wrap that box, then wrap it some more! On your first anniversary, remove the wrapping from the cake and allow it to thaw on the counter. It will be nearly as delicious and fresh as it was on your wedding day. Enjoy!

Entertainment

Now it's time to set the tone for your ceremony and reception! Music has a way of bringing life to any event and a wedding is no exception. If you're looking to save money, you can create an amazing playlist for your ceremony, cocktail hour, dinner music, and dance music. I discuss specific music selections in Chapter 15, but in this section I share some tips on booking the best entertainment for your big day that your budget allows!

Let's start with a DJ. Hiring a professional DJ company can take care of all your music needs. They are a one-stop shop when it comes to providing the audio for your ceremony, cocktail hour, and reception. The audio covers the microphones, speakers, and mixers needed to amplify the officiant and/or the couple during the ceremony and the maid of honor and best man during their speeches. We want them to be heard, and a DJ can take care of all of that for you. They can also provide all the music for the event. You pick your songs, and they play them. Finally, they serve as your emcee — the person who makes announcements and ensures everyone knows what's happening next and how they're going to get there.

The most traditional form of music at a wedding is a string trio or string quartet. There is nothing more romantic than live musicians playing during the prelude music and ceremony. If you hire live string musicians, you do not need to provide amplification or a sound system. However, a DJ can still provide the audio equipment during the ceremony, such as a speaker and microphone for the officiant. If you do want to amplify the musicians, they can provide those microphones as well.

A special touch that you can add to the ceremony is to ask a friend to sing a special song. Depending on whether they're performing with a musician or are using recorded music, a DJ can help to ensure that all the performers can be heard. If you're getting married in a building with a built-in sound system, the sound technician can provide everything you need through the venue's in-house equipment. Make sure to set up a meeting with the person running the sound for the wedding so that your vows, special music, and officiant can be heard.

For your reception, a DJ is a cost-effective way to get the party started and keep your guests on the dance floor. However, if the budget allows, hiring a band will amplify the guest experience. Live bands come in all shapes and sizes, based on your budget. They also come in every genre, including Top 40, retro, '80s covers, Motown, and so much more! It's fun to explore the options based on your favorite music. Pick a band that is going to be able to play songs that both your friends and your parents' friends will dance to. Who doesn't love to see Grandma on the dance floor cutting a rug! Everyone will be on the dance floor all night long if they know the classic hits that span multiple generations.

Once you decide on your entertainment for the reception, have fun picking your songs! If you book a DJ, they can play any song you like. If you book a band, reach out to the band leader for a copy of the songs they play. For either option, you'll need to pick the music for any of the following activities you've chosen to include: an entrance to the reception song, first dance song, father-daughter dance, mother-son dance, cake cutting, bouquet toss, garter toss, and last song. These are what we call specialty song selections.

TIP

Regarding the rest of the songs that will be played during dinner or dancing, give the DJ a list of your favorites so they can see the types of songs you like. If you pick a band, star some of your favorites from their playlist and send that to them so they can see the types of songs you like. Most importantly, please inform both the DJ and the band of the songs you do not like. The last thing you want is to have a song played at your wedding that brings back bad memories or one that you just can't stand to listen to. And remember to have fun picking your songs. You're setting the mood for your night and everything you do reflects the two of you as a couple. Let loose and show some personality with your song selections!

Transportation

Providing transportation for your wedding can be tricky to figure out because, just like the vehicles themselves, there are a lot of moving pieces. How many people need to be transported? How long do you need vehicles? What style of vehicle do you want? In this section we'll work through booking your wedding transportation to ensure everyone is safe and is where they need to be at the right time.

Let's start with some general tips in booking your guest transportation. First, providing transportation for your wedding guests is a luxury, not a requirement. If the budget allows, guests appreciate being picked up and dropped off at the end of the night. However, rideshare options are always available for your guests if the budget does not allow you to offer this luxury.

Transportation companies charge by the hour, with a minimum number of hours. This means they'll charge you by the hour for the vehicle, and larger vehicles often require a minimum of four to five hours of use. The clock starts when the vehicle leaves the garage, not when it arrives at the pickup location. This is very important when budgeting because you if you want a vehicle from 5 pm to 10 pm, that is actually 4 pm to 11 pm by the time you factor the time in transit. Another tip is to have your guests picked up and dropped off at one location. Let's say you book two hotel rooms for your guests; you can designate one of them as the main pickup and drop-off location, which will eliminate confusion on pickup times and locations.

TIP

How do you determine how many guests need to be picked up? If you're doing an RSVP card, have the guests RSVP for the transportation as well, clearly stating the location where they will be picked up and the time. Because they'll be returning this card to you, also include the details on an information card with the invitation.

Table 4-5 shows is an example you can follow to ensure you have enough transportation for your guests. Plug in your own numbers to make sure you have accounted for enough time and space. This example is based on transporting 100 guests from a hotel to the wedding, 20 minutes away and held at the same location as the reception, with a start time of 4 pm and an end time of 10 pm. For this example, you would need to book two shuttles for 11 hours each. If each shuttle is $140 per hour, the total bill plus 20% gratuity would be $3,696.

Transporting your bridal party is a fun way to keep everyone together and on time. When considering booking transportation for your bridal party, you must factor when you can arrive at the venue and where everyone is getting ready. If you have access to the venue the morning of your wedding and will be getting ready there, reach out to family and friends and ask them to transport your bridal party to the venue in the morning and get ready there. If you're not allowed into the venue until later in the day, consider transporting your bridal party to the venue in a stretch limo or party bus after you're all ready to go. If that isn't in your budget, rideshare is an acceptable option.

You've worried about how everyone else will arrive and depart the venue, but what about you? For the couple there are several things to consider as well. Do you need transportation to the church or from the church to the reception? If you can catch a ride with the bridal party, that will save you money. However, there are plenty of situations where you may need a ride to the venue, and limos are a great solution. Booking a vehicle for the couple to leave at the end of the night is always a special touch. Consider a limo or a vintage car to transport you from the reception to where you're staying on your wedding night. Splurge on this and leave in style! You'll have amazing pictures and the two of you will finally have a few minutes to yourself to begin your new life together!

TABLE 4-5 ## Guest Transportation Example

Pick up	2:00 pm	Shuttle A: Pick up 25 guests.
	2:00 pm	Shuttle B: Pick up 25 guests.
Drop off	2:20 pm	Shuttle A: Drop off 25 guests.
	2:20 pm	Shuttle B: Drop off 25 guests.
Return	2:30 pm	Both shuttles return to hotel.
Pick up	3:00 pm	Shuttle A: Pick up 25 guests.
	3:00 pm	Shuttle B: Pick up 25 guests.
Drop off	3:30 pm	Shuttle A: Drop off 25 guests.
	3:30 pm	Shuttle B: Drop off 25 guests.
Stay	4:00 pm	Both shuttles stay to return guests as needed throughout the night.
Pick up	10:00 pm	Shuttle A: Pick up 25 guests.
	10:00 pm	Shuttle B: Pick up 25 guests.
Drop off	10:20 pm	Shuttle A: Drop off 25 guests.
	10:20 pm	Shuttle B: Drop off 25 guests.
Return	10:30 pm	Both shuttles return to hotel.
Pick up	11:00 pm	Shuttle A: Pick up 25 guests.
	11:00 pm	Shuttle B: Pick up 25 guests.
Drop off	11:30 pm	Shuttle A: Drop off 25 guests.

Hotel room blocks

If you're inviting out-of-town guests or planning a destination wedding, it's always a kind gesture to offer hotel rooms for your guests. Although it isn't a requirement, it is appreciated so that your guests can stay in the same location at a discounted rate.

There are a few important tips on how to book your hotel room blocks. First, where do you start? I suggest finding a hotel no more than 20 minutes from the venue. When you find a handful of hotels, reach out to the group sales department at the hotel. They'll collect the dates that you need rooms and for approximately how many people. I understand that you may not know the number of guests until your invitations go out and your RSVPs are returned, but in the meantime, look over your guest list and count how many people are from out of town. If 100 people are from out of town, for example, you'll need about 50 rooms. The sales representative will give you a room rate at that time. Once you have researched several hotels and confirmed availability, rate, and location, then you'll have the information you need to book the perfect hotel. Make sure to book a variation of king- and queen-size rooms.

WARNING

The next step is booking the hotel rooms. There are two ways to do this. The first is what's called a *complementary hotel room block*, where the hotel gives you a certain number of rooms, such as ten, at a time. When those rooms are filled, they will give you more rooms. You are not responsible for any rooms that your guests do not book. I highly recommend going this route. The other option what's called *attrition*. This means that the hotel will give you a certain number of rooms and you are responsible for a certain percentage of those rooms. For example, if the hotel gives you 20 rooms, you'll have to book 16 of those rooms. If you only book eight rooms, then you'll be financially responsible for eight of those rooms. I do not recommend this route because of the financial risk.

Once you have your hotel in place, the sales representative will send you a contract, and when you return that they'll send you an online booking link for your guests to use when booking their hotel. This information can be included on your wedding website or information card with your invitations. Check in with your hotel contact once a week to see how many rooms have been booked. That way you can keep track of when you need to make more rooms available for your guests.

Welcome bags for your guests

There's nothing better than attending an out-of-town wedding, checking into the hotel, and receiving a special gift from the couple. Welcome bags are a perfect opportunity for you to give your guests a little insight into your relationship and the things you love. In this section we'll discuss some welcome bag options and some tips on how to get those special gifts to your guests.

>> **Location:** When creating your welcome bags, start with the location. Find special items that are staples in the area where your wedding is located. For example, a wedding held in Nashville, Tennessee, might include miniature bottles of Tennessee whiskey, Moon Pies, Goo Goo Clusters, biscuit batter, or bottles of sweet tea.

>> **Information:** Include an information card showing the schedule for the weekend and the location of the ceremony and reception. If you're providing shuttles, include the pickup times and locations as well. Also include some popular hot spots near the hotel for your guests to explore. They'll appreciate your ideas on places they need to see while in town.

>> **Savory, sweet, and practical:** I always include items that are savory and sweet, such as pretzels, popcorn, and chocolate. You never know what the cravings may be, so it's nice to include both types of snack options. On the practical side, items such as mints, hand sanitizer, and tissues are also appreciated.

>> **Thank you:** Include a general note or custom notes to your guests, thanking them for traveling to town for your special day. Let them know how you can't wait to celebrate with them and appreciate them taking time out of their busy schedule to be with you. It will make them feel so special that you took the time to thank them.

TIP

You spent all that time on these amazing welcome bags, but how do you get them to your guests? There are two ways to distribute your welcome bags at the hotel. If you want them in the rooms of your guests, the hotel can take care of this, but they will charge you a fee to do this. To avoid an additional fee, I suggest leaving the bags at the front desk, and the hotel representative can give your guests their welcome bag when they check in. Work on this project together as a couple and enjoy coming up with fun ways to welcome your guests to town.

Marriage Isn't the Only Bond You're Entering Into: Contracts

You have picked the perfect team and now it's time to make it official. In this section, we'll discuss the importance of understanding what you're signing, including all the details, the difference between deposits and retainers, and making sure that you read the fine print. I know contracts can be scary, but they're an important piece of your big day and are in place to protect both parties. Now, let's take a deep breath and work through this process together.

Understanding what you're signing

You found the perfect vendor and have reached the moment that things get serious, when they pull out the contract for you to sign. It appears time slows down; your hands start to sweat, and you wonder if you made the right decision. This is a normal reaction because you are investing in something big. If you have ever purchased anything big in life, it comes with a contract. Why is that? It's because it's a big deal, and planning a wedding is a big deal.

When you sign a contract with a vendor, you are both entering into the contract in good faith. That means they have every intention of fulfilling the contract and you have every intention of paying. When you get married, you will sign a contract with your spouse, the marriage certificate. Yes, that can be broken and so can the contract with your vendors, but only if someone didn't do what the terms of the contract stated.

WARNING

I cannot stress enough how important it is to know what you're signing. Do not skip over this part. When you sign a contract with a vendor, make sure they explain everything in the contract and that you understand it clearly. If the contract states, "If the Client (you) needs to cancel the event, all deposits and retainers are non-refundable," be certain that you're comfortable with losing your deposit or retainer.

If there is something in the contract that you do not understand, please make sure to ask the vendor to clarify. Making assumptions that you know what a vendor means does not always end well. It's important to actually read the contract and make sure you completely understand the terms before you sign the contract with the vendor.

Contracts aren't created to fit every client, so as you read through the contract, if there is something that you want to revise or amend, reach out to that vendor and see if they are willing to rewrite a certain part. Often there are slight modifications that will appease both parties, but be prepared if a vendor does not want to change something in their contract. Those items are there for a reason because at some point in their career, a past client did something that made them decide that they need to write that into their contract to protect their business. Having an open communication with a vendor about aspects of their contract that don't sit well with you will go a long way.

WARNING

I am not a lawyer, so I can't give you legal advice. My advice to you is based on my experience of negotiating and signing my clients' vendor contracts through the years. If you have a legal question that can't be answered by the vendor, I suggest reaching out to a lawyer who can advise you legally on any contract questions that you may have.

Don't forget all the details

The details are so important when you sign a contract with a vendor. Without the details, you can't understand what you're signing, as we discussed above. In this section we'll talk through the details that must be included in the contract and how to navigate the details that you don't know when you sign a contract with a vendor.

First, the contract must include the date and times, if applicable. For example, let's say you're hiring a string quartet to play the prelude music for your ceremony and to play during your ceremony. If your ceremony begins at 4 pm, the contracted time would be from 3:30 pm to 4:30 pm. If the venue allows you access to their property for 12 hours, then you will state the date and 10 am–10 pm. In situations where you don't yet know the exact times at the contract signing, include the date and an approximate timeframe, and then when you have those figured out, include that in the contract.

REMEMBER

Make sure the services provided are clearly stated in the contract or in an addendum. This is a written document included with the contract. For example, if you hire a caterer, make sure the menu and invoice are included with the contract. If the services provided sections are left very generic — like "Catering for Wedding Reception" — then what happens if you ordered beef as the main entrée, and the caterer brings chicken? It's important to get as many details as possible into the contract before you sign.

Include all the names of the parties who are entering the contract. Make sure that the actual name of the vendor, not just the company name, is included in the contract, along with their phone number, email address, and mailing address. If your parents are paying for the wedding, make sure that they are the ones who sign the contract. If you're paying for the wedding, then you will sign the contract.

The contract should include a breakdown of the payment plan. That plan should include the total price of the service, payment amounts, and the date the payments are due if multiple payments are offered. Pay close attention to whether any of those payments are nonrefundable. If there is a payment that is based on your final guest count, make sure that payment is notated as an adjustable rate and includes the date by which the final guest count must be received.

No one likes to think about the bad stuff when planning the best day of your life, but you'll want to make sure the contingency plans are included in your vendor contracts. What happens if your vendor goes out of business before your wedding? What happens if your vendor gets in a car accident on the way to your event? What happens if a pandemic hits? Make sure that your vendor has a plan for when life happens and they cannot fulfil the contract. Although we never want those things to occur, it's important to include the backup plan in the contract.

If life really hits and you or the vendor need to cancel the contract, please make sure you understand their cancellation policy. If you cancel, do you lose your money or a portion of your money? If you still have a balance due, are you required to pay a certain portion of your balance? If they cancel the contract, do they refund your money? When this situation occurs everyone wants a full refund, but that does not always happen, based on what is notated in the vendor contract. Before you sign the contract, it is very important to understand what you lose if the contract is broken.

Deposits and retainers

When COVID-19 hit, vendors in the wedding and event industry got a lesson on the difference between deposits and retainers. It's a very important one that will help you when you sign a contract with a vendor.

TIP

A retainer and a deposit are not the same. A retainer is a fee paid to hold a service, while a deposit is a fee paid towards goods or services. Deposits are refundable, while retainers are not. Make note of what the vendor states in the contract regarding whether the retainer or deposit are refundable.

This is a debate that has been going on for years and years. There seems to be confusion over what to call that initial payment you put down to hold the date with your vendor. Is it a deposit or is it a retainer? Is it refundable if either of you breech the contract or is it not? Technically, all payments should be retainers as they hold the goods or services.

When you hire a vendor and pay them money for a future event, that money is holding them from booking that date with someone else. However, that money is not simply held by the vendor until your event. Those payments go towards their operational costs leading up to your event. So if you break a contract with a vendor, that money is gone because they have used it to keep their business in business from the time you booked them until your wedding day. Therefore, many vendors say those first payments are nonrefundable.

A perfect example of a deposit that you might pay would be through your rental company or venue. They may charge you a "damage deposit," a fee collected upfront in case there is damage to the venue or the rental items. After your event, if there is no damage, that deposit will be returned. If there is damage, they will keep that fee to cover the cost of the repairs to the damaged items.

Unfortunately, I watched colleagues close their long-standing businesses because when everyone was cancelling their weddings, they lost the remaining payments and some initial payments. This caused a lot of conversation in the wedding industry because clients were wanting their first payments back when they cancelled their events. Some vendors were protected by calling them "retainers," while others were not by calling them "deposits."

REMEMBER

Regardless of where you stand in the debate, be sure that you fully understand your vendors' policies on deposits and retainers. If a vendor breaks the contract, I understand that you want your money back. If you cancel the contract, please understand your vendors' policies on what they can and will refund.

Reading the fine print

You know those little words in a contract that you don't think are important? Well, they are probably the most important words you read! In this section we'll discuss the importance of reading the fine print in your vendor contract.

TIP

Read your contracts. Then read them again. Then make sure your fiancé reads them and then reads them again. Just because you might know a vendor or maybe a friend used them in a past does not mean that you shouldn't read the contracts.

Buried inside the contract are some little words. You may even need to put glasses on to see them. Why are they so small? Why did the vendor make a special point to make them little? It's like those commercials you see where the people have been prescribed a new medication and they look so happy and then a voiceover tells you all the bad things that could happen to you if you take the medication. That voice is there to protect the large pharmaceutical company from anything that might happen to you if you take their medication.

WARNING

One thing to look out for is a few simple words called "force majeure." This is defined as any unforeseeable circumstances that prevent someone from fulfilling a contract. If a vendor has this in their contract it means that anything can happen and they are not obligated to fulfill the contract. They could be tired that day and simply don't have to show up to your wedding.

I had a client once who hired her own photographer instead of someone on our team. He had "force majeure" in his contract. That morning he woke up and texted her that he hadn't looked how far the venue was before that morning, and it was too far for him to drive so he wasn't going to come to her wedding. It's a good thing I have some amazing photographers on my team who would never do that, and we were able to get one of our photographers to her wedding.

If a vendor includes the small print that you might need a magnify glass to read, make sure that what is written does not contradict the terms that you agreed to. To clarify, make sure it is clearly written in the contract all of the services that the vendor will provide. If it does contradict what you agreed to, make sure those little words are removed before you sign the contract.

The last thing you want is to enter into a contract believing one thing and then realizing that was not the case because you skipped over reading all the little words. They are in there for a reason, and it is in your best interest to find out why so that you can protect yourself from a bad situation in the future.

Chapter **5**

All-Inclusive Wedding Planning

The hottest trend in wedding planning is what's called *all-inclusive wedding planning.* But does it actually include everything you need? The concept sounds simple enough. You hire an all-inclusive wedding planner or a venue and boom, you're done with planning. Or are you?

All-inclusive wedding planning is designed to simplify the whole process, but is it the right fit for you? What happens if they only have a certain color linen, but you don't like that color? Is only one chair "included"? How do you avoid a cookie-cutter wedding and incorporate your vision?

In this chapter, you discover everything you need to know about all-inclusive wedding planning — what's included, deciding if it's budget-friendly or a budget breaker, and how to make it your own. After you read this chapter, you'll be able to determine if all-inclusive is the right fit for your wedding planning process.

What's Actually Included?

What does *all-inclusive* mean? If you book an all-inclusive honeymoon, you expect to have your lodging, food, and beverages included in the price. It would be a disappointment if you showed up and your food and beverage was included but not your lodging. All-inclusive honeymoon destinations have been around for decades, but the wedding industry is now offering all-inclusive wedding experiences.

As a wedding planner, I offer an all-inclusive option. Let me explain why I do this. If you hire me as your planner, I assist you with booking all your vendors, among other things. Those vendor suggestions are companies I've worked with numerous times. I know the system. I know what they need, how they operate, and the product they bring to a wedding.

I care about my clients — some might even say too much, because they're often my number one, no matter what I have going on in my personal life. The vendors I suggest are like family to me. There's no hidden agenda about why I want you to book them other than that I have more confidence that your day will be perfect, as compared to working with someone I don't know.

One day I realized that I could give my clients an all-inclusive wedding planning experience because essentially that was what I was already doing for them. I was already booking their vendors for them, and now I could simplify it into one package and put a really pretty bow on it so that they didn't have to go searching for hours and hours to find vendors that they could only hope would do a good job. The main reason I offer an all-inclusive experience for my clients is that I believe it truly benefits them, and it could possibly benefit you.

TIP

As you search to see if an all-inclusive wedding planning experience is right for you, you may find different levels. It's important to make sure you understand what's included before you choose this option. "All-inclusive" typically does not include personal items like wedding attire, stationery, or custom signs. For the most part, all-inclusive wedding planning includes but is not limited to the following:

>> **Wedding planner:** An all-inclusive wedding planning experience includes a full-service wedding planner. This person or team will be with you every step of the way. They'll help you plan your wedding, book your vendors, and coordinate the day.

>> **Caterer:** Your food is included in the price — appetizers, salad, and dinner. Typically, this can be set up in stations, buffet, or plated seating. The price would also include all service and staffing fees associated with your meal.

>> **Baker:** The cake is included. You can determine if you want buttercream or fondant. You can also pick your flavors and the style of the cake design.

- » **Alcohol:** The alcohol is included and typically covers the beer and wine. Hosting liquor or a signature drink may be an additional fee.

- » **Bartender:** A licensed and insured bartender is included with all-inclusive wedding planning packages. This also includes the supplies you'll need, such as ice, napkins, cups, and mixers.

- » **Flowers:** All of your bridal flowers, ceremony, and reception flowers are included in an all-inclusive package.

- » **Decor:** Any additional decor such as lighting, draping, candles, and room accents are included. Some packages may even include a tent if you need one.

- » **Rentals:** Your tables, chairs, china, silverware, linens, and napkins are included.

- » **Entertainment:** Your ceremony musician and DJ are included. Typically, a band is an additional upgrade.

- » **Photo and video:** Photo and video are included. They also offer engagement sessions and cover the appropriate timeframe that you need for the day of your wedding. An online gallery of your photos and a highlight video are part of the package as well.

- » **Transportation:** If you want to leave in style you're in luck, as a get-a-way car is included in the price.

REMEMBER

As you research the best option for you, make sure you have all the information. The list above is to serve as a guide. Each wedding planner will offer a different package, so collect all the information to determine if it's a good fit for your budget and needs.

Budget-Friendly or Budget Breaker?

It seems so easy if everything is included in one simple package. But does it really save you money? Well, it's time to determine if it's a budget breaker or a budget-friendly option for your wedding planning process. To do so, I did a little research and found an actual all-inclusive package so that we can compare the numbers together. In this section, we're going to evaluate a real-life all-inclusive package and compare that with your budget.

Table 5-1 shows a real number based on a venue that offers this all-inclusive package. In the next table, you compare your prices with this example. Granted, I understand that each venue or planner will have their own prices, but I am just concerned about your budget. If you research your area to consider this as an option, you'll be able to input actual numbers based on your demographic. This table will help you see current prices and what is included.

TABLE 5-1

Sample All-Inclusive Package (125 Guests)

Items	Price
Catering & staff	Included
Wedding cake	Included
Groom's cake	Included
Ceremony musicians	Included
DJ	Included
Venue: 12 hours	Included
Bridal suite	Included
Groom's suite	Included
Rehearsal	Included
Venue representative	Included
Staff	Included
Design team	Included
Decor & props	Included
Flowers	Included
Sound system	Included
String Lighting	Included
Draping	Included
Bistro tables & guest tables	Included
Ceremony chairs	Included
Reception chairs	Included
Linens: Standard	Included
China, flatware, & glassware	Included
Candles & votives	Included
Limousine	Included
Sparkler exit	Included
Total price	**$32,995**

Now, I am going to add in actual numbers to our area in Table 5-2 to see if the package saves you money or costs more. Remember, this is just an example. The tables and numbers are as accurate as possible without knowing all your details.

TABLE 5-2

Breakdown of Actual Individual Costs (125 Guests)

Items	Actual Cost
Catering & staff	$8,250.00
Wedding cake	$1,250.00
Groom's cake	$250.00
Ceremony musicians	$750.00
DJ	$2,300.00
Venue: 12 hours	$6,000.00
Bridal suite	Included
Groom's suite	Included
Rehearsal	Included
Venue representative	$1,250.00
Staff	$2,000.00
Design team	$1,500.00
Decor & props	$2,500.00
Flowers	$4,000.00
Sound system	$800.00
String lighting	$1,200.00
Draping	$3,500.00
Bistro tables & guest tables	$500.00
Ceremony chairs	$500.00
Reception chairs	$500.00
Linens: Standard	$450.00
China, flatware, & glassware	$425.00
Candles & votives	$250.00
Limousine	$600.00
Sparkler exit	$75.00
Total price	**$38,350.00**

In this scenario, booking the all-inclusive option would save you money. Let me tell you one main reason why. The vendors included in the packages are regulars. They know that if the venue or planner books them on a regular basis and they keep doing a good job for their clients, it's likely they'll book them again for another event. This means the all-inclusive planner or venue gets discounts that may not be extended to you if you were to book the vendor on your own. They don't know you and don't have a relationship with you, so there's no incentive to give you a discount.

If your life is busy with work and obligations, I would highly suggest booking an all-inclusive planner or venue. However, if you're reading this book, you may want to do everything on your own. If you're using this book to guide you through the wedding planning process and you find yourself overwhelmed with the details, an all-inclusive wedding planner or venue may be just what you need to give you peace of mind, knowing that everything will be taken care of.

Making It Your Own

I hear time and again from clients who fear that booking an all-inclusive wedding planner will not allow them the ability to customize their package. This is something to watch out for if you book an all-inclusive wedding planner or wedding venue.

Remember, this is *your* wedding. This is not your wedding planner's wedding or your wedding venue's wedding. When you research an all-inclusive wedding experience, you must make sure you can customize the package within their parameters. So what does this mean? In this section, I give you some questions to ask, ideas on customization, and tips on how to adjust the price of an all-inclusive wedding planning.

You are not meant to fit into a perfect package. Every couple comes to me with different needs, different visions, and different budgets. As much as I would like to believe that I have somehow created a magic package that will fit everyone who steps into my office, I haven't.

REMEMBER

The most important thing to remember is that everything for your wedding should be customizable. Whether you pick individual vendors or a package, you need to make it your own because you don't have the same vision as the planner or venue or caterer. You have different likes and dislikes and that is okay. It's meant to be that way, so I want you to make sure your voice is heard.

Asking the right questions when meeting with an all-inclusive planner

Here are some questions to ask if you're meeting with an all-inclusive wedding planner or wedding venue to ensure customization that fits your needs.

>> **Can I customize the package?** Make sure you can make changes to the standard package to fit your needs and budget.

>> **Can I adjust the guest count?** All-inclusive packages are set up by guest brackets. If you have 50 guests, it costs this much. If you have 100 guests, it costs this much. But what if you have 80 guests? Do you pay for 20 guests you won't have?

>> **Is a wedding planner or a coordinator included?** A planner and a coordinator are two different people. A planner is with you from the beginning, planning everything from your schedule of events to hiring your vendors. A coordinator is someone who implements your plan. They are not with you during the planning process.

>> **Am I able to customize the menu?** Find out what's on the menu. Is it an actual meal or just appetizers? Make sure you know what the food options are and the parameters to customizing what is served. Catering is going to be one of your biggest expenses, so if the package includes chicken, you can't expect to serve red meat.

>> **What are the linens?** Do they include only one fabric and color? If you don't want polyester white linens, can you change them to textured light blue linens? Make sure you can design what your linens will be so you feel like the guests will see your vision.

>> **What do the china and silverware look like?** Don't get stuck with a white plate if you want something with a little flare. Are you able to customize your place setting? Is that an upgrade?

>> **How big are the guest centerpieces?** If the included centerpieces are a simple flower in a bud vase and you want a full medium-size centerpiece, make sure you can customize the size and color to fit your needs.

>> **What type of alcohol is served?** Are we talking top shelf or boxed wine here? If the alcohol selection doesn't meet your standards, can you upgrade? How much does that typically add to the overall budget?

>> **How long are the photographer and videographer booked for?** Photo and video are booked by the hour. If those hours don't fit into your timeline, make sure you can add hours if needed for an additional price.

» **Can you bring in custom items?** Make sure you can bring in favors such as koozies, cups, and napkins if you want to customize your guest bar experience. Is there a credit back for those items if you supply your own?

» **How many photographers do you have?** Do you have to use their photographer, or can you bring in your own? Is there a credit back if you're using your own photographer?

» **Can I meet with the photographers?** Seeing a photographer's work is important but meeting them in person is vital to a successful wedding. You mainly want to get a sense of their personality. It's important to make sure you like them, so you don't have to fake a smile on your wedding day. (Refer to Chapter 4 for more about this.)

» **Do I get to choose the DJ?** How many DJs do they have on their team? Do you get to pick a DJ that fits your music genre? Can you meet with that person? Can you customize the list of songs that will be played during the ceremony, cocktail hour, and reception?

» **Can I book a band?** Most packages include a DJ but what if you want a band? How many bands do they have? Is there a way to preview a band before booking? Is there an upgraded fee to hire a band over a DJ?

» **Can I book a ceremony musician?** If you know you want to book a musician for your ceremony, inquire about options. Is there a way to see their repertoire or hear them prior to the big day? Do you charge extra for that?

» **What are the getaway car options?** Is it a limo or a vintage car? Do you have the option to pick out your car? If you don't need a car, can that be removed from the price?

Looking at ways to customize an all-inclusive wedding

Customizing your all-inclusive wedding is an important piece of the wedding planning process. Like I said earlier, clients who go this route still want their vision and dreams to show through the package. Here are some ways you can customize your all-inclusive wedding experience.

» **Incorporate your colors:** Make sure your colors are allowed. If the standard linens do not match your bridesmaids' dresses, change them. Make sure your color palette is seen at your wedding.

>> **Customize the menu:** Incorporating your taste in food at your wedding is an amazing way to give your guests a little insight on what your date nights look like. Choose a menu packed with items that you enjoy eating. If you like food trucks, customize your menu with an item from a food truck. If you love pizza, do a pizza buffet.

>> **Customize the flowers:** Using your favorite flowers or color palette is a great way to bring your theme to life. Do you love daisies or roses? Then use those flowers in your centerpieces so the guests will see your favorite things.

>> **Customize the rentals:** Don't settle for the plain white plate unless you love a plain white plate. Incorporate your personal style in your dinnerware. Choose coordinating dinnerware that you would use in your house if you would be hosting a dinner party.

>> **Customize the alcohol:** If you don't like Chardonnay, then don't serve it. Serve what you like. All the guests will care about is if they get to drink for free. Serve the type of alcohol you would order if you had a night out on the town at a fancy dinner. Again, this reflects you and what you like.

>> **Customize the songs:** Music is a wonderful way to customize your wedding. Choose songs that have meaning to you for the ceremony. Choose your favorite love songs for the cocktail hour. Keep the dance floor going all night with songs you would pick if you knew no one was watching you dance. I promise, they would pick them too.

>> **Customize your getaway car:** If the options are a fleet of vintage cars, pick your favorite. It doesn't have to be just white, unless you want white. If you love a good limo, pick one to whisk you off to the honeymoon!

As I have said before, you're not going to fit into a perfect little box. Even though it's called all-inclusive, the chances of the package fitting you perfectly are slim to none, and that's okay! There are many ways to make the package your own and customize what's included.

Table 5-3 provides space for you to determine the pieces of the all-inclusive package that you need and the items that you can cut. The right of the table lists items that may be included in the price. On the left, put an X if you do *not* need that item.

You can take this list with you when you meet with an all-inclusive wedding planner or venue. Ask them to remove those items that you crossed off your list, and adjust the price. Now you can truly decide if all-inclusive it right for you and also ensure that your wedding reflects your tastes and values.

TABLE 5-3

Items You Can Cut from an All-Inclusive Package

Item you do NOT Need	Included Items
	Wedding planner
	Caterer: Appetizers
	Caterer: Dinner
	Baker: Bride's cake
	Baker: Groom's cake
	Beer
	Wine
	Signature drink
	Liquor
	Bartender
	Flowers: Bridal party
	Flowers: Ceremony
	Flowers: Reception
	Decor: Draping
	Decor: Lighting
	Rentals: Tables
	Rentals: Chairs
	Rentals: Linens
	Rentals: China, flatware
	Entertainment: Ceremony musicians
	Entertainment: DJ
	Entertainment: Band
	Entertainment: Photobooth
	Photographer
	Videographer
	Transportation: Bridal party
	Transportation: Guests
	Transportation: Getaway car

Chapter **6**

Location, Location, Location

When you think about your wedding day, what type of venue do you imagine? Do you envision a decked-out ballroom with up lighting, candles galore, and large floral centerpieces? Maybe you see a farm with a large barn, creek, and rolling hills as the backdrop. Is it a modern space with minimal sleek architecture details, simplistic florals, and white linens? Do you love exposed brick and beams with polished wood floors perfect for dancing all night long? Do you love the beach and want to marry your best friend barefoot in the sand while the sunset provides a backdrop you couldn't possibly improve on with a floral arch?

The exciting news is that the options are limitless. But that could be your greatest struggle because you can't narrow down what you want. Having so many choices can be overwhelming. In this chapter, I help you to narrow down the options to be able to pick the best venue for you and your fiancé. Specifically, I discuss how to pick the perfect venue, explore indoor and outdoor options, prepare for good and bad weather, and see if an all-inclusive wedding venue might be the best fit for you.

REMEMBER

Finding a venue is one of the most important tasks on your to-do list. I acknowledge that, and my hope is that after you read this chapter, you'll be over the moon excited about the place that you picked. After all, that venue will always hold a special place in your heart because it's where your married life began with your partner. I am looking forward to helping you find the one. You already did the hardest work — picking the actual "one" with whom you'll spend the rest of your life. Picking the venue should be easy right?

Picking Your Perfect Ceremony and Reception Venue

No matter if you book a wedding venue or host a backyard BBQ, you need a location to get married, an address that will forever be printed on your wedding invitation. A place where your greatest friends and family will meet to witness the start of your forever. Everyone has probably asked you when you're getting married. Typically the next question is where you're getting married.

You may fall anywhere on a broad spectrum: you have no idea; you have known the perfect spot since you were a kid; you attended the wedding of a friend and knew that was also going to be the spot for you. Regardless of where you are, we're going to talk through some important considerations when narrowing down the perfect venue.

Let's start with a list of determining factors that will help you narrow down your search. In my city, it seems like there are as many venue options as there are churches and bars. There's one on every corner. When a client is on a venue hunt, I go through the following points to get that list of favorites down to just a few options. My hope is that you'll be able to consider these points below to narrow down your top favorite possible venues.

>> **Availability:** First, it is available? In Chapter 1, we talked about picking the perfect date. As I said then, your date may be determined by the venue's availability. It's a classic case of supply and demand. If there aren't a lot of options or availability in your area, chances are the prices will be higher. If you live in an area with a limitless number of venue options, the prices may be lower. Most importantly, is the venue available for one of your perfect dates?

>> **Price:** Does the venue fit in your budget? Nothing good will come from touring a venue that you can't afford. Trust me, you will fall in love with it. It's like test driving a luxury car that you will never buy. Here's how it will go. You'll tour it, fall in love, possibly beg someone for a little extra money, then leave sad. I don't want any part of your process to be a disappointment, so stay away from places you can't afford.

>> **Capacity:** How many guests are you planning on inviting? The general rule of thumb is that 30% of your entire guest list will not be able to attend. There are several factors to consider, such as how many are traveling out of town, how many are local, how many are family or close friends, and how many you know for sure are not going to make it. Regardless, if your venue is too big or too small for your guest list, consider another option. You don't want a space that feels too crowded or too empty.

TIP

» When a venue tells you their capacity, make sure to clarify if that is standing or seating space. Often a venue may say they can hold 300 people but if you want a dance floor, food stations, a DJ, tables, and chairs, the real capacity is 180 people. If you have 150 people on your guest list and your guests are driving to the venue, let's factor approximately 2 people per car. You will need a parking lot to accommodate 75 parking spots. If your venue's parking lot only holds 50 cars, then you will need to figure out alternative transportation. Make sure to be clear on what your needs are and the actual capacity of the venue before you book. If you're already at max capacity before you even send your invites, you may need to consider a larger venue.

» **Location:** This is one of the most important pieces to the puzzle! First, if you're getting married at one location and hosting your reception at another location, don't pick a venue an hour away. Pick a reception venue no more than 30 minutes from your ceremony location. If your venue is far away, you will lose some of your guests for the reception and you paid money for them to be there, so I don't want that happening to you. Additionally, if you're inviting a lot of out-of-town guests, consider a venue that's close to activities in the city so your guests can explore while they're in town. Finally, make sure there are hotels close to your venue. Farm venues are often off the beaten path, so consider whether your guests will have to travel on dark country roads after your reception.

» **Atmosphere:** If you were to go out to dinner on a date night, what is your vibe? What is your house decorated like? What is your style? Pick a venue where you love the atmosphere and architecture details. Remember, everything reflects who you are as a couple. This is another way to reflect your style at your wedding. Pick a place that you enjoy being in and gives you all the feels. Additionally, make sure it does not conflict with your vision for your flowers and decor. If the carpet is red and you want pink flowers, will that conflict with your design?

» **Backup plan:** What's the backup plan if you pick an outdoor venue and it rains? Does the venue have a backup plan that isn't going to cost you a small fortune to implement? Consider all the bad things that could happen so that you're prepared to face them if you must go to plan B.

» **Food and beverage:** Does the venue have in-house catering and bartending, or do they allow you to bring in your own food and beverages? If you're looking to bring in your own catering and bartending company, make sure the venue has adequate prep areas for those vendors. Outside caterers are used to what we call a "prep kitchen." This is a kitchen space without ovens and stoves. A kitchen with ovens and stoves is known as a "catering kitchen." If you do bring in an outside caterer, make sure you understand their needs when it comes to preparing your food to ensure it's hot and ready to go for your guests. If your venue has its own catering company, ask to see sample menus to make sure you like the food options before you book with them. The same goes for bartending. Make sure you confirm with your venue if they have ice or refrigerators for storing your alcohol so that the bartender understands what they need to bring to the wedding to appropriately prep your beverages.

» **Dressing rooms:** It's important to consider where you will be getting ready on the wedding day. When looking for a venue, make sure to check out the dressing room areas for both you and your fiancé. If there are not adequate facilities — including proper lighting, air conditioning, heat, power, and restrooms — then you will need to consider an alternative space to get ready on the day of your wedding.

» **Guest mobility:** When touring a venue, consider guests who need ramps or who can't navigate stairs or a long walk from the parking lot to the ceremony and reception areas. If you do have guests in wheelchairs, make sure that the venue has appropriate pathways so they don't miss out on your big day. Also consider the lighting. Is the parking lot lit appropriately to ensure the safety of your guests returning to their vehicles at the end of the night?

» **Technology and power:** Consider your technology needs when booking a venue. Does the venue have adequate power for your DJ or band? Are there TVs if you want to play a slideshow? Does the venue have a built-in sound system or does the band need to bring their own? Is the venue able to play music if you want to make your own playlist? It's important to think through all your technology needs in order to find the perfect venue!

» **What's included:** What is included in the venue rental? Is it just the space itself or does it include tables and chairs? Does the venue have in-house vendors that provide everything you need or is it a clean slate and you must bring in everything? That's important to factor into your decision because if you have to bring everything in, you will have a higher than normal rental invoice, which may put you over budget.

» **Timeframe:** Venues are typically rented hourly. Make sure to confirm how long you have access to the venue. If the venue is available for 12 hours, does that include the vendors setting up and tearing down? That is important to communicate to your vendors to avoid additional charges from your vendors or the venue. Are you planning on getting ready there? Will the timeframe that you have the venue allow for that to happen? If you have a large bridal party, you may need to add on hours to accommodate getting ready.

» **Staff:** What kind of staff does the venue rental include? It's very important to note that all venues require a venue manager. This is the person who is onsite to make sure the power is on, to confirm there are toilet paper and paper towels in the restroom, and to ensure the safety of your guests. Often this is confused with a coordinator. As we discussed in Chapter 4, a coordinator is going to walk you through every part of your day. A venue manager is not. Make sure you understand who will be there on your wedding day and what their responsibilities are for your event.

Considering Indoor Event Venues

Without a doubt, indoor venues give you the greatest protection against Mother Nature and all she can throw at you on your wedding day. Inside, you're protected from rain, heat, cold, and wind. If you live in an area that has four seasons and the summers are hot, you're protected from melting away. The same goes if you're a bride who wants a winter wedding; an indoor location will protect you from the freezing temperatures but still allow you the chance to head outside for a few snow angel pictures.

Note: Although an indoor venue does provide the safest option for weather, it isn't foolproof. I worked with a bride who got married in the middle of our hot and muggy summer season. She checked all the boxes and booked an indoor venue. However, the air conditioner failed, and the venue turned into a hot box. Let's just say that it wasn't pretty. There wasn't a dry eye in the room. Although there was emotion and the bride was beautiful, everyone was wiping the sweat off their brow. Yes, this was a worst-case scenario, but it's a reminder that even if you have good intentions, some things are out of your control.

DON'T FLIP OUT — FLIP YOUR SPACE!

If rain or some other unforeseen circumstance forces you to use the same space for your ceremony and reception, you can flip the reception space. This means that the reception space is set up for your ceremony first and then the staff flips the space for your reception. If you find yourself in this scenario, here's a tip for you to execute this flawlessly.

Set up your ceremony where the dance floor for your reception will be. You can preset your tables off to the side and create a center aisle for your ceremony on the dance floor. After your ceremony is over, the tables can be moved into their spot and the chairs from your aisle can then be placed around your tables. The space where your chairs were is now your dance floor. This will provide a seamless transition from ceremony to reception without moving the tables and chairs multiple times.

(continued)

(continued)

The following figures show a sample floor plan set up for a ceremony (left) and then the reception set up in the exact same space post flip (right).

DJ

Ceremony

Guest Tables

Guest Tables

F
o
o
d

gifts

C

DJ

DANCE FLOOR

F
o
o
d

gifts

C

TIP

If you're looking to get married and host your reception at a single location, an indoor venue could be a great option for you to consider. If the venue has a designated ceremony location and a separate reception location, this simplifies the task of moving your guests from place to place. Additionally, an indoor reception venue with an outdoor wedding space provides you with a backup plan for rain on your big day (see the nearby sidebar, "Don't flip out — flip your space!").

Another positive trait of an indoor venue is that you have control over the ambiance. If you want a candlelit dinner, that can be accomplished by booking a dimly lit indoor space. If you want specialty lighting in an array of colors, that too can be created inside rather than outside. Indoor spaces allow you limitless options when setting the tone of the ambiance through controlled lighting.

An indoor space can also provide your guests with an architectural flair that may not be found outside. We have a venue in town that's booked for weddings often because, honestly, it's just a beautiful place. Clients don't have to do much to the space. The building alone is beautiful and that could be a positive for you as well. If you aren't a fan of over-the-top flower arrangements, seek out a venue that's architecturally stunning. Allow the building to be your decor and keep the flowers and table decor simple.

If you're someone who wants to party all night long, that's yet another reason to consider booking an indoor venue. Most outdoor venues have noise ordinance laws that must be enforced. Typically, that time is between 9 pm and 11 pm, although laws and times vary per state. Let's say you're getting married in the summer and you want those perfect sunset photos. But the sun doesn't set until late, which means you will start and end your wedding later. If you book an outdoor venue, then you might not be able to fit everything in that you want because you must stop your event when the county tells you to.

I have worked with a lot of clients who want their reception to go until 11 pm or midnight, and sometimes even later into the early morning hours. An outdoor venue is just not an option for them because I highly advise not getting in trouble with law enforcement at your wedding. An indoor venue is going to give you more flexibility to continue the party late-night if that's what your heart desires.

Often, indoor venues come with security at the main entrance that is included in your venue fee. This is especially true for venues located in a downtown setting. This is a positive to ensure those who enter are invited. No one likes a wedding crasher, so picking an indoor venue can help keep out those who aren't invited. Several of my clients who pick an outdoor venue also hire security to watch the entrance but also to ensure that those who have had a good time at their wedding stay safe.

WARNING

One downside to an indoor venue is the limitations on how many guests you can host at your wedding. As I said earlier in this chapter, it's important to narrow down your search by considering occupancy. If you invite more people than the building can hold, there's no room to expand. An outdoor venue allows room for all those guests you were certain weren't going to come who will actually be able to attend. Although there's a formula, it's only to be used as a guide. It's impossible to predict if someone will for certain attend your wedding until you receive their RSVP. Until then, you're only guessing. If you do book an indoor venue with limited space, be conservative on your guest list to ensure you will have the space you need. No one will enjoy standing room only — outside, that is!

THE PERFECT LOCATION TURNED NIGHTMARE LOCATION

I want to share a story about a client's wedding that I don't often share because it might go down in the history books as the worst wedding experience I have ever witnessed. I believe it's a valuable lesson that could help, whether you pick an indoor or an outdoor venue. In wedding planning and your marriage, communication is the key to success. If a vendor goes silent on you, this should be a concern. If your wedding is two weeks away, your vendors should be responding in a timely manner. If they aren't, I encourage you to do everything you can to reach them for your peace of mind.

The wedding location was three hours away, so most of our planning was done virtually, but there were a few site visits where I met them at the venue. Trust me when I say that nothing was out of the ordinary. The venue representative seemed to have everything in place and was responsive up until two weeks prior to the event. After calling the venue endlessly without a response, I reached out to the client, explaining my concerns. The client assured me that they knew the venue representative, and everything was fine. She was probably just busy, right?

We all get those feelings — the ones you should always listen to. Well, I had one; in my gut, I knew something wasn't right. However, I was assured that everything appeared to be normal at the venue when the client drove by to check it out. So we moved forward as planned. I was to be allowed access to the venue at 9 am on the day of the event. I was there early, but the clock seemed to be moving in slow motion.

When 9 o'clock finally rolled in, I opened the door to the venue. I was slightly surprised that the venue doors were unlocked, and no one was to be found. Due to the long drive, I had to make a pit stop at the restrooms before hitting the ground running. That was when my world stopped. The toilets were filled with cement. I wouldn't have believed it if I hadn't seen it myself. I suddenly knew today wasn't going to be a good day.

I ran to my staff yelling, "We have a problem!" They later told me I was as white as a ghost. I have made a career out of being the calm in the storm, but I had no idea how I was going to get cement out of the toilets. In eight hours, I would have 200 guests who would need to use the restroom but wouldn't be able to for the entire event.

The toilets weren't the only problem. After further exploring the venue, we quickly realized that the power had been cut to the facility. In the middle of the summer, we would have no power — no air conditioning, no lights, no running water, no microphones, no power for the band, no power for the caterer. To make matters worse, there was trash everywhere. The place was a wreck; trash cans were filled to the brim, and it smelled like rotten food.

My heart sank. I wanted to scream, to yell, to cry. I wanted to do a lot of things, but I knew in that moment, we had to try and salvage what we could for our clients' no-good, very bad day. As much as I would love to say we were able to turn it around and everything turned out perfect, it wasn't. Not only did we have a major undertaking to salvage what we could, but we had all the flowers and decor to set up as well. We were set up to fail.

The first thing I had to do was tell the client. I came up with a plan so that after I told her the bad news, I could hopefully make her happy with the amazing backup plan that I devised in five minutes. My only saving grace was that it was not going to rain. The plan was to move everything outside, using the venue facade as a backdrop, pick up a generator, and call a local portable toilet company to deliver the nicest toilets they had available. Oh, and keep the doors locked to the inside of the venue. It was a horrific site, and we didn't want anyone to see that.

We took scramble to the next level. It was mass chaos. With each step forward we took two steps back. Nothing was working right so we all had to work together to figure out how we were going to save this wedding from absolute disaster. I made the dreaded call to the client. I kept it short and to the point. My job was to ensure her that everything was going to be okay. What happened next still haunts me to this day. She was mad. Not at the venue, but at me. She screamed and told me it was all my fault. She told me I ruined her day.

Let's just be clear here, I didn't fill the toilets with cement, and I didn't cut the power and trash the place. But she needed someone to be mad at and that person was me. I was okay with carrying that for her that day but her hatred for me got worse as the day went on. It didn't matter that we completely redeemed what we could for the day; she needed to hate someone.

For the longest time, I couldn't talk about this wedding because even though it was a terrible situation, there was a lot of pain there, because I care about my clients, and I care about them having an amazing day. I also care that they like me and this one hit below the belt.

After the wedding, I wanted to figure out what happened. I investigated to determine who was responsible for the condition of the venue. It turned out that a few days prior to the wedding, the venue went bankrupt, and the bank took the building. The owners were mad, so they vandalized the building on their way out of town.

The moral of this story is that if a vendor goes silent on you, find out why. I wouldn't want something like this happening to you. This is another reason why it's important to build those relationships with your vendors so that you can have a peace of mind knowing that you'll have an amazing day because you built an amazing team.

Knowing Your Options for Outdoor Events

Outdoor venues are known for their amazing backdrops and scenic views. They're unlike any indoor venue you can book — they're ever changing with the seasons and gorgeous sunsets. I have seen some amazing views through the years. They're better than any floral arch. Who wouldn't love to overlook rolling hills or stand at the sea's edge and marry your best friend? There really is nothing better than an outdoor venue on a perfect weather day. Now for the con. There are very few perfect weather days in certain regions in a calendar year. In our minds we see it as perfect, so if you book an outdoor venue, I wish nothing but the best weather for you. But I also want you to be prepared if the weather doesn't match your picture of the perfect day.

TIP

Speaking of amazing backdrops, booking an outdoor venue can often mean spending less money on your flowers and decor. I had a client who had the ultimate view for her wedding and didn't purchase a single flower for the altar. The backdrop was the view, and with her large bridal party holding floral bouquets, that was all she needed. It was beautiful!

Another positive to an outdoor venue is the somewhat limitless number of guests you can invite. I say somewhat because you might be limited on parking or a venue's policy, but for the most part, the sky's the limit on how many guests you can have outside. You don't have the pressure of having to narrow down your guest list if you don't want to and can afford to invite everyone you know. You know those people you don't really want to invite but feel obligated to? Guess what; they can come too!

WARNING

Perhaps the most obvious downside to an outdoor venue is the possibility of inclement weather. You must have a backup plan. Plan B doesn't have to be a bad thing; it can be just as beautiful as Plan A. My main concern is that you're prepared. It shouldn't deter you from booking an outdoor venue; it just needs to be something you consider. Often clients believe that the flowers and decor can be set up extremely last minute. As much as I would love to say that's true, it isn't. There's a time in the day where we make a call on the weather and implement either Plan A or Plan B, for multiple reasons. For instance, if you have hired a rental company to set up the chairs at 8 am, and it's raining, they will not set those up because the chairs will get ruined.

WARNING

A common issue with outdoor venues is appropriate restrooms, walkways, driveways, and wheelchair accessibility. Plenty of outdoor venues have this taken care of, but when I'm searching for a client's perfect venue, I always consider these common issues. In the south, surrounded by farms, the venue may have a pretty barn, but the parking is in a field, or the restroom is a restroom trailer. Yes, these can be executed flawlessly, but I just want to make you aware of what your venue offers. If you have several guests who can't navigate uneven terrain, then you may want to cross that option off your list to ensure the safety of those you love.

WHEN TO IMPLEMENT YOUR BACKUP PLAN

Here's my advice if you wake up on your wedding day and it's raining but you believe the weather will move out before your wedding begins. Make the call on your plan no later than three hours before the start of your wedding. If it looks like it might rain during your wedding and you're within three hours of starting, set up Plan B. If a vendor is hired to be there for setup at 9 am, they may not be able to adapt their schedule on the day of your wedding due to the other deliveries on their schedule. Have some help ready to set up the chairs and decor last minute, even if you paid the vendor to do it.

Suppose you hired a florist and told them to set up your arch at 10 am. It's raining at 10 am and your decor will get ruined in the rain. But it looks like the weather will be perfect when your wedding begins at 4 pm. Your florist can get everything prepped and ready at the hired time and then your bridal party can help move those pieces into the appropriate spot closer to your wedding start time.

Let me explain why I say three hours. I don't know who you have setting up those items, but I would assume they're people in your wedding or at least people who need to get ready for your wedding. Pictures usually begin two hours before your wedding so this allows them time to set up and be ready to go by the start of photos. This will also allow the photographer enough time to take photos of your flowers and decor. Additionally, your guests will start arriving thirty minutes before the ceremony begins. This is why it's important that you make the call no later than three hours before your wedding. That way the flowers, decor, and music can be set up before your guests arrive. Finally, if there's a chance of rain within three hours of your wedding start time, set up for Plan B.

Taking cover from sun and rain: Tents and coverage

If your outdoor venue doesn't have an indoor space, then you will need to consider booking a tent. A tent is your protection from the sun and rain. It can also serve as a backup ceremony location if your day is a complete washout.

Tents come in all shapes and sizes. The main two are frame tents and pole tents. I have also seen clients get creative and book a carnival tent for their reception.

>> **Frame tent:** A frame tent has all its supportive poles on the perimeter, with the frame on the ceiling of the tent. This leaves a completely open space on the floor of the tent.

>> **Pole tent:** A pole tent has supportive poles typically every 20 feet running through the tent.

Figure 6-1 shows a frame tent compared to a pole tent. Something to remember if you book a pole tent is that you will have to plan your setup around the poles, especially your dance floor.

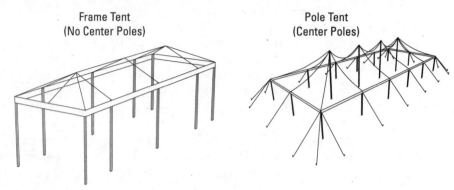

Frame Tent
(No Center Poles)

Pole Tent
(Center Poles)

FIGURE 6-1:
Frame Tent
versus Pole Tent

Here are some simple rules to follow when planning the size of your tent.

10 x 10 feet of space for every guest table with ten people per table.

10 x 10 feet of space for the DJ.

16 x 20 feet of space for a band.

10 x 10 feet of space for food tables, beverage tables, and gift tables.

20 x 20 feet of space for the bar.

10 x 10 feet of space for the cake.

12 x 12 feet of space for every 100 guests for the dance floor. If you have 200 guests, you will need 24 x 24 feet of space.

Figure 6-2 shows an example for you to use as a tool. I usually get out the old-fashioned paper and pen and draw this grid until I get the right size. Each box represents 10 by 10 feet of space. For this example, I used 200 people, a DJ, two food tables, one beverage table, one check-in table, one cake table, one bar, and a dance floor. For this example, you would need a 60-foot by 80-foot tent. This is another reason why a frame tent is easier to plan because you don't have poles in the way of your floor-plan spacing.

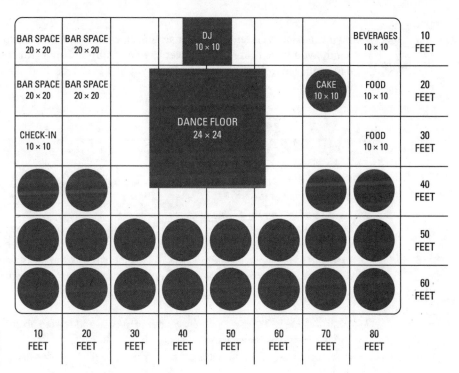

TIP

Your tent must be secured to the ground, either staking it into the ground or by weights, which can be water tanks or actual weights. Check in with your venue to confirm if your tent can be staked or if it needs to be weighted. If your tent is going over grass, confirm that there are no utility lines running where your tent needs to be set up. If your tent is going on concrete, you will need to have it weighted down with a weight source. I am going to share with you one of my favorite client stories to stress the importance of weighting or staking your tent. It is a must!

Wind: It's a four-letter word for a reason

I'm from the south and most would say southern women aren't supposed to cuss, but in weddings, "wind" is my favorite cuss word. Every bride thinks about rain on her wedding day but wind is often overlooked. Wind can potentially affect your wedding more than rain. We know when rain is coming but you can't predict wind.

If it's a windy day, your veil might be sticking straight up while you walk down the aisle. Those candles that you planned on lighting won't stay lit and your tall centerpieces keep falling over. Mother Nature doesn't care whether she got an invite to attend your wedding. I have seen time and time again how wind affects weddings.

TIP

If you're booking a tent, consider adding sidewalls that can roll up. That way if it's windy, you have more control over the environment under the tent. If it's a nice day, you can roll them up. At least you'll have a backup plan to fight those windy days.

THE AMAZING FLYING TENTS

I have seen pretty much everything when it comes to weddings, but I'll always remember this as one of the craziest experiences I've ever had.

My client had booked a venue with an incredible 360-degree view of the surrounding hills. It was picture perfect. My client had two tents out front of the venue for the guests to sit and have dinner. As I pulled in, I saw that something didn't seem right. The tents were set up on concrete, so the tent company had weighted them down, but the tents appeared to be floating just slightly off the ground.

It was a rather windy day. Our crew got out of the van and started unloading the flowers and decor. As we headed into the venue, which had a carriage house feel, we heard a strange sound. At the time, we thought maybe it was the tent flaps hitting the side of the building. It was rather windy that day, so that seemed logical.

We checked in with the venue manager and started working on setting up the lighting, tables, chairs, decor, and flowers. While we were inside working on those pieces, the sounds from outside seemed to be getting stronger. We kept looking outside to make sure the tents were staying put. They were weighted but they were moving slightly. We reached out to the tent company, who assured us those tents weren't going anywhere.

Until they did. I will never forget this moment. I was hanging the string lights inside the venue when all of a sudden I heard the loudest sound I have ever heard. And then someone outside yelled, "The tent is on the roof!" The venue manager came running into where I was working and said a few choice words, but the main point he was trying to convey was that I needed to get that tent off the roof!

I immediately dropped everything and ran outside. In my mind, I was singlehandedly going to remove the tent from the roof, as if I had somehow turned into Wonder Woman and was going to fly above the venue and pull the tent slowly to the ground. And then everyone would clap and smile, and we would just go on with our day.

Well, that wasn't the case. When I got outside, I turned around to see a heaping pile of bent metal on the roof that vaguely resembled a tent. Additionally, at the beginning of the day there were two tents, but now I saw only one tent.

We immediately needed to get on the roof because there was a pole sticking straight up that was about to break though the upstairs window. It took as many hands as we could grab to stabilize the ball of metal on the roof until the tent company could come back and get the tent off the roof. Once on the roof, we realized that the second tent had lifted like a kite and was about a hundred yards down the hill. It didn't look salvageable but at least we knew where it landed.

I had never seen anything like it! I had to call the tent company. That was a fun phone call. "This is Sarah, the wedding planner. Um, both tents you put up this morning just flew away. Oh, and one of them is on the roof of the venue. When do you think you might be able to come back?" I say this jokingly as if I was calm, but this wasn't a calm phone call. Everyone knew we needed all the help we could get immediately, and we also needed two brand new tents.

When the tent company arrived, they too were in complete shock. They quickly met us on the roof to work together to lower the tent to the ground. It was all hands, feet, arms, and legs on deck, but we were able to get that tent off the roof. The tent company removed the damaged tents, brought us two new tents, secured those and then secured them again, and my client and all her guests had no idea the morning we had. In the end, my client had her perfect day up on a hill.

The moral of this story is that wind can quickly change your plans. It's often forgotten, so I encourage you to consider a backup plan for our little four-letter word and make sure those tents are secured! Tents can quickly turn into large kites, and I don't want that happening to you.

Considering an All-Inclusive Wedding Venue: Pros and Cons

The hottest trend in wedding planning is booking an all-inclusive wedding venue. It seems simple, right? Everything you need is in one pretty little package.

There are several perks to booking an all-inclusive venue. If you have a busy life, this may be the perfect fit. Often at all-inclusive venues, you will have one company to communicate with, one contract, and one bill. Picking your vendors and sorting through the good one, bad ones, and who can provide exactly what you need obviously takes some time. It will consume most of your time through the planning process so booking an all-inclusive venue should help you save the time you will spend on the research.

The con is that even though you saved the time, you may not like the vendor options that the all-inclusive venue offers. It's important when booking an all-inclusive venue that you understand what you can alter from the set package. If you love a particular photographer, can you hire them? Does that mean you get money off the all-inclusive package or is there a loss? If the package includes a DJ but you want a band, can you upgrade, or get a credit back for the DJ and book your own entertainment?

As discussed in Chapter 5, an all-inclusive wedding venue should save you money. The main reason is that the vendors the venue is using often provide a custom price that may be less than if you book them on their own. There is loyalty between the venue and the vendor for being a part of their all-inclusive package because they're given a higher chance that they will be booked for your wedding. You benefit from that relationship as opposed to hiring each vendor on your own.

REMEMBER

Most all-inclusive venues are booked based on your projected guest count. Therefore, it's important to make sure you know an approximate guest count before you start touring venues. Confirm with your venue that you can adjust the price up or down based on your final RSVP. If you contract at 200 people, what happens if you end up with 150 people? Can you adjust down, or do you lose the money you spent on the 50 people who aren't attending?

In wedding planning there will be variable costs and fixed costs. A variable cost is a vendor whose pricing is based on your guest count, such as your rentals, caterers, florist, baker, and bartender. They're providing products where the quantity changes based on your final guest count. A fixed cost is a vendor whose pricing is not dependent on your guest count, such as your photographer, videographer, DJ or band, venue, and wedding planner. Whether you have 50 people or 200 people, their services and prices don't change. If the all-inclusive venue allows you to adjust up or down, make sure the variable costs reflect that.

If you're planning a destination wedding, an all-inclusive venue could be the perfect option for your wedding. It can be challenging to hire vendors in an area you're unfamiliar with. Working with an all-inclusive venue for a destination wedding will provide you with vendors in that area who do a wonderful job at serving brides in that location. Again, the venue does the vetting of vendors so you can feel confident in booking a stellar vendor.

Often, all-inclusive venues in a destination location offer lodging. The price is at a group rate that's less than if your guests booked their own lodging online. A benefit to this is saving your guests money in their travel expenses but also your guests will all be in one place. It maximizes the experience for your guests as they will be able to see you and your fiancé during the entire wedding weekend. This is different than a venue that's booked for one day. In that situation, you will most likely see the guests who aren't in the wedding only on your wedding day.

Another positive to all-inclusive wedding venues is that most come with an in-house coordinator to ensure a smooth day for all in attendance. This means there will be someone on site to make sure your ceremony starts on time, the guests are seated, the bridal party comes in at the right time and in the right order, the transition to the reception runs smoothly, dinner is served, the cake is cut, the toast and special dances happen. As a reminder, a coordinator is different than a venue manager, so it's important that you understand what that person's responsibilities will be for your wedding.

All-inclusive venues also have every piece of the puzzle that you need, such as an in-house rental company, caterer, photographer, videographer, baker, bartender, entertainment, and more. This is a wonderful positive to booking an all-inclusive venue because you don't have to worry about who's going to do what. It simplifies the process and makes the vendor communication so much easier.

When I meet with a client who is considering an all-inclusive venue, the one thing I hear over and over again is that they're afraid they will lose the ability to customize their event. This can be a downside to booking an all-inclusive venue because you may feel like you're getting a cookie-cutter wedding like all the other weddings at the venue.

It is important when considering an all-inclusive venue that you can customize your event. Remember, everything reflects your relationship, and it is important to add your personal touches to the wedding. This can be done at an all-inclusive venue, so make certain you know which items you can customize so that your experience there will feel special and uniquely yours.

Chapter **7**

Inviting Friends and Family

t is officially time to organize your guest list and start spreading the news! So many pieces to your wedding planning puzzle will be affected by the number of people you'll have at your wedding. Up until this point, it's been okay to have a rough idea of how many guests will attend, but now is the time to set that list in stone.

In this chapter, I discuss the different sizes of weddings, how to organize your guest list, several ways to invite your guests, and the information they need to know along the way. By the end of this chapter, you'll have all the tools you need to ensure your guests are finalized, organized, and informed on the details of your day, in the right way.

Deciding What Size Really Matters

During the COVID-19 pandemic, wedding sizes drastically changed across the United States. Most couples were forced to change attendance numbers due to state, county, or venue regulations. Additionally, the situation forced everyone to reconsider their priorities. We've been accustomed to larger weddings but hardly hear of small weddings — until recently. To us, a wedding is a big deal, and we want all our favorite people with us to celebrate. But when we couldn't, we had to accept the fact that our big wedding was now going to be a small wedding.

Weddings can come in all shapes and sizes. In picking the size of your wedding, it really comes down to what's most important to you. Have you always dreamed of having a large wedding and you have the budget to make that happen? Would you rather save money and buy a house and just have a few of your closest friends and family witness your marriage? What is your dream size? What do you envision when you think about your wedding day? In the following sections I explain the different sizes and share some pro tips so that no matter what size is best for you, you'll be able to maximize your budget and make the best selections for your big day.

Micro wedding: An intimate affair

A micro wedding is an intimate wedding with no more than 50 guests. Micro weddings have all the major activities that a larger wedding would have. The only difference is the lower number of guests.

REMEMBER

A micro wedding is different than an elopement. An elopement does not have all the activities that a traditional wedding has, such as dinner, dancing, or a reception. Elopements are all about the ceremony and possibly a cake cutting or refreshments. Some photographers have "elopement photo packages." There are also venues that host elopements. Those packages are less expensive due to the timing of the event. Traditionally, elopements don't last longer than two hours.

A SMALLER WEDDING DOESN'T ALWAYS MEAN LESS EXPENSIVE

Let's start with the first myth: that a smaller wedding costs less than a larger wedding. Overall, in general, yes, a smaller wedding will cost less because you have fewer variable costs. However, the price per person may be higher than a large wedding due to the fixed costs. That is important to note because I often hear, "Well, it's going to be a small wedding, so we don't have a big budget." Remember, a fixed-cost vendor is not going to price their services based on whether you have 50 people or 200 people. They're providing a service that is not affected by the size of your event. This is why smaller weddings can often have a higher cost per person.

There are many benefits to hosting a micro wedding. In general, you do save money on the overall event because you don't have as many people to feed, provide a place to sit, and give them a beverage. They're often held at an intimate location that wouldn't be able to accommodate a big wedding. This allows you the opportunity to find a hidden gem for your venue. Additionally, if it isn't an official venue, you may be able to save money on a larger venue cost.

TIP

I want you to consider a smaller venue for several reasons, but mostly on financial and practical grounds. Remember, it doesn't matter to a fixed-cost vendor if you have 50 people or 200 people. If the venue costs $5,000, for example, and you have 50 people, then the price per person works out to $100. If your venue costs $5,000 and you have 200 people, the price per person is $25. That's a big difference, so finding a more intimate venue, possibly off the radar of traditional venues, will lower your price per person.

The greatest benefit to hosting a micro wedding is the ability for each of your guests to have an authentic experience. For micro weddings, you don't have to worry about not spending some time with each guest. Due to the smaller size, you'll have a more personal experience for your wedding, like you do at a rehearsal dinner or a dinner party at your home. You get to spend more time with your guests and that's a very special characteristic of a smaller versus a larger wedding. I'll never forget how at my wedding I didn't even see several people who attended, including close family. Not until I got the pictures back from the photographer did I realize there were so many people I didn't even get the chance to say hello to. I was so sad about that because obviously they were important to me, and I wanted to spend time with them but didn't get the opportunity because of the size of the wedding.

Medium wedding: It's "just right"

A medium wedding is one with 50–150 guests. Medium weddings are the most popular size when it comes to guest count. They allow you to invite your closest friends and family with a little room for other guests you may feel obligated to invite.

A medium wedding could be a great fit for you because you get to invite those you want to be with you, but it isn't a budget buster. A medium-sized wedding will still give an intimate feel and connection with your guests and won't feel too big or too small.

REMEMBER

For a medium-sized wedding, the general rule is 25 percent your family, 25 percent your fiancé's family, with 50 percent left for your friends. I understand this percentage will change slightly for a larger family, but the main point is that you have the room to spread the guest list out evenly between your families and friends.

Medium weddings also allow you to pick a smaller venue for the reception. Hopefully, this will save you some money as well! If you end up on the higher side of 150 people, pick a place that can accommodate up to 180 people seated. That will allow enough room for tables, chairs, and a dance floor.

Large wedding: Go big or go home

A large wedding is a wedding with 150 or more guests. There's no limit to who you invite if you're hosting a large wedding: family, friends, coworkers, neighbors, childhood friends, even the person who delivers your mail if you want! There's no need to stress over who makes the cut.

It goes without saying that large weddings are the most expensive due to having the highest number of people in attendance. There are more mouths to feed, sit at a table, and keep those beverages flowing. You'll also need a larger venue to make sure you have enough space and parking to accommodate all your guests.

REMEMBER

This size often requires additional staff from either your wedding planner, caterer, or bartender to ensure everyone is served in a timely manner. Therefore, it is important to know your guest size when picking your vendors because if you're hosting a large wedding, you need to make sure your vendors are comfortable with the additional people to take care of.

The sky's the limit when it comes to large weddings. They often include all the bells and whistles regarding the extras such as a photobooth, champagne fountain, chocolate fountain, party favors, or even fireworks. Remember, if you're planning a large wedding, be sure you have a budget. It's easy to get carried away with large weddings and end up way over budget. Keep that at the front of your planning so that you aren't overspending when all is said and done.

Organizing Your Guest List

I'm a girl who loves a good spreadsheet. It makes me feel organized and in control of whatever data I'm collecting. Maybe you love it like me, or maybe it's the last thing you ever want to do. Either way, it's an important step in the planning process. The great news about organizing your guest list is that you'll now have the names and addresses of everyone important to you. When was the last time you asked for someone's mailing address? I'm certain it's been a minute. Don't worry; that's normal.

In this section, we'll work together on determining who's on the list and how to organize it. Regardless of whether you're collecting email addresses or mailing addresses, there's information you need to start collecting to ensure a smooth planning process. Having this information will allow you to send out your invites, collect RSVPs, and figure out your floor plan.

Deciding who's invited

The first step in setting up your guest list is determining who's invited. This decision is determined by your budget and what size wedding is perfect for you as a couple. If you have a limitless budget, you could potentially have a limitless guest list. If you have a smaller budget, you'll only be able to invite the number of people who fit within that budget.

I created Table 7-1 to illustrate three main points. Variable versus fixed costs makes a difference to your price-per-person cost, how to determine how many people you can invite, and how to find your cost per person. Please know that I understand wedding costs vary geographically. Some areas in the United States and across the world cost more than others. This table is to be used as a sample to help you fill in your own table and create your numbers.

TABLE 7-1 **Sample Cost Per Person**

		50 Guests	100 Guests	150 Guests	200 Guests
Fixed Cost	Photographer	$5,000	$5,000	$5,000	$5,000
	Videographer	$2,800	$2,800	$2,800	$2,800
	Planner	$3,000	$3,000	$3,000	$3,000
	Venue	$6,500	$6,500	$6,500	$6,500
	DJ	$1,500	$1,500	$1,500	$1,500
	Officiant	$500	$500	$500	$500
Variable Cost	Catering	$3,000	$6,000	$9,000	$12,000
	Bartending	$825	$1,650	$2,475	$3,300
	Rentals	$750	$1,500	$2,250	$3,000
	Flowers	$1,250	$2,500	$3,750	$5,000
Price/Person		$502.50	$309.50	$245.17	$213.00
Total Budget		$25,125	$30,950	$36,775	$42,600

If you consider the national average of $250–$300 per person, that would help you determine your budget. If you have $15,000 to spend on your wedding, you could host approximately 60 guests. If you have $50,000, that allows for 200 guests. Obviously, there are pieces to the sample shown in this table that you won't need, but if you look at the average cost per person on a national level, that gives you a range of how many people you can invite. It's always better to over-estimate than underestimate when it comes to planning your guest list and budget.

Now that you have your guest count, you can invite up to 30% more because you can safely assume that not everyone you invite will be able to attend. If you can afford to host 60 guests, you can invite approximately 78 people. If you can afford to host 200 guests, you can invite approximately 260 people. Again, this is to be used as a guide and not an absolute. It's a formula to give you a starting point to help you determine your guest list size, price per person, and total budget.

Once you've calculated an approximant guest count based on what you can afford, it is time to sit down as a couple and select those people you want to have with you on your wedding day. This part of the planning process can cause some tension, so I want you to acknowledge that. You're both loyal to your people but the main thing to remember is that you're a team. Together you're working to blend your lives and pick the people who get to be with you and celebrate your love.

It is easy to fall down the rabbit hole of inviting just this one person, and this other person, and then this one other person, and before you know it you've invited an extra 50 people. I always tell my clients that if they feel like they can't hand a guest and their plus-one $300 and ask them to come, then they should make the cut.

Setting up your guest list

When you have that sacred list of names, it's time to start collecting their personal information. Reach out to the guests you know, and your fiancé should do the same. You need to collect their name and their plus-one's name, the street address, city, and zip code. If you're sending out your invites electronically, you'll need to collect their email address or phone number.

You don't want to do this more than once, so it's important to input your guests' information the way you want their names printed on the invitation envelope or place card. Table 7-2 shows how to set up your file electronically.

TABLE 7-2   ## Sample Electronic Guest List Setup

Guest Name	Children/Plus-One	Address	City	State	Zip
Mr. & Mrs. John Doe		1234 Street Name	City	State	Zip
Mr. & Mrs. John Doe	Jo, John	1234 Street Name	City	State	Zip
Mr. John Doe	Mrs. Jane Smith	1234 Street Name	City	State	Zip
Mr. John Doe	Miss Jane Doe	1234 Street Name	City	State	Zip
Miss Jane Doe	Guest	1234 Street Name	City	State	Zip

REMEMBER

When you enter your guest names into an electronic format, make sure you type it *exactly* how you want it printed — including the punctuation. Here are some of the most important formatting tips to remember:

>> Include the (.) after Mr., Mrs., or Ms.

>> Spell out the entire state name rather than using the two-letter postal abbreviation.

>> For children, list only the first names, no last names.

>> Include apartment or unit numbers at the end of the address. Do not put them in a separate column.

The main reason to set up your guest list in this format is due to electronic merging. If we simplify the format, there's less risk that the merging of your guest list will omit an important piece of information. For example, if you add another column for an apartment number, there's a higher chance that the apartment number will be forgotten, and your guest will not receive the invitation.

Now let's discuss the proper way to address a married couple, someone with children, two single guests, and a single guest who you give a plus-one to.

>> **Married couple:** A married opposite-sex couple with the same last name should be addressed as Mr. and Mrs. and the Mr.'s first and last name. This example would be Mr. and Mrs. John Doe. If the couple has different last names, they would be listed as Mr. John Doe and Mrs. Jane Smith. The exception to this rule is if one is a Dr. The Dr. should be first. If the male is a Dr., it would be Dr. & Mrs. John Doe. If the female is a Dr., it would be Dr. & Mr. John Doe.

If you're inviting a married same-sex couple, you'll need to confirm if they have combined their names. If they have, they would be listed in the first column together in the first column. If they don't combine their names, you can list them formally in the first column with an "and" between their names.

>> **A guest with children:** You'll list the guest's formal first and last name in the first column and list only the children's first names in the second column. There's no need to include the last name. Some children come from blended families, or their parents have a different last name. This format prevents the child being addressed by the wrong last name.

>> **Two guests coming together:** If you're inviting a non-married couple, you'll list them separately between column one and two. There isn't a proper order to listing those names. Typically, the person you know will be listed in the first column. If you know both single guests, they can be listed how you deem appropriate.

>> **Single guest plus-one:** If you're inviting a single person and letting them bring someone but you don't know their name, they can be listed in the first column and "Guest" listed in the second column.

Getting the Word Out

Well, friend, it's time to pick your invitation format and let your guests know the details they need to be able to attend your wedding. Regardless of which format best fits your style, there are certain things your guests need to know to be able to attend and get to your wedding location. In this section, I cover setting up a website, creating your Save-the-Dates, invitation must-haves, collecting RSVPs, and determining whether to use traditional mail or email.

REMEMBER

Your invitations are a first glimpse into who you are as a couple that your guests will see. They set the tone for what your wedding will look and feel like.

Sharing updates on a wedding website

Wedding websites are a perfect outlet to get information to your guests without spending additional money on paper information. These can be used to share your story, list your registry, share last minute changes or updates, and collect online RSVPs.

TIP

There are many resources online for creating your wedding website. If you do create one, make sure to establish a custom URL, which can be created in the settings of your website building format. This is important because it will allow you to set up a simple website address rather then a long standard website filled with all kinds of symbols, letters, and numbers that will prove tricky for your guests to find. Making a custom website URL allows you to say something like: www. johnandjanedoe.com. It will be easier for your guests to find your website and will look prettier on a printed invitation.

TIP

Another thing I want you to consider is making your website password protected. This is a short password, often your wedding date, that only the people who have received your website information know. Once you publish your website, anyone can search your names and find all your wedding information. They learn the date, time, location, and additional details about your day that you may not want them to know. Protecting your website with a password gives you the ability to control who can see your personal information.

A special piece to creating a wedding website is that it gives you a place to share your love story. With a formal invitation, no one knows your story. The wedding website is the perfect place to share how you met and got engaged. Remember, there will likely be people at your wedding who don't know this information, so a website allows you to share more information than they would get from a traditional wedding invitation.

Wedding websites are also the perfect place to share your wedding registry, transportation information, specific addresses to your venue, planned activities for the wedding, and your bridal party information. It really is a limitless platform to impart information they wouldn't normally see on a formal invitation. Use this platform to let your guests into your story.

Asking people to save the date

Save-the-Date cards are sent to your guests before you send out formal invitations to make sure they hold your date on their social calendar. They can be sent any point during your journey, but if you do decide to use them, make sure your guests receive them at least six months prior to your wedding.

Save-the-Dates are typically less formal than your invitation. They're often printed on postcard-style paper or a refrigerator magnet. It's also fun to use a picture of the two of you in your design. If you're getting married in the spring or summer, consider using your Save-the-Date as your holiday card. You need to include your wedding date, city, and wedding website, and let your guests know that a formal invitation will arrive later. By the time you send out your Save-the-Dates, you need to know your wedding date and city.

Including the city of your wedding is important for those who need to travel to have adequate time to plan airfare and hotel rooms. Prior to sending your Save-the-Dates. It's best to secure your hotel room blocks and build your wedding website. That way when your guests receive them, they can start planning their accommodations for your big day.

Figure 7-1 is an example I created to show the important information that needs to be included. Have fun with the design. Use a picture from your engagement session or keep it simple, like the sample here. The design options are limitless, but use the Save-the-Dates as the first time you set the tone of your wedding.

FIGURE 7-1:
Sample
Save-the-Date.

Sending the all-important wedding invitations

Even though digital invitations are gaining popularity, sending a formal invitation is never going to go out of style. A formal invitation is as classic as it gets when it comes to determining the best format for inviting your guests. It's a staple in the wedding planning process and I'm going to help you determine who is inviting your guests, learn the format protocol, and explore different printing types. There's something exciting about seeing your names printed together on a piece of paper. so this part should be fun!

Let's first address the timing. Formal invitations should be mailed 6–8 weeks prior to your wedding. This allows your guests enough time to RSVP without giving them too much time to place your invitation on their counter and forget about it. With that being said, make sure you start designing them and send them to the printer with enough time for you to put them together in that timeframe.

TIP

I also advise you to order about 10% more invitations and envelopes than you actually need. This will ensure you have enough for any guests you originally omitted or errors while addressing the envelopes. Another important thing to remember is that there is a difference between invite totals and guest totals. If you're anticipating 200 guests, you won't need to order 200 invitations. Make sure to check your list to confirm the number of invitations, not guests, that you need to order.

TIP

Once you receive your invitations and envelopes, take one invite, RSVP card, any additional information cards and envelopes to the post office to confirm how much your postage will be. If you're asking your guests to return an RSVP card, don't forget to buy those stamps and put them on the RSVP card or envelope, as well as the stamp for the outside envelope. This way your guests can easily return the RSVP card without searching around their home for a stamp.

One of my clients forgot to put stamps on her RSVP envelopes, so few guests returned them. Another client didn't put enough postage on the outside envelope, which meant a lot of her invitations never made it to her guests. To make matters worse, some of her guests had to pay the additional postage to receive their invite. I don't want that happening to you, so take the extra step to ensure you have calculated the postage correctly.

Who's doing the inviting

The first step in designing your invitations is to determine who is inviting your guests to your wedding. Traditionally, the host or the person who is inviting is the one who is paying the bill. It could be your family, or maybe you and your fiancé are paying for your wedding. There are several different scenarios, so I created a few samples to help you determine who's inviting your guests.

For these examples, the bride's name is Jane Smith, the groom is John Doe, the bride's parents are Mr. & Mrs. Adam Smith, and the groom's parents are Mr. & Mrs. Mark Doe.

Bride's Parents

Mr. & Mrs. Adam Smith

Request the honor of your company

at the marriage of their daughter

Jane Smith

To

Mr. John Doe

Groom's Parents

Mr. & Mrs. Mark Doe

Request the honor of your company

at the marriage of their son

Mr. John Doe

To

Jane Smith

Both Parents

Mr. & Mrs. Adam Smith and Mr. & Mrs. Mark Doe

Request the honor of your company

at the marriage of their children

Miss Jane Smith

To

Mr. John Doe

Bride's Parents with Acknowledgment of the Groom's Parents

Mr. & Mrs. Adam Smith

Request the honor of your company

at the marriage of their daughter

Jane Smith

To

Mr. John Doe

Son of Mr. & Mrs. Mark Doe

The Couple

Miss Jane Smith

and

Mr. John Doe

Request the honor of your company at their marriage

The Couple and Parents

Together with their parents

Mr. & Mrs. Adam Smith and Mr. & Mrs. Mark Doe

Miss Jane Smith

and

Mr. John Doe

Request the honor of your company at their marriage

Invitation Format Protocol

Regardless of whether you're sending digital or print invitations, it's important to make sure your guests have all the information they need to know so that they can make it to your wedding location, arrive on time, and know what's in store for the event.

REMEMBER

Your invitation should include the following:

>> The host names

>> The invitation to attend the wedding

>> Your name and fiancé's name

>> The date, year, and time of the ceremony

>> The location of the ceremony

>> The location of the reception

>> A notation of a dress code

>> Your wedding website or additional information

As discussed above, it's important to make sure your guests know who the host is for your wedding. This is the person, family, or couple who is inviting your guests to attend.

Next, you need to formally invite them to attend. I have created a few examples to consider. Customize any or create your own to fit your style and feel.

You are cordially invited to celebrate the marriage of

The honor of your presence is requested at the marriage of

You are cordially invited to attend the wedding of

You are invited to celebrate in the marriage of

Request the pleasure of your company at the celebration of

Joyfully request the pleasure of your company at

You are invited to witness the exchange of vows and rings of

You are invited to celebrate the marriage of

With joyful hearts, we invite you to celebrate the marriage of

It would be our honor to have you witness the marriage of

We are getting married and invite you to witness

Please join us in celebration of

You are invited to our beginning

Cheer and celebrate as we say I Do

Don't forget to include your names. You'll need to include your first and last names, with one exception. If your parents are hosting and you share the same last name with them, your invitation needs to include only your first name and middle name. Here's example of this:

Mr. & Mrs. Adam Smith

Request the honor of your company

at the marriage of their daughter

Miss Jane Elizabeth

To

Mr. John Doe

When you inform your guests of the date, year, and time, you begin with the ceremony start time. Your guests will start arriving 30 minutes before your start time. A formal version will have everything spelled out, while a less formal invitation will use the number characters. I've included a few examples to consider for your invitations.

The Formal Version

The first of January

Two thousand and twenty-two

At half past four in the afternoon

Semi Formal Version

January first

Two thousand and twenty-two

4:30 pm

Least Formal Version

January 1, 2022

4:30 pm

Next, list the location of the ceremony. You should include the name of the venue (if there is one) and the physical address. This is necessary for locations that are not easily found on an internet search engine. It's not important to list the city code, simply the name of the venue, address, city, and state.

If your ceremony and reception are being held at the same location, inform your guests at the bottom of your invitation by saying, "Dinner and dancing to follow," or "Reception to follow." Let guests know what to expect. If you aren't serving dinner and are instead hosting desserts and cocktails, consider saying, "Desserts and cocktails to follow." This will let your guests know that they will not be served an actual meal and will know that they need to eat before or after your reception.

If your reception is located at another location, you'll need to include that information on your invite. If the reception is immediately following the ceremony at another location, there's no need to list the time. You'll simply put "Reception to follow at" and then the name and address of the venue. If there is a time gap between the start of your ceremony and your reception start time, you'll need to include the time with the venue name and address. Here are a few examples to help you fill in the appropriate information for your wedding.

Reception Immediately Following the Ceremony at Another Location

Ceremony location

Ceremony address

Ceremony city & state

Reception to follow at

Reception location

Reception address

Reception city & state

Reception Following the Ceremony Later at Another Location

Ceremony location

Ceremony address

Ceremony city & state

Reception will begin at 5:00 pm

Reception location

Reception address

Reception city & state

Advising your guests about what to wear is a good idea, for many reasons. Most importantly, if you're hosting an outdoor event, you should inform your guests that all wedding activities will be outside. That way they'll be prepared, for example, for a warm fall day with a chilly night and will know they need to bring a jacket or sweater for when the sun sets.

If you'd like to specify a dress code at your wedding, some popular tiers are Black Tie, Semiformal, Cocktail Attire, or Casual.

>> **Black tie:** Formal long dresses for women and tuxedos for men.

>> **Semiformal:** Formal long dresses or formal short dresses for women. Tuxedos or suits for men.

>> **Cocktail attire:** A short cocktail dress for women and a suit for men.

>> **Casual:** A sundress for women and a blazer with khakis or jeans for men.

The last piece of the puzzle is to share your wedding website with your guests. This will be your catchall for communicating your registry, accommodations, weekend activities, and last-minute changes or updates as needed. You can simply put, "For more information visit" and then list your website. This is why it's important to create your own personal URL so that it's easy to read on your invitations. If you created a password-protected website, include that under your website address.

For more information visit

www.johnandjane.com

passcode: 12345

Printing types

Now that you have the content of your invitation ready to go, it's time to think about the printing style. There are many online resources that will print your invitations for you, or you can work with a custom invitation company near you. If you pick a company in your area, they'll be able to show you paper samples, printing types, and design options. It's a wonderful way to touch and feel your actual invitation or sample before you buy.

TIP

If you decide to work with an invitation company online, the number of options may feel overwhelming when trying to decide which one is best for you. I encourage you to get out ever invitation you have every received and pick out those you love. You may be surprised with a trend in the ones you prefer. What were the designs? Is the text flat print, raised print, or engraved print? Additionally, if you do work with an online invitation company, ask them if they're able to send you a sample invite before they formally go to print.

In this section, I want to introduce you to a few different printing types so you understand what these mean and can determine your printing style.

>> **Digital or flat print:** This is the most popular way to print your invitations. Digital printing is limitless on the number of colors you can use and your design options. It's the most cost-effective way to print your invitations. The printing style is in the name: it's completely flat without raised elements.

>> **Foil stamping:** Using a foil detail on your invitations is a cost-effective way to add some pizzaz without breaking the budget. Several online companies now offer foil details with their flat printing services.

>> **Spot color:** Spot color is when your invitations are printed one color at a time to create a vibrant finish. There is consistency between each invitation. The spot colors are Cyan, Magenta, Yellow, and Black.

>> **Thermography:** Thermography is raised print on your invitation created with a custom plate and heat to raise the print off the page. It's the type of printing where you can run your fingers across the invitation and feel the font above the paper.

>> **Embossed or engraved:** This style is opposite of thermography as the print is created on a custom plate and pressed into your invitation to create an impression. The font is lower than the paper, like engraving.

>> **Letter press:** This style is like thermography and embossed in that a custom plate is created and ink is placed on your invitation, but the final product is flat. There is no raised or engraved effect.

>> **Laser cut:** This style offers the most flare at the highest price. It doesn't involve ink but rather materials such as paper, metal, or wood where the design is cut out with a laser to give your invitation a wow factor. It's an impressive way to invite your guests or add a special flare to a standard invitation.

Getting a headcount with RSVPs

Let's face it, we have tried our best to predict if your guests are going to reply yes or no. But I can tell you from experience that guests are often unpredictable. Up until this point, it has all been what you believe to be truth when it comes to your guests' responses, but now is the time to get those firm commitments or regrets. Those responses will affect your final payments, floor plans, and setups. I don't want you paying for one more guest than you need to.

Gathering your guests' responses can be a bit frustrating. As much as you would like to believe that everyone will respond, often that is not the case. I have seen it time and time again where clients are scrambling to get answers from their guests. I mean, you have made it simple for them to respond but not all of them will, so I want to give you a heads up on that so you're prepared to avoid the frustration.

If you're not a lover of spreadsheets like I am, delegate this part of your process to a person in your life who is. By the end of this section, you'll be able to give your caterer, bartender, rental company, baker, and florist an exact head count to avoid overpaying.

Let's chat about what needs to be on your RSVP card.

>> **The RSVP date:** This is the date by which your guests should postmark their response. If it is January 1, they have until that date to get it in the mail. Expect the responses to arrive in your mailbox a few days after that date.

>> **Accept or decline:** We will create a section on your RSVP card where your guests will accept (yes) or decline (no) the invitation to your wedding. I suggest designing multiple lines where they can write in the names of every person who is coming, along with this instruction: "Please list all guest names." This will help you get an exact count of who's coming. The (M) is the start of Mr., Mrs., Ms. or Miss.

>> **Menu selection:** If you're doing a plated seated meal where your guests select their meal, you'll collect that information on the RSVP card. Again, it is important to make sure you know which guest has picked which entrée selection. (Figure 7-2 shows an example to illustrate my suggestion.)

>> **Adding something fun:** Consider adding something fun to your RSVP card to engage with your guests. Have them request a song for the reception. Ask them to write how you all met or know each other. Ask them marriage advice. It is a way to make them feel special and included in your wedding planning and you may have a few laughs along the way which is a good thing!

Figure 7-2 is a sample RSVP card for you to use as a template to design your own based on the information you need to get from your guests.

Deciding on an RSVP date

The first step in determining your RSVP date is to make sure you know when your vendors need that number. There are certain deadlines that may determine this date. An example would be if your caterer needs your final guest count by 14 days out from your event. You'll want to make sure to set that date with enough time for you to collect those responses, organize them, and get them that final number before their deadline.

FIGURE 7-2:
Sample
RSVP Card

For our clients, I set the RSVP date four weeks before their wedding date. This allows enough time to receive all the RSVPs, follow up with the guests who haven't responded, organize the list, and give those final numbers to the vendors who need them two weeks before their wedding.

Once that number is given to the vendors that need it, there are no more changes. That doesn't mean that there won't be changes, because managing all your guests' schedules can be a big task. Some guests will say they can come and then back out. The same will be true for those who RSVP no and then show up on the day of your wedding.

When those situations occur, reach out to the vendors that are affected by the change to see if they can accommodate. Generally speaking, those last-minute changes seem to work themselves out naturally. One person will back out, another will come. If you're communicating those changes with your vendors, you'll be taken care of. Don't wait until the last minute to update them on ten changes. Inform them as they come in so everyone can stay up on the changes they need to know so they can make your event a success.

TIP

Before you send out your invitations, consider giving each guest's envelope a number for your RSVP cards that correlates with a number in your electronic guest list file. I can't tell you how many times guests return the RSVP card with a yes or no but no name. If you number the cards, that will help you determine who returned the response even if they don't fill in their name.

Organizing responses

The first step in organizing your responses is deciding on an RSVP return address. If you're sending them by mail, where are they going? Are your parents going to collect the RSVPs? Do you want them to come to your home? The address of whoever is collecting those responses needs to be on the RSVP card or envelope. Consider using your last names followed by "wedding" and then the address, such as "The Smith Williams Wedding." That way the return address doesn't specify who the responses are going to.

TIP

When we created your guest list, I had you create an electronic file with your guest names and addresses. You'll use that same file and now add another column to include "RSVP." In this column I want you to input the numbers, not a yes or no. If a married couple RSVPs that they're both coming, you'll input "2" in that column. If a married couple RSVPs to say they're not coming, you'll input "0." Table 7-3 is a visual example of how to set up your RSVP list.

TABLE 7-3   ## Sample Guest RSVP Setup

Guest Name	Address	City	State	Zip	RSVP
Mr. & Mrs. John Doe	1234 Street Name	City	State	Zip	2

TIP

The reason to input a number and not a yes or no is so that at the bottom of that column, you can formulate the file to add up all the numbers in that column. This will give you a total number of guests attending. Additionally, you can data-sort that column so that those guests who can't attend will be at the bottom of your list. That way you can always view the guests who are attending first.

It's good to get into the habit of entering those responses as soon as you get them. It's always fun to find an RSVP card in the mail instead of a bill, right? That is a good thing, so make a habit of staying on top of the responses as they come in. This will also help you see how your guest count is shaping up as you go rather than being surprised in the end by your actual numbers.

As soon as the day ends on your RSVP date, I give you permission to reach out to your guests via email, phone, or social media. You gave them until that date to respond and you haven't heard from them, so now is the time to find out their response. Divide and conquer the list based on your friends and family and your fiancé's friends and family. You take your friends or assign this to your maid of honor, and your fiancé can do the same with his best man. Give the family to your parents or a close friend who knows the people you haven't heard from. You want an answer either way so that you don't have to pay for one more guest than you need to.

Tracking menu selections

The only reason you need to track guests' menu selection is if you're doing a plated seated meal, which is different than a buffet. A plated seated meal is when you offer your guests a selection of entrées and the caterer brings them their selection.

If you're offering your guests this option, you'll add multiple columns to the top of your guest file that list the selections. For example, across the top, after RSVP, you'll enter "chicken," "beef," "vegetarian." You'll do this for the same reason you're doing the RSVP formatting — to keep careful track of specifics.

Once you receive the RSVP, you'll input the number into each column. That way you can total the sum of that entire column at the bottom of your file. When you view your guest list file, you'll see at the bottom that you have, for instance, 20 beef, 50 chicken, and 10 vegetarian meals selected.

Let's say a married couple RSVPs that they want chicken and beef. So you would find their name in the file and input a "1" under chicken and a "1" under beef. Table 7-4 is a visual example of how to set up your guest menu selections.

TABLE 7-4   **Sample Guest Menu Selection Setup**

Guest Name	Address	City	State	Zip	RSVP	Chicken	Beef	Veg.
Mr. & Mrs. John Doe	1234 Street Name	City	State	Zip	2	1	1	0

REMEMBER

For a plated seated meal, you'll need to print place cards. We'll discuss in detail soon about formatting those cards. The caterer will need to know how many entrée selections will be at each table. For example, you'll tell the caterer, "Table one has five chicken entrées, four beef entrées, and one vegetarian entrée." As we continue in our guest list organization, we'll add a final column titled "Table number."

To mail or to email?

That is the question! What is best for you? Do you prefer a modern digital format or a traditional print format? In this section we are going to discuss a few pros and cons to a digital format versus good old-fashioned paper.

A digital format is faster than sending snail mail if you're short on time. If it's through social media or email, chances are you already have the contact information ready to go for your guests. You won't have to ask for mailing addresses and although some of your guests may move during your planning process, personal email addresses tend to stay the same.

A digital format is eco-friendly and saves on printing and paper cost. Additionally, you won't have to figure out the correct postage and save that money too! If you're looking for a simple way to save money on your wedding, consider a digital format.

You won't have to worry about printing or shipping delays. The only downside to the delivery is the infamous junk mail folder. It's the black hole of the digital format. The best chance of not ending up in a guest's junk mailbox is sending individual emails as opposed to using a mass email marketing tool. Often the bounce rate is higher even if you have sent them an email in the past because their email host may see you as someone who shouldn't get into their inbox even if you're best friends.

Another pro to digital is an instant RSVP response that is already formatted for you. National wedding websites also offer digital invitations and RSVP responses. If keeping up with the RSVPs sounds daunting, consider a one-stop-shop wedding website that will collect all the information you need for you.

On the other hand, paper invitations offer something magical that you can't receive in your inbox. Imagine your guest opening their actual mailboxes and seeing a beautiful invitation. They will thank you that it isn't a bill. In fact, even better, it's an invitation to attend a free event! Printed invitations are something your guests can tangibly see and feel. You can't get that from a digital format.

A paper invitation also gives your guests something to keep in their memory box. You too will have a copy to hold onto forever. Digital formats will eventually go away, never to be seen again. If you're excited about having something for your keepsake box regardless of whether your guests keep it, a paper invite is what you need.

TIP

Although it might be hard to imagine, you'll have guests who aren't online. You could also print a formal paper invitation but ask your guest to RSVP via email or electronically. If you do this, create a separate email account that's only for your RSVPs. This account will only have your RSVPs and not your junk mail. For those guests who aren't online, reach out to them to receive their response or include a separate card for them to RSVP via phone.

The downside to paper RSVPs is the time it takes to collect all the responses and organize them. Additionally, sometimes getting a response from a guest feels impossible. No matter how many ways you try, they just won't respond. It can be frustrating, and you may feel like a digital format would be easier for everyone, but what do you really want?

Providing Helpful Handouts

Stationery and printed materials for your wedding provide the guests with a keepsake of your wedding and information they need to know. Planning those elements to your big day can seem overwhelming. What do you need to have? What can you do without?

The list for your stationery needs may seem a mile long but we are going to narrow down the list to those items that will be given to your guests specifically on the wedding day or just after your big day. In this section, we'll discuss the essential handouts and those that you may choose to integrate into your wedding day. We'll work on the content of your wedding program, menu, place cards, and thank-you cards.

When I got married, I didn't do a wedding program. I know, shocking . . . the wedding planner didn't have a program at her own wedding? First, I was so busy being a mom, planning my clients' weddings, and running several businesses that my own wedding and the things that needed to get done kept getting pushed to the back burner. To me, the little things didn't matter. All I cared about was having a marriage that lasted. My perspective had changed. The program seemed to be the least important thing about my wedding day. To others in attendance, that was not the case. I remember guests and family making comments to me about not having one. I cannot tell you if the flowers were on the table or if the candles were lit but I can tell you that it bothered guests that I didn't have a program. As a reminder, I'm someone who cares about what others think about me, so of course this bothered me. Did a piece of paper matter to my husband and me? No. Did that piece of paper matter to others? Yes. I had to let that one go, but the point of telling that story is to show there are essential printed materials that need to be a part of your wedding day for certain reasons. Other pieces are up to you if you decide to have them or not.

A guide to your wedding: Programs

Programs are not a requirement at your wedding, especially if you're hosting a small, intimate, short wedding ceremony. But they're greatly appreciated for your guests to read and follow during your ceremony. They're also a keepsake for your family and friends who witnessed your marriage.

If you're planning a long ceremony with elements that involve guests participating, such as a community hymn, reading, or scripture, then they need to be a part of your stationery items on your big day. Programs are the roadmap for your guests to follow during your ceremony.

Another scenario that would prove to be helpful for your guests and a reason to have programs is if your reception is located at a separate location from your ceremony. This will allow you the perfect space to note directions from the ceremony site to the reception venue.

All in all, if you want them, have them. If they aren't the most important thing to you, then save the time and money and put that into something else for your big day. If you do decide to have programs for your wedding ceremony, you'll find here the information that needs to be included and how you can use them to celebrate those you have lost along the way.

What to include

Your wedding program should include your names, and the date, time, and location of your wedding. This is a stamp in time that will always mark the important details that some may eventually forget.

TIP

A special touch to a wedding program is to include a message from you and your fiancé. In this message, you'll thank your guests for being there and share how excited you are to marry your best friend. It's also a wonderful outlet to use to thank the family and friends who have helped you get to this day. Let them know how much they mean to you and that without them, the day wouldn't have been so wonderful.

Next up is the order of your ceremony. You'll include your prelude music titles, processional order of your bridal party with the song selections, content of your ceremony, and the recessional. If there are parts in your ceremony where the guests will repeat or recite, you'll list those as well in this section.

Don't forget your bridal party! The list should include the names of your officiant, bridesmaids, groomsmen, flower girl, ring bearer, hostess or ushers, parents, and grandparents. It is also nice to include the names of any musicians who are performing in your wedding. I have also had clients who listed the relation of their bridal party. This is where both sides come together so it is special to notate how you know your bridal party (for example, "Maid of Honor: Jane Smith, College Roommate").

Lastly, if your guests need instruction on how to get to the reception or you want them to participate in a grand exit from the church, the program is a perfect place to mention this information. For example, if you want your guests to line up outside the church after your ceremony for your exit you could say, "At the end of the ceremony, please join us in the front of the church for our send-off. Grab some bubbles on the way and we will see you soon."

Remembering those we lost

A wedding day is filled with emotion. Adding to the emotion is the void of those you love who can't be with you on the biggest day in your life. That void should be acknowledged to honor them and who they are to you as a person.

A wedding program is a perfect place to honor those you love who have passed away. You would begin with a statement of acknowledgement, like: "We lovingly remember and honor our loved ones who have gone before us and are with us in spirit today." This would then be followed by the names of those who have passed away and their relation to you.

If you have an element of your wedding that was designed specifically for those you have lost, the program is a perfect place to notate that. For example, if you have a special floral arrangement at the altar you could say, "The flowers on the altar are in loving memory of our loved ones." Another example would be if you left a seat at the front open for that person, you could say, "The seat at the front of the church is left open but not empty as we know they are with us today."

There are several ways that you can acknowledge your loved ones if you don't have a printed wedding program. Most popular is designating a memory table at your ceremony. This table is filled with pictures of those who have gone before us with an acknowledgment of their relation to you. It is a wonderful way for your guests to see those you love who can't be with you.

If you're hosting an outdoor wedding, hanging wind chimes is a beautiful way to celebrate those you love. I had a client one time who hung wind chimes and they played through the entire ceremony. We knew that person was with us on that day. It was a beautiful moment I will never forget.

Another special way to honor your loved one is to carry them with you. Purchase a small locket and put their picture in it and give it to your florist to put into your bouquet. If they're family, wearing their wedding rings or jewelry is a special way to honor them. If they have a handkerchief, you could wrap that around your bouquet stems or carry it with you in case you need to wipe a few tears.

In some cases, the traditional moments such as the father walking in the bride or sharing a father-daughter dance sadly aren't possible. Although they cannot be replaced, consider asking a brother, uncle, or close friend to assume the duties of your father. It doesn't mean they take their place in your heart; it only means they support you during this time in your life.

Regardless of what feels right to you, take time to honor those you love during your wedding day. Their lives are to be acknowledged and celebrated.

Teasing the tastebuds: Menus

Printed menus are optional at your wedding but add a special touch to your table setting and reception. If you're hosting a plated seated meal, they're not essential because your guests already preselected their dinner on the RSVP card. If you're hosting a buffet or stations meal, it's a nice touch to include a menu so your guests know what their options will be.

Regardless, your guests will want to know what they're eating for dinner. There are some important pieces to include on a printed or displayed menu to make sure your guests know what's for dinner. A menu is also a great place to notate dietary restrictions, such as gluten-free or vegetarian options.

As with the program, you'll want to include your names, date, and location. A menu is also a perfect place to send a message of appreciation to your guests. You can thank them for being with you and traveling to be a part of your special day. Let them know how much you appreciate them and that you can't wait to see them soon.

When designing your menu, reach out to your caterer to receive a detailed description of each item. This is not the ingredients list but rather the main details of the dish, similar to what you would read in a menu at a restaurant. Instead of saying "chicken and potatoes," get those yummy descriptions from your caterer: "Pan-fried fillet of chicken with caramelized onions, mushrooms, and garlic mashed potatoes.

When you have the fancy way of describing the dishes, organize them in this order:

Appetizers, Hors d'oeuvres, or First Course

Salad or Second Course

Entrée or Main Course

Dessert

It's also appropriate to include your bar selections on your printed menu. This will help avoid lines at your bar because your guests will be able to see their options before they go to the bar and ask the bartender what's available. If you're serving wine during dinner, this should be noted as well. Including nonalcoholic beverages is also helpful for guests who don't drink alcohol or who have children with them at your reception.

Menus can also serve to inform your guests about the schedule of the reception. After you list your menu items, you can include a general schedule or program.

This doesn't have to be a detailed timeline, just a general order so your guests know what's in store for the night, for example:

Bridal Party Introductions

Welcome & Prayer

Dinner

Cake Cutting & Toasts

Dancing

Exit at 10:00 pm

Boy, girl, boy, girl: Place cards

Place cards are an important piece to a seamless event if you're offering a plated seated meal for your guests. The caterer must know where your guests are seated so that they can give them the meal that they picked on the RSVP card. In this section, I'm going to give you some tips on how to execute place cards so that your dinner service is done in a timely manner.

Let's discuss the difference between place cards and escort cards. Place cards notate guest's name, table number, and entrée selection. An escort card includes the guest's name and table number. Place cards are printed individually per guest or couple, while escort cards may be displayed for your guest to see rather than printing actual cards.

The first step in a seamless dinner experience is to formalize your floor plan and number your tables. It's easier for guests to navigate the reception if your tables are in some consecutive order. Therefore, I want you to number the tables on your floor plan first before you start placing guests at the tables.

Now for the fun part that will change a million times until you lock it in. Table 7-5 lists a few standard table sizes and how many guests can fit at each table. If you're using round or rectangular tables, I suggest using paper and pencil to draw your floor plan so you can add guests' names to the tables, erase them, move them to another table, and do that over and over until you have everyone in their spot.

TIP

When you're picking a seat for each guest, consider where you and your partner are sitting in the room and who needs to sit closest to you. If you're doing a head table, decide with your fiancé whether you'll allow the spouses or guests of your bridal party to sit at the head table. If they aren't allowed to sit at the head table, consider placing them close to the head table.

TABLE 7-5

Table Sizes and Guest Capacity

Table Size	Guest Capacity
30" Round Table	2 People
48" Round Table	4–6 People
60" Round Table	6–10 People
72" Round Table	10–12 People
48" x 48" Rectangle Table	4 People
30" x 72" Rectangle Table	6–8 People with 2 on the end
30" x 96" Rectangle Table	8–10 People with 2 on the end

After you have drawn out your floor plan and selected a seat for each guest, we'll return to your master guest list document and add an additional column called "Table." When you input each guest table number into the column, write out "Table" and then the number. If your guest is seated at table one, for example, you would write in that column "Table One."

I want you to do this so that when you merge the file into a format to print the place cards, it will already be spelled out for you instead of having to input numbers. Certain fonts and calligraphy make it difficult to read the numbers, so spelling them out omits a guest going to table 7 when they're supposed to be at table 1.

It is appropriate and cost effective if you combine a couple on one place card. There's no need to print Mr. Smith and Mrs. Smith on separate cards. You can simply say, "Mr. & Mrs. Adam Smith — Table One."

Now add a column to your guest list document and title it "Dinner Selection." Go through your list and input the combined dinner selection correlating to your guests. For the example above, Mr. Smith selected Chicken while Mrs. Smith selected Beef. In this column, you'll write out, "Chicken & Beef." If there are more than two entrée selections — for example, a family of five — you would write their entrées and include the number per entrée, such as "Two Chicken, Three Beef."

When you merge your file and print them on your place cards, they should read in this order:

Mr. & Mrs. Adam Smith

Table One

Chicken & Beef

It is not imperative to assign a seat at that table for each guest. All you need to do is assign them a table. The caterer who is serving the plated meal will send their staff to each table prior to dinner service to confirm the entrée selections of your guests. The caterer will then place them in order based on where they're seated for the most efficient dinner service.

If you do not want to print the guest's entrée selection on each card, then you'll need to color-code them for the caterer. If the place card says, "Mr. & Mrs. Adam Smith — Table One" then after you get all your place cards printed, you'll add a sticker or marking to the card to designate an entrée selection, such as green for chicken and red for beef. The colors don't matter as long as you inform the caterer on your choices.

Showing gratitude: Thank-You Cards

Sending a thank-you note may feel like a lost art or unnecessary, but I encourage you to take the time to do this for your guests. It's an important part of your wedding planning process. Will it be expected? Possibly not. Will it be appreciated? Yes! Your guests have traveled to be with you on your big day and if they took the time to send or give you a gift or attend your wedding, you should thank them appropriately.

TIP

You are about to be showered with gifts and parties. My tip is to send your thank-you notes as you go. If a guest attends a shower or party several months before the wedding, send them a thank-you note at that time. If a guest sends you a gift before your wedding day, send them a thank-you note. Don't wait until after your wedding to send all your thank-you notes. They'll pile up quickly and, trust me, you won't want to do it as life gets busy.

Regardless of gift status, every guest should receive a thank-you note for being a part of your big day. On top of that, if someone sent you an engagement gift, shower gift, and wedding gift, they should receive three separate thank-you cards. Each gift should be specifically acknowledged. If someone took the time and money to buy you a gift, you should take the time to thank them.

Thank-you notes should be sent within three weeks of the event. If too much time passes, the chances that you'll send a thank-you note decrease. It may also feel like old news or not genuine if you send a thank-you note six months after your wedding.

In this section, we're going to discuss how you should keep track of your gifts and talk about what to say to your guests to show your appreciation.

Keeping track of your gifts

It's important to keep track of the gifts you have received along your planning journey. The last thing you want is to thank a guest for a gift that another guest gave you. How awkward would that be?

TIP

The first step in keeping up with your gifts is to take good notes. If you're having a party, you won't remember later who gave you which gift, so assign a friend during the party to write down the gift and the person who gave it to you. That way when you go to write your thank-you notes, you'll have an accurate master list.

When your wedding is over, sit down with your spouse (hey, I just said spouse!) and one person opens the gifts while the other writes down the name of the person who gave the gift and what they gave you. This is always a fun time to spend together and be grateful for what you have been given.

Keeping track of your gifts can be done in your master guest list file, or you can create a separate file that's only for gifts. I suggest keeping this in the master list so you can make sure to send a card to every guest who attended and not just those who gave you a gift. This can be accomplished by adding a column called "Gift."

The next column will be named "Event." If a guest gave you "Gift A" at your bridal shower, in this column you'd write "Bridal Shower." The same goes for gifts given at your wedding. That would be listed as "Gift B" and then "Wedding."

The final column in your master guest list will be named "Thank-You Note." When you send a thank-you note, enter an X or a check mark in that column. It's important to note if you have sent your guest a thank-you note because, again, it will be difficult to remember who you have or haven't sent a note to.

Keeping track of this along the way will help you avoid missing a thank-you note. I don't want you to be sitting at a family event years later and someone gives you the stink face for not sending them a thank-you note. Trust me, they will know if you did.

Knowing what to say

There is a simple format to writing your thank-you notes. If you aren't the best at coming up with what to say, I'm here to help! In this section, I'll share the format to make your thank-you notes special for your guests.

There are five simple steps to writing the perfect thank-you note. Follow this template to save time so you can get those thank-you notes in the mail as soon as possible.

1. **Address the person to whom you're sending the thank-you note by name.**

If it's a couple, you can address them by their formal or last name. Just as in writing a letter to someone, it's important to include their name.

2. **Express your gratitude for the gift.**

If they attended your wedding, make sure to let them know how much you appreciate that. If they didn't send you a gift but attended your wedding, let them know how much you appreciate their presence on your big day.

3. **Make sure to mention what they gave you.**

This is another reason why it's important to keep an accurate record of the gift and the person who gave it to you. It will feel personal to them if you acknowledge the specific gift they gave you rather than saying, "Thank you for the gift."

4. **Let them know what you plan to do with the gift they gave you.**

This is especially true for those who gave you money. Yes, their individual monetary gift alone may not buy you a house, but if you're using your collective monetary gifts from your wedding you could say, "Thank you for your generous gift. Our wedding funds will go towards the down payment on our new home."

5. **Finally, close with your final appreciation and hope for the future.**

For some guests who attend your wedding, you may not see them for a while. Mentioning the future lets them know that you appreciate them in your life and want to see them again.

Here's a sample thank-you note designed to save you time and help you create your own personalized version. Regardless, take the time so send thank-you notes to your guests. I know it takes a lot of time and you might not be excited about this part of the planning process, but it's an important part!

Dear Shannon,

Thank you for attending our wedding. We truly enjoyed seeing you on our big day. We love the beautiful picture frame you gave us. When we get our pictures back from the photographer, we will use it in our dining room. Thank you for your support as we begin our life together. We hope to see you again soon.

All the best,

Sarah and Clayton

Chapter **8**

Adding Special Touches with Flowers

After the planning logistics are finished, it's time to start designing all the pretty things. In this chapter, you get to play around with flowers! Because I'm a florist, this is hands down my favorite part of the process for my clients.

In this chapter, you find out how to design your bridal party flowers, as well as the ceremony and reception atmosphere. Those are the main three parts to your day and where to add flowers or decor to create your dream wedding day.

Maybe you're highly allergic or just don't care for flowers. Don't worry, we can still be friends. This chapter is mainly focused on setting the atmosphere with flowers, but I also share tips on how to use nonfloral decor to spruce up your day.

First Things First: Determining Your Style

The first step is determining your style. When I sit down with a client, I ask them to bring their inspiration photos. Those can be created online or in a document. The main point of me asking them to do this is so that I can visually see their vision.

I see a wedding in my head way before the wedding day. For those who don't plan wedding florals every day, visualizing what it will look like will be a challenge. That is ok and completely normal. It's hard to communicate your vision adequately in words alone. Therefore, finding those images that display your vision is an important part of the planning process.

If you're planning on hiring a florist, take those images with you. They will be able to see a pattern of what you're picking. You may not see it but if you look at all your inspiration photos, chances are they're similar. It's a natural thing that happens when you turn to visuals. You start to create your vision without knowing you're even doing it.

I don't want you to focus on the colors when you pick out inspiration photos. Focus on the events, floral arrangements, bouquets, and atmospheres that you enjoy. All the colors can be changed to fit your palate. Often clients get locked in on a color rather than a design. My focus is looking at the structure of a bouquet. Is it whimsical or classic? Do they pick simple floral arrangements or elaborate?

If you're planning on producing your own flowers and decor, I still want you to explore visual inspiration. This will help you formalize what you want for your big day. Search for a local class hosted by a florist and learn the tips and tricks of making floral arrangements so that you'll have the knowledge you need to be able to create what you want. They'll be able to help you prep your flowers properly so that they last all weekend.

REMEMBER

Your flower order needs to be finalized three weeks prior to your wedding. This means that you have the final guest count, and you know how many table arrangements you'll need. If you hire a florist, this allows them enough time to place your flower order with their distributor. If you're ordering your flowers online, this allows enough time for your flowers to arrive a few days before your wedding.

TIP

If you're producing your own flowers for a Saturday wedding, have your flowers arrive on the Thursday before your wedding. This will allow enough time for your flowers to properly open so that they will be beautiful on your wedding day. Certain floral arrangements, those designed in water, can be produced two days before your event. If you're creating something that is not in a water source, such as a floral arch, those need to be produced within three hours of the start of your wedding.

Wearing and Carrying Floral Accents

The bridal florals are important because you'll have them with you for your photos with your bridal party or fiancé. They may even be the only visual decor you have at your ceremony. If you don't use a lot of florals at your ceremony, when your bridal party stands up at the altar, the magic happens because they're holding beautiful flowers or decor.

In this section, I walk you through what your bridal florals consist of and explain what each person in your bridal party should carry or wear. The bridal flowers or decor are different than the flowers at your ceremony or reception. They're the ones you and your bridal party wear or carry during the ceremony.

REMEMBER

The bridal florals should be designed to coordinate with each other. What do I mean by this? Your bouquet, bridesmaids' bouquets, boutonnieres, and corsages should coordinate with each other. This will give you a uniform look in your photos. Your bouquet or boutonniere can be different than your bridal party flowers but, collectively, they work together to create the overall feel of your bridal flowers.

Choosing the perfect bridal bouquets

Focus on the bridal bouquet first. Determining what you're going to carry will set the tone for your additional bridal floral needs. This is where I am going to give you permission to splurge (assuming you like flowers, of course). Your bouquet should be special. It can be completely different than your bridesmaids' bouquets or it can be a larger version of theirs. Either way, make it special and pamper yourself a bit.

Following is a list and description of the different types of bouquets I get asked to design the most. These are terms that will be helpful for you to know if you hire a florist.

>> **Hand-tied:** A hand-tied bouquet has more to do with the way it's constructed rather than the shape of the bouquet. A florist will design the bouquet and simply tie the stems together, leaving the stems exposed in a loose form.

>> **Nosegay:** A nosegay bouquet is the smallest bouquet besides holding single stems of flowers. Nosegay bouquets are perfect for mothers, flower girls, or attendants.

>> **Pageant:** A pageant bouquet is designed to rest on the arm of the person who is caring it. This style will have you channel your inner beauty queen and pageant wave by the end of the day. Calla lilies are perfect for this type of bouquet because they're long and rest nicely on your arm.

>> **Cascading:** A cascading bouquet is designed so that the flowers flow or cascade towards the ground. It's a dramatic statement and difficult to produce because flowers are going in different directions.

>> **Round:** A round bouquet is a classic style where all your flowers work together to form a ball or round shape. Hydrangea and roses are perfect for this style because they're naturally rounded when placed together.

>> **Whimsical:** A whimsical bouquet is designed to be free in form. There is no particular shape. Often whimsical bouquets include a lot of greenery and a variation of flower types. They're also great bouquets to implement natural elements such as wheat, wildflowers, or succulents.

>> **Pomander:** A pomander bouquet is designed to be a complete circle or ball of flowers. It isn't carried by hand but rather on your wrist. It's constructed with floral foam in the middle that is hidden by the flowers.

>> **Floral wreath:** A floral wreath is designed to be worn on your head. It's often constructed with greenery and floral wire and accented with flowers. A flowing ribbon can be added to cascade down your back.

REMEMBER

When designing your bouquet, think about your dress. They should work together. If your dress is simple, consider a bouquet with several variations of flowers. If your dress is elaborate, consider a bouquet that is simple in nature. Bring a picture of yourself in your dress to your florist to ensure they work together and don't fight each other.

I also want you to consider your size in comparison to your bouquet size. If you're petite, you won't need a large, over-the-top bouquet. You want to be seen and, let's face it, bouquets can be heavy. If you pick a large bouquet, you won't be able to carry it around all day.

Bring on the bridesmaids' bouquets

Designing your bridesmaids' bouquets or what they're going to carry is a great way to add some personal flair to your big day. These are your most important people. Give them something beautiful to hold in their hands if the budget allows.

TIP

If you need to save some money, you don't need to give them bouquets. Consider using ribbon, lanterns, or paper pompoms. Giving them something to hold will help them feel comfortable while standing at the altar in front of your guests.

WARNING

Before you design your bridesmaids' bouquets, check in with your squad and make sure there aren't any allergies to flowers. The last thing you want is for a bridesmaid to have an allergic reaction to something you placed in her hand. Once you've been given the green light, it's time to design.

Here are some things to consider when designing the perfect bridesmaids' bouquets.

>> **Your bouquet:** Traditionally the bridesmaid's bouquet should have one type of flower that you have in your bouquet. If your bouquet has roses, theirs should as well. The bouquets do not have to match yours exactly, but they should coordinate to give an overall image of unity.

>> **The dress:** Consider their dresses. This is another reason why we plan the flowers and decor later in the process, so you can coordinate their flowers with their attire. Pick flower colors that complement their dresses. Additionally, the flower colors and their dresses can work together in the overall theme. Let's say your colors are blue and yellow. Blue flowers are hard to find and often expensive, so pick a blue dress and use their flowers to bring in the yellow.

>> **The size:** Bridesmaids' bouquets don't have to be large to make a big impact. Simple smaller bouquets can save you money without taking away from the impact of flowers at your wedding. If you have a large bridal party, consider smaller bouquets. When all your bridesmaids are standing with you at the altar, smaller bouquets will have a large presence. If you have a smaller bridal party, design a bouquet slightly smaller than yours.

>> **The style:** Just as listed above, what type of style do you want for your bridesmaids? Do you want theirs to be completely different than yours or have the same style just smaller? Remember they should complement yours. Even if they're completely different, they should work together.

Stick a pin in it: Boutonnieres

A *boutonniere* is a small flower worn on the left lapel of a jacket or sport coat and secured with a small pin. Boutonnieres have traditionally been worn by the groom, fathers, grandfathers, groomsmen, ushers, ring bearers, and officiants, but any member of the wedding party who will be wearing a tuxedo or a suit can wear a boutonniere.

The boutonniere often includes a few small flowers with a greenery accent. Traditionally, they're designed to complement the bride's bouquet. If you have roses in your bouquet, consider a spray rose, which is a smaller version of a rose for the boutonniere. The color should also match or coordinate with the other bridal flowers but not contrast with the color of the men's suits or tuxedo.

TIP

Consider sprucing up the groom's boutonniere and make his slightly different than everyone else. This could be done by quantity or color. If the boutonnieres have two flowers, give the groom three. If the boutonnieres are white, give the groom's a pop of color that coordinates with the florals or theme of the wedding.

TIP

Make sure to check in with your officiant about whether they're comfortable wearing a boutonniere before your purchase one. If your officiant is wearing a robe, they will likely not want to wear a boutonniere. If they're not wearing a jacket, they may also opt out of wearing a boutonniere.

Simple and elegant: Corsages

A *corsage* is a small flower worn by the women in your bridal party. This should include the mothers, grandmothers, attendants, and female officiant. It's slightly bigger than a traditional boutonniere and can be pinned on or worn on the wrist.

A BOUTONNIERE WITH A POCKET SQUARE — YAY OR NAY?

A question I get asked time and time again is whether the men should wear a boutonniere if they're wearing a pocket square. Honestly, it depends on the design. If the pocket square is elaborate, there's no need for a boutonniere. If you want both, keep the pocket square simple in design. Boutonnieres are fragile and often end up broken by the end of the night. If you choose both, then when the boutonniere has seen better days, it can be removed, and the pocket square will still allow those special people to be noticed.

Make sure to check in with the women who will be wearing corsages to see if they want a pinned or wrist corsage. Wrist corsages can be made into pinned corsages on the day of the wedding, but it's difficult to make a pinned corsage into a wrist corsage last minute. It's better to find out their preference before you order your corsages.

Corsages often include small flowers with greenery accents. Traditionally, they're designed to complement the bride's bouquet. If you have ranunculus in your bouquet, consider ranunculus for the corsages. They should also coordinate with the colors used in the bridal flowers and themes.

If the women in your bridal party do not want a pinned corsage, consider miniature bouquets for them to carry or a magnet corsage to avoid damage to their clothing. They can coordinate with the bridesmaids' bouquets and look wonderful in photos.

So sweet: Flowers for flower girls and ring bearers

When planning your bridal party flowers, don't forget to consider the little ones. They're special people in your life and giving them something to hold or wear on your wedding day will make them feel so special.

Let's address one thing first. Despite the name, the ring bearer should never carry the actual rings. Those should be held by your maid/matron of honor or best man. You may feel as though the ring bearer is more responsible than the people who are standing by your side, but the real rings should not be given to our little friends. Instead, purchase fake rings and secure them to a pillow. Or send him down the aisle with a briefcase that says, "ring police."

Flower girls and ring bearers vary in age across the board. Typically, they're between one and ten years old. It's important to consider what they can manage on your big day. Their age will make a difference about whether they need flowers or if they will stand next to you at the altar. Every child is different, so you'll need to access their level of participation based on their maturity level.

Ask the parents of your flower girl and ring bearer to sit up front. If they're in the wedding, assign someone to take care of them before and during the wedding if they're younger. That way, if they start to get fussy, that person can take them away from the ceremony.

The age of your little friends will help you determine what to purchase for their flowers. Ring bearers traditionally get a boutonniere like the groomsmen. Just know that it may get damaged quickly, so only give it to them right before the ceremony begins.

TIP

Flower girls often carry baskets of rose petals to throw down the aisle before the bride enters the ceremony. However, some venues don't allow rose petals on the aisle. If that is your case, consider a crown of baby's breath or flowers. Ask their moms to measure the circumference of their head and give that measurement to the florist to ensure their flower crown will fit them appropriately.

Recognizing the attendants and ushers

Attendants are those people assigned to watch over the guestbook or pass out programs. They're not a bridesmaids or groomsmen, but they're still important people in your life, and you want them to be involved. Those people would also include readers, singers, or performers at your wedding ceremony. Ushers are those individuals who escort your guests to their seats at the ceremony.

Order a corsage or boutonniere for those who are in your wedding in any way. This will make them feel special that they were considered in your bridal flower order.

Sprucing Up the Ceremony Space

The ceremony is the first experience your guests will have at your wedding. This is where you begin to set the tone for the rest of the night. A lot of attention is placed on the reception, but you wouldn't have a reception without a ceremony, so it's to be celebrated.

Before you start designing your ceremony, you need to check in with your venue and make sure you know the policies for decorating. If you're hosting your wedding in a church, it's important to know what they allow. Are you allowed to put flowers on the altar, aisle, entryway or front doors? The last thing I want for you is to order ceremony flowers that can't be used because the church or venue doesn't allow it.

Churches often have their own in-house florist who produces the flowers for the church each week. If this is the case for you, reach out to the church florist to ensure your colors are represented in the flowers they create. This will save you the cost of purchasing flowers, but you want them to coordinate with your attire and bouquets if possible.

If you're booking a venue that hosts numerous weddings on a weekend, reach out to your venue contact and see if you can connect with the other couples and split the cost of your flowers. Selecting a neutral floral arrangement that will work with all the weddings that weekend may save you some money if you can split those costs.

If you're booking a florist for your ceremony and reception, ask them if they have done a wedding at your venue. If they haven't, there's nothing to worry about. Request a site visit to tour the venues with your florist so they can help you create your vision. It's a helpful part of the process so that your florist will know the load-in/load-out procedures and the measurements of the areas you want adorned with flowers.

REMEMBER

The first step in planning your ceremony flowers is to consider the type of ceremony you're hosting. If your wedding is traditional and structured, your flowers should reflect that. If your wedding is fluid and spiritual, consider whimsical flowers. Regardless of where your concept falls, your ceremony flowers can stand alone and don't have to match your reception flowers.

In this section, we'll discuss all the elements to designing a perfect ceremony atmosphere. Although flower design is ever changing, decorating your ceremony is the first reflection of your relationship that your guests will experience. My job will be to help you know the essentials so that you can create your perfect setting.

Adorning the altar

Your altar is a sacred place. No matter if you're hosting a religious or nonreligious wedding, it's the place where you'll exchange your vows and commit to each other for the rest of your life. When planning your altar or backdrop flowers, remember that those decorations will always be behind you in your photos.

Most couples use a picture from the wedding to decorate their home. What do you want that photo of you kissing to look like? Do you want a beautiful centerpiece sitting on an altar? Do you envision a floral arch backdrop filled with hydrangeas, roses, and greenery? Maybe it's a cross with flowers and draping fabrics.

This is where searching for inspiration photos will be extremely helpful. You may not know what you want, but searching for ideas and saving the images of backdrops or altar decor that you like will help you narrow down your search and communicate that vision to your florist.

If you're planning an outdoor wedding, consider how mobile your backdrop may be when you're designing it. If it were to rain, could the backdrop be moved easily to a covered location? Will it fit under the covered location? Will it withstand strong winds on a windy day?

TIP

When designing your altar backdrop, make sure it's tall enough to be seen behind you. Most arches and backdrops need to be at least eight feet tall. Another thing to consider is what is sticking out of your flower arrangements. Remember, those will be behind you and may cause strange things to appear in your photos. What is that behind the bride's head?

Decorating the aisle

Your aisle is the pathway that lines your forever. It's an important part of your big day. Don't forget to consider how you'll decorate that pathway to reflect your relationship. There will be photos of you going down the aisle and returning, so it's important to consider its design in your floral planning.

Your venue may be stunning enough that you don't need to spend money on the aisle, but if you need to spruce up your venue a bit, I am here to help you pick the perfect flowers or decorations for your aisle.

The first thing I often hear is that a client wants to add a runner to an aisle. A runner is a cost-effective way to dress up your aisle. However, they do not work at an outdoor location if your aisle is grass, which makes them impossible to navigate in heels. It's easy for someone to poke a hole in the runner while finding their seat or, worse, you could get stuck while walking down the aisle.

TIP

If you're getting married in a place where an aisle runner will work, a tip is to use ribbon or greenery to block off the aisle to your guests and have them enter their seats from the side. Just prior to the bridal party entrance, have someone remove the ribbon so that your aisle runner remains beautiful until the moment you walk down the aisle. If you don't, it will have footprints and markings from the guests who entered before you.

Simple flowers or greenery can go a long way when it comes to decorating your aisle. There's no need to decorate each aisle entrance unless you have the budget to do that. If you decorate every other pew and stand in the back, that will be enough flowers to project the appearance of having every pew decorated. Another simple decoration is rose petals on the aisle. That will give you a romantic setting without having to put anything on your pews or chairs.

TIP

If you need to reserve rows for close family and friends, those can be done with floral accents on the end of your aisle. Make sure to let your family know that they need to sit in the rows that have flowers on the end of the aisle. If you need to save money, decorate the first four rows at your ceremony. When a photographer goes down the aisle to get photos, they typically only capture the first four rows. Decorating the front rows will give the appearance in your photos that every pew was decorated. If flowers won't work for your budget or venue policy, lanterns or potted plants placed on the ground can adorn an aisle without breaking the budget.

Make sure to check with your venue on their aisle policies to ensure that you can implement your design plan. Take a picture of the chairs or pews along with you when you meet with the florist so they'll know how to secure your pew markers, the flowers on the ends of your aisle.

Candles are also a beautiful addition to the aisle. However, I want to let you know a few things about open flame on the aisle. First, make sure your venue allows it if you want the real deal. If they don't, consider LED candles. If you do design an aisle full of candles, make sure they're placed far enough away from the guests who are sitting in the pews. You also need to make sure that your aisle is wider than a normal aisle width.

I once sent a bride down an aisle full of candles. Before she went down the aisle, I reminded her of the candles and made sure she knew they were there. But in the moment, she slowed to a snail's pace — while wearing the biggest dress I had ever seen! I don't think I have ever been as nervous watching a bride walk down the aisle. Thankfully, she didn't catch on fire, but it was a terrifying possibility, and one I will never experience again. If a bride wants candles on her aisle, I now always suggest LED candles to avoid a very bad accident — one I don't want to happen to you!

Additional decor

Now that you have thought about your altar and aisle flowers, it's time to consider additional places to decorate. When you tour your venue, consider those places that need a little sprucing up.

Are there stairs at your ceremony location? Stairs are the perfect place to add greenery. They can also serve as a backdrop for bridal party photos prior to your ceremony and for family photos after your ceremony.

TIP

If you're getting married and hosting your reception at the same location, consider floral arrangements that can be used at the ceremony and moved to the reception or cocktail hour. That will help you cut down on the overall costs of your flowers.

If your church or ceremony location is hard to find, think about adding something near the main entrance of the driveway for your guests to see. This can be as simple as a sign with balloons or a fun marquee. I mean, who wouldn't love to see their name in lights?

Guestbook table

The guestbook table is a small vignette inside the big picture. It's the perfect place to show your personality and give your guests insight into your relationship. The guestbook table reflects who you are as a couple. You could design a theme to decorate the guestbook table based on your favorite things as a couple.

Do you love to travel? If you do, have your guests sign a world map that you can hang in your home as your guest book. Additionally, you could add a small suitcase as your card box. You could also add a floral arrangement constructed inside a globe or small suitcase.

Do you enjoy wine? Have your guests sign messages on wine bottles that you'll enjoy at a later date. You could put signs on them for the milestone anniversary years (1 year, 5 years, 10 years, 15 years — and beyond for a really good bottle that's likely to last). When you and your spouse get to that anniversary, you open the bottle, drink the wine, and read the well wishes written on the side by your guests.

Do you love a good date night together? Place a book on the guestbook table and ask your guests to sign it and give you date night ideas. Or have them write date night ideas on tokens and place them in a jar. That way when you're looking for an idea, you can grab a coin out of the collection. You could also design a floral arrangement out of a popcorn box, wine bottle, or a simple container with candles.

Do you love to celebrate birthdays? I don't know about you, but I love birthdays! You could print a custom calendar with your photos and have your guests sign their name on their birthday. Not only is it a fun way to commemorate your love of birthdays, but you'll also know your guests' birthdays in case you want to send them a card. You could design an arrangement that mimics a birthday cake or a floral arrangement in a present box.

Do you love to cook together? Have your guests sign a recipe book and ask them to bring their favorite recipe with them to your reception. You can let them know on either your information card or wedding website. When you're trying to figure out what to have for dinner, pull out the book and cook a favorite recipe from a guest. You could design floral arrangements or tealight candles in measuring cups or get out your mixer and fill it with flowers.

Regardless of what you pick, let it reflect your relationship and what you enjoy doing together. There are a few things to remember when setting up your guest-book table. Always remember a picture of you and your fiancé. Make sure there is a sign instructing your guests on what you want them to do. Have someone remove your guestbook five minutes before your ceremony begins so that the guests can sit down in time to start the wedding. You can always move your guestbook to the reception if it doesn't get signed in time.

Front doors

The front doors are the first thing your guests see if you're getting married in a church or other house of worship. They welcome your guests to your celebration but are often forgotten. If you're getting married outside, you can still create an entrance even if your venue doesn't have physical doors.

In this section we'll explore a few options for a church setting and an outdoor location to create a formal entrance to your ceremony. It's important to let your florist know what the entrance looks like if you're getting married in a church.

You also need to confirm with the church that you can hang items on the front door. How can you do that? Do they require a particular brand of hanging strips, suction cups, or wreath hangers? This is important to know so that your florist isn't surprised, and left without the ability to hang your beautiful arrangements.

If your entrance has stairs leading to the front door, consider sprucing them up with greenery, garlands, lanterns, or candles. Again, you can use this space for photos with your bridal party before the wedding, with guests after the wedding when you make your grand exit, and combined family photos if the interior of your church is dark.

If you're hosting an outdoor wedding, you could rent doors or search your local building supply store for vintage doors and create your own entrance. You can also create an entrance with pipe, drape, and floral garlands. It's a perfect way to designate an entrance to your ceremony at an outdoor location.

Whichever you choose, remember that every part of your decor can be used as a backdrop for photos. Adding these vignettes to blank slate venues gives you the ability to customize your decor to your vision. Reflect who you are as a couple and your style from the first guest impression.

Creating a Festive Feel at the Reception

We picked your bridal party flowers, set the mood with your ceremony flowers, and now is the time to create a reception vibe that will make your guests want to party all night long. Choosing your reception flowers and decor is an important reflection of your theme and style.

When you think about your reception, what do you see? What do you want your guests to experience? When they walk into the room, what do you want them to see? Do you envision a dimly lit room with tall, extravagant floral arrangements and candles galore? Do you imagine greenery and natural elements? Do you see a modern, vibrant space that exudes your happiness?

I have challenged you to search for images that reflect your style, and the reception ambiance is no exception. There are so many options when it comes to decorating your reception, which can make narrowing down your vision difficult. Make sure to save all the images you love and rely on your florist to put them all together into one reflection of your style.

When you're planning your reception decor, it's so important to understand your reception's decor policy. If it's a blank slate, are you allowed to bring in all your decor? If you're at a historic venue, are you allowed to change the decor or space in anyway? If you picked an all-inclusive venue, how much can you customize to reflect your style and vision?

In this section we're going to discuss the elements that you may consider decorating at your reception. Use this as a guide to follow to ensure you haven't forgotten anything. If you're booking a florist, it will help you organize your thoughts so you can go in prepared with what you need for your venue space.

Cocktail hour

The cocktail hour is designed to be a buffer for your guests between your ceremony and reception. Guests are often served beverages and appetizers while you're busy taking photos. If you're seeing each other before the wedding, you can attend the cocktail hour. This will give you an opportunity to mingle with your guests before the reception begins. Either way, it's designed to be an in-between where the party gets started.

The cocktail hour is held near the reception space but typically in a separate area. That means it needs to be considered when planning your florals and decor. The florals are typically on the lighter side because the guests will only be in this space for a short period of time. If you need to save some money, the cocktail hour is the perfect place to do that.

If you're doing place cards, you'll need a table where those can be displayed at the cocktail hour. A simple floral arrangement with a sign explaining to guests that they need to pick up their place cards for the reception is all you need. If you're doing escort cards, you can place those on that table as well, or create a custom sign with the table numbers and guest names. That can be located near the entrance of the reception so your guests can look at the seating assignments prior to entering the reception.

A cocktail hour isn't complete without a bar. The bar top is a great place to decorate with floral garlands or floral arrangements flanking each side. Create a custom bar menu and place that on the bar. If you're serving a signature drink, have fun with the drink names. I love rosé so my signature drink would be called "Rosé all day with Sarah."

If you're serving appetizers, you'll need to order bistro tables for your guests. This will give them a place to set down their drink while they enjoy their appetizers. A simple floral arrangement and votive candles is all you need. There isn't a lot of space, so keep the florals simple to leave room for plates and beverages.

Setting the perfect table

Have you ever attended a dinner party or gone on a date night to a fancy restaurant? There is something so beautiful about a formal table setting with a floral arrangement. You know you're experiencing something special, a table set for royalty. If you can deck out your guest tables with china and floral arrangements, I am here to help you pick the perfect table setting for your reception.

Time and time again I've had clients who walked into their reception and saw the sparkling china and melted right there on the floor. It's simply a showstopper. Make sure to reach out to your caterer to see if they offer tableware with their dinner service. Often caterers have their own tableware to deck out your tables. And the best news — they will set it up for you. If they don't offer that service, you can rent the items you need from your rental company and then ask the caterer to place those items on the table.

Schedule a meeting at your rental company's showroom where they can set up a mock table to include your linen selection and all tableware. Seeing it in person is valuable so that you can adjust your selections right there in the showroom. If you're setting your table, you'll need to select a linen, cloth napkin, china, silverware, and glassware.

If you decide to set your table with the serving essentials, you can use Figure 8-1 as a guide. There may be pieces that you don't need depending on what you're serving, but you'll be able to take the basics and customize it to fit your needs.

Sample Formal Dinner Table Set Up

PLACE CARD

DESSERT FORK

WATER GLASS

WINE GLASS OR
CHAMPAGNE FLUTE

BREAD PLATE & KNIFE

NAPKIN &
MENU

SALAD FORK

SALAD KNIFE

FIGURE 8-1:
Sample table
setting.

DINNER FORK

DESSERT KNIFE

DINNER PLATE

Sweetheart table

A sweetheart table is a smaller table where only the bride and groom sit. You don't have any bridal party with you. This one is only for the two of you to share. It's a perfect way to enjoy your first dinner together.

When it comes to decorating, this table stands alone. You can rent an upgraded linen to make it stand out. You could also pick another color, different than your guests' tablecloths. This is your table to feature at your reception, so the options are limitless and don't have to match your guest selections.

This table should be placed where it will be visible to all your guests. You may also consider a small riser to elevate your table for all to see. Adding specialty lighting through your rental company or venue is another way to highlight your table.

Another fun accent is adding unique custom chairs or a vintage loveseat to the table decor. If you're using chairs, you could even add florals or your initials. This makes a great photo op for your photographer to grab during the reception.

Don't forget the front of the table, which is often adorned with a greenery garland or custom sign. You could also add a sign with a custom monogram to the front of your table and then use it on the front door of your new home together.

If you're not seated close to your guests, create a custom backdrop to compose the perfect picture for you to look back and remember your perfect night. When you're finished with dinner, ask someone to move your table and utilize the backdrop as a photobooth for your guests.

TIP

Separating yourself at dinner from your guests gives you the best shot at getting a little bit of time together before the next activity. Although guests will come up and speak to you at dinner, a sweetheart table can provide you with a little time to enjoy together. Take that time because the party is about to begin.

Head table

A head table is a table where all your bridal party sit together. This can be set up as one long table or a cluster of smaller tables within the same section. If you sit with the bridal party at the head table, you'll be in the middle or on the end of the table.

It's important to discuss with your fiancé if you prefer the head table to be only the bridesmaids and groomsmen or if you'll allow their spouses and dates to sit with them. If you choose to include their significant others, make sure you confirm the number of people with your bridal party so that you have enough chairs at the head table. You're typically the last ones in the room, and I would hate for you to enter and realize there are no seats left at the head table due to your bridal party's plus-ones.

REMEMBER

If you're sitting at the head table with the bridal party, you'll sit on the side where you're facing your guests. Traditionally, your maid/matron of honor or best man will sit the closest to you at the table. After that, your bridal party may sit wherever they would like.

Just like for a sweetheart table, consider different chairs for this one than the guests' chairs, and mark your chairs with a floral accent or custom sign. This also helps avoid having to move anyone who's not supposed to be in your seats so that you have a seat when you enter the reception.

Guest tables

The first thing to consider when you're designing your table arrangements is the height and size. Guests will sit at their table for an extended period. It will be their "home base," and they'll be talking to the other guests they're sitting with. When you consider the height of the arrangements, remember not to block your guests from seeing one another at the table.

If you want tall arrangements, have your florist create them in either a clear vase or a thin base so your guests can enjoy your beautiful centerpieces but also the people around them. It's uncomfortable for guests to have to peer around the floral arrangements to speak to someone. They may or may not know who they're sitting with, so you want to create a comfortable environment for them to get to know each other.

Another thing to consider is the size. If you're seating the max capacity of guests at your tables; setting the china, silverware, and glassware; and adding candles, consider a smaller arrangement so that everything will fit on the table. If you're not setting your table with the china, silverware, and glassware, consider a wider centerpiece that will fill the table.

If you're booking a florist, take your inspiration photos with you so they can design the perfect centerpiece that reflects your style and vision. There are also several possibilities for a designer to deck your tables with nonfloral elements, such as candles and vases. If you're a DIY bride, resource local forums and purchase your centerpieces from other brides who are selling their nonfloral centerpieces.

Check-in table

The check-in table is the first stop your guests will make when they enter the reception. Remember when you picked a theme for your guestbook table at the ceremony? The check-in table design should also reflect your relationship. It's also a nice touch to include your favorite photos from your engagement session, the actual engagement moment, or photos while you were dating. A simple floral arrangement is a perfect edition to your check-in table. You could also bring an arrangement from the church to the reception and place it on the check-in table to repurpose and use again.

There are a few essentials that need to be included on your check-in table. Some of these items are dependent on whether you're including them at your wedding, but here is your checklist to create the perfect check-in table.

>> **The location:** The check-in table needs to be located where all your guests can see it. This can be in the cocktail hour area, outside the reception space, or inside the reception space.

>> **The guestbook:** Remember when we pulled the guestbook from the ceremony five minutes before your ceremony began? The guestbook needs to return to the check-in table at the reception so that guests who didn't get to sign it prior to your wedding will be able to do so at the reception.

>> **The card box:** The guests who bring you cards will need a place to put them on the check-in table. Assign someone to make sure that all your cards end up in the designated location at the end of the night. Whether that location is in your personal bags or given to your parents, ask one person to collect those cards for you to keep them safe.

>> **A place for presents:** Whether or not you registered for gifts, someone is going to bring you a present. It's important to have a place for those to go and the perfect spot is the check-in table.

>> **The place cards or table seating:** If you're printing place cards or designating table assignments, those need to be displayed either at your cocktail hour or on your check-in table.

Room accents

Now that you have the essential tables decorated, we can think about your room accents. Room accents are enhancements to your reception venue and your guest experience. I am going to give you a list of room accents to consider when planning your reception decor.

>> **Cake or dessert tables:** Not everyone loves cake. If you do, your cake table should stand out like your sweetheart table. For those who are looking to give guests an alternative sweet experience, consider a dessert table filled with favorites such as doughnuts, cookies, mini pies, cupcakes, or shooters. Another guest favorite is a chocolate fountain with all the dippables, such as strawberries, bananas, cookies, and more for your guests to enjoy.

>> **Specialty lighting:** Your ambiance can be created with lighting alone. If you have a clear-top tent, add string lights to lend a starry night feel to your reception. Up lighting — light that shines up the wall — enhances any reception space. Create a custom monogram and hire a lighting company or resource your DJ to shine that monogram on a wall or dance floor.

>> **Lounge seating:** Bringing in lounge furniture through your rental company can create a wonderful atmosphere that all your guests will enjoy. Lounge seating is the perfect accent to be placed around your dance floor perimeter. For those who want to take a break from the dance floor but stay connected to the party, lounge seating provides them that space to catch their breath. Lounge seating can also help divide your reception space into different areas. This creates visual interest and an interesting space to relax other than your dinner tables.

- » **Floral backdrop:** Floral backdrops are a perfect way to bring in something beautiful to a reception venue. They can serve multiple purposes. If you need to flip your space, they can be your ceremony backdrop, your sweetheart table backdrop, or your photobooth backdrop.

- » **Draping:** The use of draping at your reception can transform your space. I have seen it time and time again where a client books a simple reception venue, and we add all the pretty with draping and lighting. It's amazing how you can create your own ambiance through draping.

Sample Flower Order

Throughout this chapter, I discussed several ways that you can decorate your wedding day with flowers. In this last section, I thought it would be helpful to show you a sample flower order and also provide an easy table for you to use when you first visit your florist.

Table 8-1 is an example from a client's wedding. In the first column, I listed the item categories the client wanted. In the second column, I listed the type of flower. In the third column, I list the amount that I needed. You can use this table as a sample to create your own flower order.

TABLE 8-1

Flower Order Breakdown Example

Flower Categories	Type of Flower	Amount
Bride's bouquet (1)	Eucalyptus seeded	1 bunch
	White roses	12 stems
	White peony	10 stems
Bridesmaids' bouquets (9)	Eucalyptus seeded	5 bunches
	White roses (5 each)	45 stems
	White peony (5 each)	45 stems
Boutonnieres (15)	White ranunculus	30 stems
	Eucalyptus seeded	1 bunch
Corsages (5)	White spray roses	5 stems
Flower girls (2)	Baby's breath	2 bunches
	White roses	5 stems

Flower Categories	Type of Flower	Amount
Arch altar (1)	Jackson vine	1 box
	Eucalyptus seeded	10 bunches
	White hydrangea	20 stems
	White roses	20 stems
Aisle	White rose petals	6 bunches
Cocktail hour bistros (6)	White roses	18 stems
Bar garland	Eucalyptus seeded	10 bunches
Guest centerpieces (13)	Eucalyptus seeded	13 bunches
	White hydrangea (3)	39 stems
	White roses (8)	104 stems
Head table	Eucalyptus seeded	12 bunches

After I write out the order and determine how many types or flowers and the quantity I need per arrangement, I develop my flower order. To be able to know how many flowers you need to order, ask you supplier to tell you the bunch brakes. Flower bundles come in different sizes, or breaks, so if you need 200 stems of roses, for example, and the bunch breaks are in 25, you'll need to order 8 bunches.

Table 8-2 is the final flower order for this client. The totals are based on how many stems of each type I needed, divided by the bunch amount. Compare these tables to help you order the flowers you need for you wedding.

TABLE 8-2 **Sample Flower Order**

Flower Type	How Many Stems	Bunch Break	How Many Bunches to Order
Baby's breath	20	10	2
Eucalyptus seeded	510	10	51
Jackson vine	1	1	1
White hydrangea	59	1	59
White peony	55	5	11
White ranunculus	30	10	3
White roses	329	25	14
White spray roses	5	10	1

Regardless of whether you're producing your own flowers or hiring a florist, it's important to have the knowledge of what you want and need for your wedding flowers.

TIP

I created Table 8-3 for you to fill in and take with you to your meeting with your florist. This will help you think through your bridal floral needs so that you don't forget anyone. The first column is a list of people in your bridal party who may need flowers. The second column is for you to fill in the appropriate number that you need.

TABLE 8-3

How Many Bridal Flowers Do You Need?

Bridal Party Type	How Many Do You Need?
Bride's bouquet	
Bridesmaids' bouquets	
Boutonnieres: groom, fathers, grandfathers, groomsmen, ring bearer, ushers, male officiant, women in the bridal party wearing a suit or tux	
Corsages: mothers, grandmothers, attendants, female officiant	
Flower girl	

Style Icon

Chapter **9**

In Pursuit of Your Dream Dress

Have you been dreaming of the perfect dress since you were a little girl? You know the color, the style, and whether you want to wear a veil. Or maybe you fear the attention being on you and have put dress shopping on the back burner because the pressure of picking the perfect dress is too much to handle. I understand both sides of the coin and I'm here to help you pick out the perfect dress you have been dreaming of your entire life, or eliminate the stress you're feeling about making the right decision.

In this chapter, you determine what that perfect dress looks like for you. What color will it be? What will the silhouette be? Will you have a long or short train? Will you wear a veil? What will you wear under your dress? Will you have something old, something new, something borrowed, something blue? We will also discuss how to preserve your dress.

And because picking the dress is only one piece of the pie, you'll also figure out your accessories, decide how you'll wear your hair. and determine your makeup needs. In the end, I truly want you to feel amazing! If you're the type of person who forgets to put yourself on the list of things to take care of, now is your time to feel special. If you have skipped to this part of the book and this is the first time we're meeting because you're so excited about your dress, read this chapter and enjoy picking your perfect dress, and then go back to the parts you skipped. I look forward to helping you feel like the style icon you are.

Selecting the Perfect Dress

Oh my goodness, the pressure, right? The perfect dress — what does that even mean? Everyone will be looking at you and it must be just right, right? Remember in the introduction where we talked about the word "perfect"? So many factors go into making something perfect. I don't want any part of your wedding planning experience to be stressful. I want you to release the pressure you have been carrying to pick the perfect dress. It only needs to be perfect for *you*.

MY OWN DREAM DRESS STORY

To prove that I'm a normal person who is on your side and can relate, I want to share a personal story with you. Let's just say, my hope is that this story lightens the stress and pressure of picking your perfect dress.

When I got remarried, I was a single mother to three girls and over 40 years old. The dress was the very last thing I wanted to do. I had set in my mind that there was no way I'd look remotely pretty on my wedding day. Remember, I have spent my entire career being the person who moves all the pieces but isn't seen. Now, it was my turn to be seen and I was terrified.

I started my journey to finding the perfect dress online. I saved dresses that I loved and after I did that for a while, I found my style because it kept coming up in the inspiration photos. I don't love my arms, so I knew I wanted long sleeves. I don't love my tummy because I've had three kids, so I didn't want anything too form fitting. I also didn't want a ballgown because I felt I was too old for that.

I found a dress that I loved, but I loved it on a model with a perfect body. I had no idea how it would look on my non-model body. I searched the designer's website and found a store near me that carried that dress. I felt as if that would be a great place at least to start. When I reached out to the bridal store in town, they said they had the dress, so I set up an appointment to try it on.

Initially, I thought, I'll just run down there and try it on real quick to see how it looks on my body. That was really the true test. I quietly mentioned that to one of my brides-maids and she loudly responded, "We are all going with you!" Here's the thing: I wasn't a typical bride. I didn't have a single shower, no one threw us any parties, I didn't go on a bachelorette trip or have any brunches. So, to think about having my friends there to help me pick out my dress was far off my radar.

I went along with my friend's suggestion and asked my bridesmaids if anyone would be interested in coming to my appointment. Thankfully, several wanted to come, my kids were there, and my mom and future sister-in-law came into town. This was the ultimate uncomfortable situation for me. It was like an out-of-body experience that anyone would even consider being with me, but they were.

We walked into the bridal store and the owner sat us all down to talk about my style. I will never forget when she asked me, "What is important to you with your wedding dress?" I didn't have the typical response as I said, "I don't really care, I just want a marriage that lasts forever." After a little pushing on her end, I finally came up with, "I guess it would be nice if I was able to feel pretty on my wedding day."

We started trying on dresses, not my dream dress but other dresses in the store. Here's the thing: at one point in my life, I was in Miss America on national television. I used to wear amazing designer dresses and had no problem being in the spotlight. However, trying on those dresses and having to walk out of the dressing room with my family and friends staring at me was too much to handle.

I finally couldn't take it anymore and asked the owner if I could just try on the dress that I picked out online. This was my last shot. If this one didn't work, I was just going to wear something I already had in my closet. She took me back to the dressing room, and just stepping into the dress, I knew it was the one.

I was excited to show my squad! The dress had a low back and I was wearing my grandma panties, which showed out of the back of the dress. My friends were invited into the dressing room to see me in this dress. Instantly, they all said, "YES!" It got a little dusty in there because I was truly shocked at how pretty I felt in that dress. And then in that moment, one of my best friends said, "Sarah, your panties are on inside out."

Only a best friend can bring you back to reality in a way that makes you truly appreciate a moment. In that instant, I released all the pressure I put on myself to look pretty. My husband's friends are all younger than me and I was carrying this high expectation to have the body I had twenty years earlier. The reality was, I needed to be happy in my own skin.

Now, to add fuel to the fire. My husband and I had to postpone our wedding due to COVID. In that year, I got very sick and had to have my appendix removed and had a full hysterectomy four weeks before our wedding. Under my dress, I was bandaged from surgery and wasn't cleared to do any physical activity until eight weeks after our wedding.

The reason I'm telling you this story is so that you can keep perspective through your entire planning journey. Yes, I found the dress that made me feel pretty. But several factors (including a pandemic and my own medical issues) prevented me from having the dress fit perfectly on my wedding day, the way I imagined it would while standing in that dressing room. But my hope is still that my marriage will last a lifetime — just as I told the shop owner.

Gathering floral and decor inspiration

The first step in picking your perfect dress is to gather as much inspiration through photos as you can. Just as we did with your flowers, I want you to start looking at dresses. You will soon see a trend in your dress styles and that will help you narrow down your dream dress.

REMEMBER

I will say one thing about looking online: it is important to see how a dress actually looks on your body. I can't tell you the number of brides I have worked with who were certain they wanted a particular style. Once they put it on, they saw that it didn't fit their body type. Gathering inspiration is your starting point but not the end. Those inspiration photos will also help your stylist assist you in finding the perfect dress.

I had a bride who was certain that she wanted a lace gown. She was one of those who had dreamed about it her entire life. When we got into the store to try on all the lace gowns, they completely ate up her small frame. In the end, she picked a simple satin gown. That was what looked the best on her and made her feel beautiful. It's funny how you can have one thing in your mind and end up with a completely different style. Just remember to enjoy the process of trying on dresses. I am certain you'll find the one.

TIP

Here's my advice to you. Pick a dress that looks good on you now. What makes you feel good today? I don't advise going on a crazy diet to fit into a dress. Don't let losing weight determine which dress you pick. Pick a dress that makes you feel like the rock star that you are right now.

All shades of white

You may be a traditional bride and only want white or ivory for your big day, but if you want to spice things up a bit, wedding dresses come in an array of colors to fit your needs. When you pick your dress color, think about the bridal party attire, your theme, the time of year, and your traditions. In this section, we'll look at these elements to help you pick the perfect shade of whatever color you'd like.

>> **Bridal party:** Consider your bridal party colors when you are picking your dress colors. If they're in ivory or champagne, you may want to be in pure white. If you're wearing a vibrant color, make sure it doesn't clash with your bridal party attire.

>> **The theme:** If you're getting married in a church, white is always best. However, if your setting and theme are outdoors, you may want to consider an option other than white. If you're going bold with color, make sure your dress color coordinates with your decor.

>> **Time of year:** The time of year you're getting married could also help determine what color you want your dress to be. A spring bride may consider a blush wedding dress, while emerald green or bright white could work for a winter wedding.

>> **Your traditions:** Your culture and traditions may play a big part in picking your wedding dress color. There may be certain colors set in history that must be worn at your wedding. Picking your dress color may already be decided for you based on your traditions and culture.

No matter which color you select, it's fun to explore the meaning behind your color. You may be sticking with white or ivory, but if you're picking a bridal party color, you may consider the meaning. Table 9-1 lists the color and the meaning. Use this as a tool to bring special meaning to your big day.

TABLE 9-1

Dress Colors and Meanings

Color	Meaning
White	Purity
Ivory	Integrity
Red	Passion
Lavender	Beauty
Orange	Joy
Peach	Renewal
Silver	Poise
Gray	Calm
Blue	Peace
Pink	Femininity
Green	Stability
Black	Strength

Complement your silhouette, neckline, and arms

It is important to consider your body when picking your perfect dress. We all have one and it's only ours. Your body can't be compared to the model who wears your dress. Her body is different than yours, no matter what shape or size you are. The fact is, we all come in different shapes and sizes, so considering the most flattering silhouette will help you feel beautiful on your big day.

Silhouettes

In this section we will discuss dress styles, your silhouette, flattering options for your body type, necklines, and how to flatter your arms. First, let's discuss dress styles. Table 9-2 is a list of standard dress styles and their descriptions so you can pursue the right one for you.

TABLE 9-2

Dress Styles

Type	Description
Mermaid	A dress that clings tight to your hips and flares out just below the knee
A-line	A fitted bodice that highlights your narrowest point with a gradually flared skirt
Sheath	A fitted, straight-cut dress with no waistline seam
Ball gown	A tight fit around the bodice with a large flare out at your waistline like a princess
Separates	A two-piece wedding dress combo with a crop top and skirt
Strapless	Any dress that stays put around the upper body without shoulder straps or other visible means of support
Trumpet	A dress fitted through your torso, and hips that flares out around mid-thigh
Backless	Any dress that features an open back with a keyhole, cutout, or low back
Fit and flare	A form-fitting dress around your bodice that flares out below your hips
Slip	A loose-fitting silhouette with thin straps
Sleeveless	Any dress without sleeves
Empire	A dress with a raised waistline

Caroline and Audie
Summer wedding

Colors/Theme:
Natural elements; nude, camel, blush

Best Part

We enjoyed our food and cake tastings. I also loved dress shopping and final fittings. Our planner was the best part because she took away the stress of the details so we could enjoy our day.

Lesson Learned

In a few years you're not going to remember every little detail that you stressed over. You're going to remember the way you felt and the experience you had with you friends and family, so enjoy!

Piece of Advice

Buy more alcohol than you think you'll need!

Kristin and Chad
Spring wedding

Colors/Theme:
Lots of natural greenery; white, cream, gold accents

Best Part

Having a coordinator/planner on your big day is a *must*! Our sweet Sarah was on top of it. Chad and I never felt lost, rushed, or stressed. The very second our ceremony ended, she had drinks in our hands, which was much needed after a day full of nerves. She guided us through each part of the night to ensure we didn't miss a beat, and was super thoughtful throughout. She even helped pack our things from the bridal suite at the end of the night, so we could soak up every last minute with our guests.

Lesson Learned

Ask for what you want. Ask if "this" has been done before, or if "this" is possible. Whether it's a unique room setup that aligns with your vision, personalized exit line props, or goofy mix 'n' match pictures with the bridal party, there will be so many ideas swirling around in your head (and your planner's) that can make your day even more perfect, if you just ask!

Piece of Advice

Something *will* go wrong, whether big or small. Just prepare yourself for that now. You'll be glad you did.

Kelly and Brandon
Spring wedding

Colors/Theme:
Neutrals with lots of greenery

Best Part

How easy and fun Sarah made the entire process. She truly made it stress free. Hiring her was the best decision, as we both have really high-stress jobs, and she totally listened to our vision and made it all happen.

Lesson Learned

Stay true to what you all want and what will make the day most memorable. The little things that don't really matter can unnecessarily stress you out.

Piece of Advice

Try to remember what the day is actually about. You and your significant other are getting married! That's where a planner really helps.

PHOTOGRAPHY: NYK + CALI PHOTOGRAPHY
PLANNING, FLOWERS, AND DECOR: SARAH LIZABETH EVENTS

Grace and Jack
Summer wedding

Colors/Theme:
Elegant but whimsical; whites, greens, pops of blush and peach

Best Part

The best part of the planning process was meeting and selecting the people who would be a part of our day. The relationships mattered to us because these were the people who would bear witness to our marriage and ultimately who we would share our lives with. We felt so lucky to find people who shared our vision and invested in our story.

Lesson Learned

Make decisions and let them go. It is so easy to second-guess all of your choices, and there will be things you look back on that you might tweak, but you can't control everything. Always look forward in the planning progress and take it in small bite-size pieces.

Piece of Advice

Take a deep breath! The details matter, but they aren't everything. Have *fun*. We look back so fondly on our wedding because we made sure we had fun, and when you're having fun, your guests will too! If you want a full dance floor, be on the dance floor. Your guests want to be where you are!

PHOTOGRAPHY: KELLI LYNN PHOTOGRAPHY / KELLI LYNN WELLMA

Anna and Bradley
Fall wedding

Colors/Theme:
English garden in a historical Southern mansion; neutral palette

Best Part

Creating mood boards and thinking of little details for the big day!

Lesson Learned

The small details won't matter nearly as much as you think. No one will

Piece of Advice

Make sure you, as the bride and groom, are prioritizing the things

Britney and Vincent
Summer wedding

Colors/Theme
Navy blue, ivory, rose gold

Best Part

For us, everything was exciting, and Sarah made it feel as though our wedding was the only one going on

Lesson Learned

Throughout the planning process, I think we both learned patience and to

Piece of Advice

Nothing is perfect, but enjoy it all! You can't control it someone doesn't RSVP

Makenzie & Greer
Spring wedding

Colors/Theme:
Blue, greenery, neutrals

Best Part

Envisioning what that day would look like and watching it all come to life.

Lesson Learned

Trust Sarah to take care of everything that day! (But seriously, she was an angel the day of and made it so easy to enjoy the day.)

Piece of Advice

When the big day comes, enjoy every minute of that day with your new spouse.

Emily and Adam
Summer wedding

Colors/Theme:
Rustic vintage; neutral with pops of color

Best Part

Getting to spend time with family and friends throughout the entire process. I loved going to meetings with my mom, bridesmaids shopping with my closest friends, and seeing family at wedding showers. I loved celebrating with friends and family near and far, and I especially liked watching two families become one.

Lesson Learned

Everyone is going to have an opinion about everything, but it's *your* day. Make sure you stay true to yourself and you as a couple. Your day will remain timeless because it's what you love.

Piece of Advice

Something is probably going to go awry on your wedding day. Hopefully it's nothing big, but the most important thing is that at the end of your wedding day, you and your spouse will be married.

Penelope and Andrew
Spring wedding

Colors/Theme:
Backyard garden/pool party; blue, blush

Best Part

For us, having a planner to act as "boots on the ground" (we were planning a destination wedding from thousands of miles away), with years of expertise and knowledge of all the local vendors, who could help us both anticipate and solve problems quickly and calmly, made the wedding planning process truly enjoyable. Having a wedding planner made the act of planning our wedding something fun, rather than something to be feared.

Lesson Learned

There is almost always a solution. Most of the problems that seem like crises won't be remembered once the wedding is over.

Piece of Advice

The day after your wedding, after the dust settles, find some time to sit together to recap the day. This will help cement memories from what can be a whirlwind experience. If you wrote your own vows, keep a copy of them and reread them to each other! I was so emotionally overwhelmed during our ceremony that I missed a lot of what Andrew said to me; hearing it again the next day made it all the more special.

PHOTOGRAPHY: CHAD ERICKSON

PLANNING, FLOWERS, AND DECOR: SARAH LIZABETH EVENTS

Grace and Daniel
Spring wedding

Colors/Themes
Light blue, light pink, white, gold

Best Part

The best part of the wedding planning process was how seamless it was! Sarah kept us on task as the months flew by, so I never felt like we were behind or had to quickly make decisions.

Lesson Learned

A lesson I learned was that communication is key. Listening to your partner and making sure their ideas for the wedding are implemented throughout the process is very important. Things my husband wanted that I wasn't too sure about ended up being some of my favorite details from our wedding!

Piece of Advice

Find a planner or day-of person you trust and release all control. They've got you and will make your day so much less stressful and enjoyable. On the day of the wedding, you don't want to be bogged down with decisions and making sure everything arrives on time. All that matters is getting to the end of that aisle to your husband!

PHOTOGRAPHY: LAUREN ATHALIA PHOTOGRAPHY
PLANNING, FLOWERS, AND DECOR: SARAH LIZABETH EVENTS

Lindsay & CJ
Summer wedding

Colors/Themes:
Neutrals, greens

Best Part

My mom and dad were just amazing throughout the wedding planning process. We planned our wedding in five months, which isn't a lot of time, especially in Nashville where vendors are booked so quickly. My fiancé also lived in another state at the time, so wasn't able to be there for all the planning. Between my mom and Sarah (and my dad being the expert taste-tester) we were able to pull off the most beautiful wedding. Getting to spend so much time with my parents (even in a few tense moments) was a time that I will cherish forever.

Lesson Learned

Something will go wrong. You can plan and plan and plan, but then you need to let some things go. There are a few things I might have changed, but it is also those things that go not quite like you planned that make the process and wedding day memorable. When the power went out minutes before I was supposed to walk down the aisle, I could have let that ruin the whole experience for me. But I cannot tell you how many times people have brought up our wedding with fondness, laughing about how hot it was in that church in the middle of August with no AC. (Apparently one of the groomsman was holding a battery-operated fan while we were up there.) I was marrying my best friend that day and nothing was going to stop me!

Piece of Advice

My dad called the day after our wedding and asked if we could do it again, and I told him that would be amazing if he was paying! My husband and I look back on the almost eight years since our wedding day and remember how much fun we had with all our friends and family, but also how much we don't remember. The pictures are amazing and we cherish them, but we wish we had taken a video as we were leaving in the limo. Do yourself a favor and take a video or write down your favorite memories!

Kelly Mae and Brandon
Fall wedding

Colors/Theme:
Classic; white with hints of greenery

Best Part

The whole process was laid out perfectly, so I always knew what the next steps were. It really made the whole wedding planning process not overwhelming.

Lesson Learned

I learned that you need to have clear communication. It's your one day, and you need to make sure all your wants and dreams are communicated.

Piece of Advice

They are the experts and have all the knowledge and connections. Also, on your wedding day, whatever happens, happens, and you will have the absolute best day of your life!

PHOTOGRAPHY: NATHAN WESTERFIELD
PLANNING, FLOWERS, AND DECOR: SARAH LIZABETH EVENTS

Emily and Ben
Spring wedding

Colors/Theme
Neutrals, blues, greens

Best Part

Having a planner to manage the nitty-gritty details.

Lesson Learned

There are so many options and ways to use your budget. So figuring out high-priority items early on is important.

Piece of Advice

Sometimes easier said than done, but try not to plan around other people.

Alex and Rachel
Summer wedding

Colors/Theme:
White, gold, neutral

Best Part

The best part of our wedding planning process was hiring a professional wedding planner who took care of every detail of our day. It was such a relief to know that everything would be done and done well, but still being able to share our preferences and have input. We never once worried about a vendor, a decoration, or the flow of the whole event because we knew it would be perfect under the direction of Sarah and her team! This allowed us and our families to be fully present during our engagement season and the day of the wedding without a single worry.

Lesson Learned

Set a budget and decide what items are the most important to you and your spouse. Put your budget towards those things first, and then be willing to be flexible on the smaller details.

Piece of Advice

Make sure you keep the purpose of the day at the forefront of your mind. At the end of your wedding day after all the guests leave, you will be married to your spouse! That is the most important thing. Everything else will fall into place. Most guests will not remember if you had chicken or pasta, what color the table runners were, or if the ring bearer wouldn't walk down the aisle. Don't sweat those small things. Take the time to enjoy the planning process and your day, but also be sure to keep things in perspective on what is really important.

PHOTOGRAPHY: MELANIE GRADY PHOTOGRAPHY
PLANNING, FLOWERS, AND DECOR: SARAH LIZABETH EVENTS

Lauren and Lindsey
Fall wedding

Colors/Theme:
Greenery; white, light pink, gray, crimson

Best Part

The best part was making the ceremony personal for us. We wanted the ceremony to reflect many different things about our marriage, love for one another, and the values we both hold together as a couple. There is definitely a classic way to plan a wedding ceremony, and we held to those pieces, and getting to add in what really represented us as a couple was really fun and special. Lauren's parents were also an incredible part of the whole process. We planned our wedding in about three months, and we absolutely could not have done it without them.

Lesson Learned

Don't let making decisions (because there are a lot of them!) steal your joy from the engagement season. Don't be afraid to ask for help, and don't be afraid to let people help you! Your tribe of people want this day and this marriage to be amazing, so let them help you and be a part of that process!

Piece of Advice

Everything goes so quickly in the planning and the big day, even if you have a long engagement. The wedding day can feel like a blur in hindsight. Stay present, and be in the moment. Give yourself grace to leave all the planning behind you and enjoy being pampered and taken care of. Later in the reception my husband and I walked out into the field past the tent where everyone was dancing and just took a moment to look at all the people there celebrating us. We really wanted to take that sight in, and I'm so glad we have that moment as a memory.

PHOTOGRAPHY: LOVE IS A BIG DEAL
PLANNING, FLOWERS, AND DECOR: SARAH LIZABETH EVENTS

Emily and Drew
Summer wedding

Colors/Theme:
Earthy; light blue and neutrals with a pop of bright pink/coral flowers

Best Part

Watching all of our small decisions and ideas finally come together for the big day. You spend so much time picking decorations, linens, flower types and colors, ceremony music, dresses and ties, and so on, so when you see the finished product it is beyond exciting to see your dream come to life!

Lesson Learned

Try not to stress too much. Whatever happens on the wedding day is going to happen. Be open to going with the flow. You will have an amazing day no matter what because you are marrying the love of your life and celebrating with your favorite people.

Piece of Advice

This day is about you and your future spouse. Make decisions that will help the two of you have the most memorable and fun day celebrating your love for one another. Do not let other people persuade you into compromising or changing your vision of your special day. Also, remember to eat, drink, and take a moment to soak it all in! And hire a wedding planner or day-of coordinator. You need someone to help keep things organized and running smoothly so you are able to enjoy being a bride!

PHOTOGRAPHY: LOVE IS A BIG DEAL
PLANNING, FLOWERS, AND DECOR: SARAH LIZABETH EVENTS

I created Figure 9-1 as a visual of these various wedding dress styles.

Mermaid

Backless

Empire Waist

Sleeveless

Separates

Trumpet

Sheath

A-line

Ball Gown

Fit & Flare

Slip

Strapless

FIGURE 9-1:
Visualize the perfect style for you to become a style icon.

Reproduced with permission of April Jae

Now that you know the standard dress styles, let's talk about some standard silhouettes. Table 9-3 lists the types of silhouettes and their descriptions. Make sure to consider where you are physically today, not in the future. Dresses can be altered and yes, you may lose weight, but your body type won't typically change drastically.

TABLE 9-3   ## Standard Silhouettes

Type	Description
Rectangle, straight, or banana	Your waist measurements are about the same as your hip or bust, and your shoulders and hips are about the same width.
Triangle, pear	Your shoulders and bust are narrower than your hips.
Spoon	Your hips are larger than your bust or the rest of your body.
Hourglass	Your bust measurements are slightly larger than your hips.
Inverted triangle or apple	Your shoulders and bust are larger than your relatively narrow hips.
Round or oval	Your bust is larger than the rest of your body, your hips are narrow, and your torso is fuller.
Diamond	You have broader hips than shoulders, a narrow bust, and a fuller waistline.
Athletic	Your body is muscular and not curvy.
Petite	Your height is less than 5 foot 4.
Tall	Your height is taller than 5 foot 8.

Body type

We have discussed dress styles and your body shape, and now it's time to put the two of those together to get you to the end goal of the best wedding dress ever! To do so, I created Table 9-4 to compare the style with the body shape. Find your match and you'll be closer to the end goal of becoming the style icon that I know you are!

Necklines

An important piece in picking your perfect dress is to consider the neckline. There are several options when it comes to picking your neckline. One thing to consider is how you'll wear your hair on your wedding day. Does that vision complement the neckline of your dress? Table 9-5 is a list of necklines and their descriptions.

TABLE 9-4   # Matching Dress Styles with Body Shape

Dress Style	Body Shape
Mermaid	Hourglass
A-line	Hourglass, pear
Sheath	Hourglass, slim, and petite
Ball gown	Pear, tall, slim, and hourglass
Separates	Small waist
Strapless	Balanced, hourglass
Trumpet	Inverted triangle
Backless	Anyone with a great back
Fit and flare	Straight, tall
Slip	Tall and slim
Sleeveless	Anyone who loves their arms and neckline

TABLE 9-5   # Dress Necklines

Type	Description
V-neck	A neckline in a V that gives the illusion of a longer torso
Boatneck	A wide, high, scooped neckline that provides support and coverage
Scoop	A U-shaped neckline that is universally flattering
Jewel	Similar to a T-shirt without sleeves; flattering for smaller body types
Queen Anne	A high collar with a dipped neckline in a V-neck, sweetheart, or scoop
Off the shoulder	A style designed to highlight your shoulders or collarbones, perfect for hiding your arms without full coverage
One shoulder	Neckline on one side, leaving the other side exposed
Portrait	Similar to off-shoulder but built with additional fabric from shoulder to shoulder
Plunging	A neckline that plunges down to your torso, great for long-sleeved dresses
Illusion	A deep neckline with a transparent piece of fabric, perfect for those wanting the plunging look without all the skin showing
Halter	A neckline that goes around the back of your neck, designed to show off your shoulders
Square	A neckline with a square, wide cut that accentuates your neck and bust while slimming your shoulders

(continued)

TABLE 9-5 *(continued)*

Type	Description
Sweetheart	A neckline that resembles a heart and gives you a longer, leaner appearance
High neck	A neckline that hits at the base of your neck and provides the most coverage
Straight	A clean-line, strapless neckline that accentuates your collarbones and provides full coverage
Strapless	A neckline without straps or sleeves
Cowl neck	A neckline with folded fabric in the front

Figure 9-2 provides a visual of these dress necklines. Use it as inspiration to determine your perfect style.

Sleeves

I am not a lover of my arms. I tend to carry my weight in my upper body. Trust me, I have always dreamed of wearing a sleeveless dress, but my arms are my archnemesis. If you're in a different scenario, congratulations, I am officially jealous! However, if, like me, you don't love your arms, I have some flattering options for you so that your arms don't steal the joy of feeling amazing in your wedding dress.

First, if you want camouflage but don't want to feel fully covered up, consider a transparent fabric over your arms. On my wedding day, I opted for long sleeves but with cutouts, so I didn't feel completely covered up. Long sleeves aren't always the best option, especially if you're getting married in the summer.

TIP

Although a long-sleeved dress is very elegant, you can also cover those arms with a three-quarter or half sleeve. You can still feel amazing even if you aren't wearing a sleeveless dress. The important thing is to pick a dress that flatters your body, not the model's body. Embrace where you are on your physical journey and pick a dress that makes you feel beautiful, because you are!

Thinking about the train and veil

Trains and veils are an important piece in completing your look. A train and a veil make any white dress officially bridal. But are they for you? In this section, I cover the different types of trains and veils to see if they are the right fit for you.

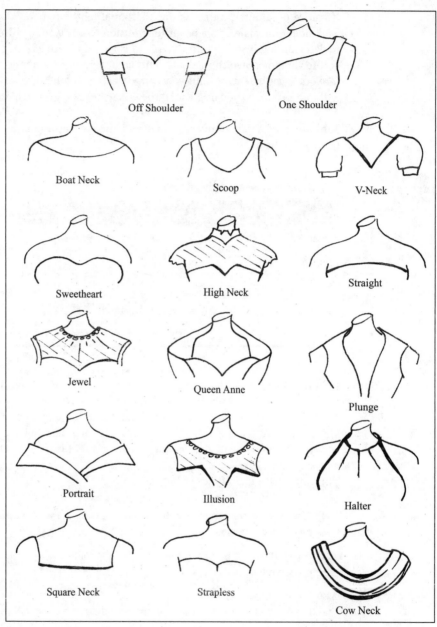

FIGURE 9-2: Which one of the necklines is your perfect style?

If you're unfamiliar, a *train* is the additional fabric that trails behind you as you walk down the aisle. It's a beautiful addition to any wedding dress. The first step in determining if it's right for you is to consider where you're getting married. If you're walking down the aisle at a church or venue, a train might be a good choice for you. If you're saying your vows on a beach, you might want to consider a dress without a train, so you don't drag the entire beach with you along the way.

Table 9-6 lists the standard trains and their descriptions to determine which train you'll be on!

Wedding Dress Train Styles

Type	Description
Sweep	6 inches to 1 foot beyond the hem
Chapel	2 feet beyond the hem
Semi-cathedral	5 feet beyond the hem
Cathedral	7+ feet beyond the hem
Detachable	Any length that is removable

TIP

If you pick a dress with a train, make sure to take someone with you to your final fitting to learn how to bustle your train before your reception. Go ahead and take a video so you don't forget. If you're hiring a wedding planner, they can take care of making sure your bustle is perfect. However, it's hard to bustle your own dress, so delegate someone in your squad to take on that task.

There are three main types of bustles.

>> **American:** Several hooks scatted on the outside of the dress allow the train to be lifted and hooked.

>> **Australian:** The fabric is gathered down the middle of the dress, creating a ruched effect.

>> **French:** Small hooks are scattered on the underside of the dress and when they're hooked, the fabric lies on the outside of the dress in layers.

The train and the veil should work together to create the perfect look for your big day. To veil or not to veil, that is the question. Whether you think a veil is old-fashioned or a must-have fashion statement, in this section we'll talk through the different types of veils to complement your dress perfectly.

TIP

If your wedding is outside, I would highly recommend a shorter veil. Just like tents, veils can easily pick up with the wind. I have seen time and again where the veil is standing straight up due to wind while the bride is walking down the aisle.

Table 9-7 is a list of a few standard veil types and their descriptions so you can make the right choice on which veil will be perfect for you.

TABLE 9-7   **Veil Types and Descriptions**

Type	Description
Cathedral	Fabric that drapes all the way to the floor and extends three yards or more in length. The most royal style of veil.
Elbow	Typically, 25 inches in length resting right at your elbow.
Chapel	Like the cathedral veil but approximately two yards in length.
Birdcage	A 9-inch piece of netting that drapes off the side of your head.
Waltz	This style falls between your knees and ankles. Often, you'll see this style clipped to the bottom of an updo hairstyle.
Blusher	A short, single layer of fabric, the blusher is worn over the face before the ceremony and flipped over the head. A real wedding tradition!
Shoulder	This style extends to your shoulders and can be worn with a blusher.
Fingertip	This style extends to your fingertips and is popular with ballgowns.
Double tier	Multiple-layered fabric usually with a blusher and veil combination.

Trains and veils are the quintessential way to enhance your wedding dress. Often these pieces make a bride feel like a bride ready to walk down the aisle. Enjoy trying on different options to create your perfect look. They are all so different and enhance your dress to provide the perfect pairing like fine wine and gourmet cheese.

Figure 9-3 provides a visual of how much of a train you want and the length of your veil. Be inspired, this is your time to officially feel bridal.

FIGURE 9-3:
Complete your ultimate bridal look with the perfect train and veil.

Underneath It All: Picking the Proper Undergarments

If you read the earlier sidebar about my own wedding dress experience, you know that I tried on my wedding dresses and my bridesmaids pointed out the fact that my underwear was inside out. Although the dress may be fabulous, it is also important to consider what's underneath your dress. Maybe you need everything to stay in place or maybe you need the illusion of wearing nothing at all. For me, I would choose to have everything tucked and slimmed where needed. I wouldn't care how uncomfortable I was if the outside looked good. Can you relate?

The first step in picking the undergarments is to consider your dress style. What are the areas that are exposed and what are the areas where enhancements will not be seen? The last thing you want is for your undergarments to show on your wedding day. Inside out or right side in, those need to be kept a mystery.

TIP

Start shopping for your undergarments after your first formal dress fitting. This way, you'll be able to see any alterations that will be done to your dress that may limit your selection. For example, with a low-back dress, how long will you go? If you go too low, the high-waisted, suck-everything-in garment that many of us love will not work.

REMEMBER

When you venture out to find the perfect undergarments, make sure they're breathable. Additionally, make sure you can use the bathroom when needed. For some, that may look like having to take off your entire dress, while others can lift their dress, with some assistance from a best friend, to potty. Trust me, you'll need to use the restroom at some point in the day even if you think you can hold it.

Do you need a bra? If you have a plunging neckline, your seamstress can sew cups into your dress to keep everything from plunging out. If you have a strapless dress, consider a strapless bra. There are several dresses out there where the top of the dress is made with a thick fabric where you don't need to wear a bra. Working with a seamstress will help you find the perfect solution for your upper half and what you need to wear underneath it all.

If you do need a bra for your wedding dress, I put together a list of dress styles and bra suggestions in Table 9-8.

If you can wear shapewear under your dress, that is always a popular selection and there are several online stores where you can get a built-in bra and panties all in one. Shapewear can provide a slimming effect while providing you the support you need on top.

AVOIDING A WARDROBE MALFUNCTION

I had a bride one time who was taking pictures with her husband outside the church with all her guests lined up for their send-off. They got to the end of the crowd and the photographer told them to stop and for the groom to dip the bride. Everyone was going to cheer, and it was going to be a perfect picture. Well, when the groom dipped the bride back, everything up top fell right out for all to see. There she was being dipped in front of all her guests who saw all her things. There was nothing left for the imagination. How mortifying!

My advice to help avoid this type of disaster is to move in your dress. Make sure everything stays where it is designed to stay so that you don't have a wardrobe malfunction in front of grandpa and your childhood youth group leader.

TABLE 9-8   **Dress Styles and Bra Types**

Type of Dress Style	Bra Type
Halter	A strapless or convertible bra
Deep V or plunging	A low-cut bra or have your seamstress sew cups into your dress
Strapless	A strapless bra or corset/bustier bra, depending on how low the back of your dress is
Backless	Adhesive cups or have your seamstress sew cups into your dress
Sheath	Shapewear that provides the illusion of wearing nothing under your dress

TIP

No matter your selection, practice moving or dancing in your dress to make sure that everything stays where it is supposed to stay, and you can't see what's underneath your dress. The point of shapewear is to create an illusion so if it can be seen either through your dress or when you move, that defeats the point.

From Head to Toe

Making you a style icon means every part of your look needs to be considered, including what you wear on your head and your feet. If you aren't wearing a veil, it's important to consider an accessory on your head. In this section, we discuss options for you to consider from head to toe to complete the perfect look.

Headpieces

Let's start with the top! Headpieces can be combined with a veil or stand alone. You may even wear a veil for your ceremony but want to add something different for the reception and remove your veil. Table 9-9 was created to give you some inspiration on what to wear on your head if you're looking for an alternative option to a veil or an addition to a veil.

TABLE 9-9   **Headpiece Options and Descriptions**

Type of Headpiece	Description
Fascinator	A lightweight decorative headpiece made with fabric, beads, or feathers and attached to a hair clip or comb. These can also be birdcage veils.
Hair clip	A clip that has beads or flowers for pulling back a portion of your hair.
Flowers	A flower wreath that is worn on your head or single flowers that are pinned into your hair with a bobby pin.
Headband	A headband with beads, fabric, or flowers that is worn on the crown of your head.
Hair ribbons	Decorative ribbons that are used throughout your hair with a woven appearance.
Tiara or crown	A crown with jewels or beads that is worn on the crown of your head. The most royal way to celebrate your day.
Hair comb	Like a clip, a comb has plastic or metal teeth that go downward into your hair, either on the side or the back.
Hat	A decorative or boho accent to spice up the traditional bridal look with a more retro vibe.
Hair pin	A single pin with beads or flowers that can be worn anywhere on your head.

Shoes

When it's time to pick your shoes, it is important to consider the ground you're walking on. Heels are great for an indoor venue but not for an outdoor venue on grass, sand, or stone. It's also important to consider your pain tolerance. I can't tell you the last time I worked with a bride who didn't switch into a more comfortable footwear option for her reception. If you can wear heels all day, I commend you! Those days are long gone for me.

REMEMBER

Pick out your wedding shoes before your first dress fitting. That way the seamstress will be able to hem your dress appropriately. If you're planning to change into a more comfortable option for the reception, bring those too so that the seamstress knows the length of the bustle. If you're wearing six-inch heels for your ceremony and flip-flops for your reception, that will make a big difference!

The best way to add height and navigate rough terrain is with a wedge or block-style shoe. You are more balanced, and you'll still have the look of a stiletto without the fear of falling or being in pain by the time you say "I Do." This is coming from someone who prefers flip-flops or tennis shoes to heels, but if you can rock some stilettos, do it! If not, a wedge can provide you the comfort and stability you need to make it down the aisle.

Whatever your decision, invest in your shoe material. Shoes can be an expensive part of your wardrobe, but you'll get what you pay for. Choosing genuine materials will save your feet from blisters. A less expensive material can often leave brides in a lot of pain. Yes, you can always just take your shoes off if you're in pain but let's try and avoid being a barefoot bride.

TIP

From the moment your wedding shoes arrive, start wearing them around the house to break them in. Cook dinner in them occasionally. This will help tremendously to avoid blisters and painful feet later on. The last thing you want is a blister on your wedding day.

TIP

To be able to dance the night away, consider switching your ceremony shoes to either flats, wedges, tennis shoes, or boots. Brides often wait until after their first dance or special dance and then the heels come off and the comfort goes on so they can dance the night away pain free. It's okay to do this on your big day. I give you permission to embrace the comfort and dance all night long.

Something old, new, borrowed, blue

You have probably heard the old saying "Something old, something new, something borrowed, something blue, and a sixpence in her shoe." I absolutely love this tradition. Don't worry, if you don't want to do this — it doesn't mean your marriage is doomed.

This custom dates back to the Victorian era, where the "somethings" were given to the bride as good luck on her wedding day and in her marriage. The tradition has adapted to where the bride typically provides her own "somethings" now, but if you're into wedding traditions, this one is a must-have for your big day.

>> **Something old:** This represents your family heritages, given by a family member, or something to remember a loved one who has passed away. An example of this is a locket or bracelet from a relative. If you want to remember someone who has passed away, consider wrapping your bouquet in one of their handkerchiefs or carrying a locket with their picture.

>> **Something new:** This represents your new life with your spouse. Most brides choose to consider their wedding rings or their dress as their something new.

>> **Something borrowed:** This is something borrowed from a happily married relative or friend, to symbolize conveying their happiness in marriage to you. Examples are jewelry, a dress, a veil, a handkerchief, shoes, or a garter.

>> **Something blue:** Blue symbolizes love and faithfulness. Often the bride will carry blue in her bouquet or wear blue shoes. Another option would be a blue garter, or a blue ribbon sewn in the underside of your dress.

>> **Sixpence for your shoe:** This symbolizes wealth for the couple. Who doesn't want that? Many companies sell sixpence online just so brides can put them inside a shoe on their wedding day. I may even buy one just to wear in my shoe every day!

Whether or not you participate in this tradition, I wish many blessings, happiness, faithfulness, and prosperity for your new life together. That is what this is all about and why I'm excited to be a part of your journey.

PRESERVING YOUR MEMORIES

After all the planning, the wedding day is over. Besides the memories you hold in your heart forever, there are several ways to preserve the tangible items you'll have. Remember I told you to take mental pictures along the way during your day? That will help with the memories, but what about those pieces you want to keep with you forever — what do you do with those?

Following are some ideas on how you can hold on to those tangible memories a little longer, and potentially pass them on to your children one day. Here are some of my favorite ways to preserve your wedding day.

- **Your dress:** Preserving your dress is important if you want to give it to someone else one day. Fabrics will fade, discolor, and disintegrate with time. It is important to reach out to a respectable, professional dress preserver in your area. We have all heard the horror stories of companies that don't actually preserve the bride's dress but instead put an alternative dress into the box. Make sure you can see your dress through a clear panel when you get it back from the dress preserver. The last thing you want is to open that box for your daughter one day and your dress is gone. This has actually happened, and I want you to be protected from that. A unique way to remember your dress is to have a piece of it made into jewelry. There are several online stores that will create a beautiful necklace or bracelet encapsulating your dress forever.

- **Your flowers:** There are companies that will freeze-dry your entire bouquet to be displayed in a case. One of my favorite ideas is to dry or press your flowers and put some in acrylic or in a small necklace that you can wear. To dry your flowers, hang your bouquet in a dark closet upside down to allow the flowers to dry out and keep

(continued)

(continued)

their form. You can place them into a vase when they are completely dry. You can also press certain types of flowers (the less chunky ones without a thick core). To press them, you can buy a flower press online, or just grab a notebook or newspaper and put the flowers in between the pages individually. Set something heavy on top, like a stack of books, and wait two to four weeks. You can put pressed flowers into a frame or acrylic box to display in your home. Another idea is to put your preserved flowers into a clear plastic ornament and hang them on your tree each year.

- **Your invitations:** Consider framing your wedding invitation and displaying it on the wall or a side table in your home. You can also combine this with other items from your day and display them in a shadow box.

- **Your photos:** You are about to have the most amazing photos! Consider displaying them in your home to remember your wedding day. On those rough days we call life, remember one of the best days of your life together. It's hard to forget when you can see them displayed in your home.

- **Your cake:** When you cut your cake, you'll cut the bottom layers, leaving the smallest layer, the top, uncut so that you can save it for your first anniversary. When you receive that top cake layer, leave it in the box and put it in your freezer for a few hours. (Freezing it first will make it more manageable.) Then remove it from the freezer, take it out of the box, and wrap it in layers of plastic wrap. Put your cake back in the box and wrap the box in several more layers of plastic wrap. Keep the wrapped box in the freezer until your first anniversary. On your anniversary, place your cake on the counter to thaw. Then enjoy a piece of cake that is as good as it was on your wedding day!

- **Your first dance:** Play your first dance song and dance in your kitchen regularly. It is a special way to take you back to that moment on your big day. Consider framing the lyrics to your first dance and display them in your home. On rough days, read those lyrics to remember the commitment you made to each other.

- **Your vows:** You vows can be preserved after your wedding day. You can print them and frame them in your home. I have also seen them printed on a towel, pillow, blanket, or journal. Spreading reminders throughout your home is a great way to remember your wedding day.

- **Your guestbook:** Displaying your guestbook in your home is a great way to remember those who were with you on your wedding day. Never again in your life will all those people be in the same place at the same time. It's always fun to look back at that years later and remember those who were with you. You'll be amazed at how much your life and relationships will change through the years.

- **Live event painting:** A newer trend in wedding planning is to hire an artist who will paint a live portrait of your wedding day. This is one of my favorite ways to remember your day forever. Displaying this beautiful piece of art in your home will take you back to that moment each time you see it.

Picking the Perfect Hairstyle

Your hairstyle is an important element of your big day. There are many things to consider when determining the perfect style. In this section, we'll discuss a few things to consider so you feel confident with your selection on your big day.

First, let's consider how your hair naturally reacts to weather. If you're getting ready for a summer date with your fiancé, what does your hair naturally do in the humidity? Do you struggle with creating the perfect look and then you walk outside and feel like a melting popsicle, or like you just got zapped with some high voltage? If it rains, how does your hair behave? If you aren't even leaving your house, do your curls hold up or quickly fade away?

Consider the time of year and the atmosphere when picking your perfect hairstyle. What does your hair naturally do during that time of year? What atmospheric setback will you be up against? Wind, rain, heat? How will your hairstyle that you paid a lot of money for withstand those conditions? Don't rely on hairspray and bobby pins alone. Pick something that will hold up based on your hair sustainability.

Another piece to picking the perfect hairstyle is to consider your dress style. Does your dress look best with your hair down or up? Do you have a dress where any hairstyle will work? Table 9-10 is designed to give you inspiration on how to perfectly pair your dress with your hair.

REMEMBER

One more thing to consider is the shape of your face. Just as our bodies come in all shapes and sizes, so do our face structures. When picking your hairstyle, make sure that it complements your face. Below I have listed the standard face structures and the hairstyles that complement them.

>> **Oval face:** If you have an oval face, you're in luck! Almost any style works with your face structure. Choose a timeless and classic look to complement it. Enjoy having a lot of options.

>> **Long face:** If your face structure is long, consider wearing your hair down with loose curls. Stay away from sleek updos or buns.

>> **Diamond-shaped face:** If you have a diamond-shaped face, consider soft curls or a loose updo.

>> **Round face:** If you have a round face, consider a half up, half down hairstyle or a sleek updo. The focus should be on keeping your hair behind your ears.

TABLE 9-10   **Dress Necklines with Hairstyles**

Type	Description
V-neck	Hair down or sleek updo
Boatneck	Low bun or half up, half down
Scoop	Low bun or half up, half down
Jewel	Hair down, updo, or half up, half down
Queen Anne	Updo
Off the shoulder	Hair down
One shoulder	Hair on the opposite side of the one shoulder, either down or in an updo
Portrait	Hair down
Plunging	Hair down or sleek updo
Illusion	Updo, either loose or sleek
Halter	Loose updo
Square	Bun or curled ponytail
Sweetheart	Updo, down, or half up, half down
High neck	Sleek updo
Straight	Sleek ponytail or bun
Strapless	Updo, down, or half up, half down
Cowl neck	Updo, down, or half up, half down

» **Heart-shaped face:** If you have a heart-shaped face, consider a side part and a soft updo.

» **Square face:** If your face structure is square, consider minimizing the volume of your hairstyle with a lose updo or sleek down hairstyle.

TIP

Have you thought about asking your fiancé how they love the way you wear your hair? If not, ask them. They may have an opinion and if you don't care either way, wear your hair the way they love the most. After all, we all just want to be the most beautiful person to our spouse on the wedding day.

No matter your decision, schedule an appointment for a trial run with your hairstylist. This is a wonderful time to adjust what you have in your mind with reality. We don't like surprises on wedding day, so it's important to test out your perfect hairstyle to make sure it complements your dress and face shape. This will ensure a perfect day so that you can feel amazing with your selection.

Makeup: How Much Is Too Much?

It's true, sometimes less is more when it comes to makeup. Whenever my daughter is playing with makeup, she comes out with the biggest smile, so proud of her bright red lipstick, blue eyeshadow, and foundation that makes her look like a ghost. As her momma, I let her know that less is more and ask her to wash her face. I know I steal the joy right out of her, which breaks my heart, but I'm looking out for her own good.

The same is true for you. It's important to consider how much is too much makeup and what the perfect selection is for you. Do you normally wear a lot of makeup? What is your fiancé used to seeing? My husband doesn't love when I wear a lot of makeup. If I had shown up on our wedding day with a ton of makeup, he wouldn't have recognized me. In this section, I'm going to share some tips and tricks on determining your perfect makeup style for the big day.

>> **Your style:** If you were going out on the town with your fiancé, how would you wear your makeup? It's important to figure out your normal date night makeup and then enhance it slightly for your wedding day. We want your fiancé to recognize you. There's no need to add a ton of makeup just because it's your wedding day. This is not the time to transform yourself into someone you're not. However, there will be pictures, and this is an important event, so a slight enhancement — not a complete transformation — is appropriate.

>> **Waterproof:** Oh my goodness, news flash: you may cry on your wedding day. Just in case it starts to get a little dusty in the room, use waterproof makeup, mascara especially. The last thing we want are racoon eyes on your big day. (I can see all the memes now!) Protect yourself from your emotions with waterproof makeup.

>> **Contour:** If I could, I would contour everything on me. I love it, but it can also go bad if you aren't careful. I'm a fan of adding some contouring to your wedding makeup. Who doesn't love defined cheek bones? Just be subtle with the contour. It's designed to enhance your natural features.

>> **Eyelashes:** I love eyelashes and would highly recommend them for your wedding. They take your natural eyes to the next appropriate level. Consider using individual lashes rather than a strip of lashes. Our eyelashes aren't strips, they're individual sections, so individual lashes will create a more natural enhancement to your eyes.

>> **Foundation match:** Just as in building a strong house, the foundation makeup you pick is so important. We have all seen the foundation that doesn't match any other part of your body. A makeup artist can help you pick the perfect shade, but if you're doing your own makeup, try a few shades to find the perfect match to your neck. Use long-lasting foundation because your wedding day will be a long day. If you're using a makeup artist, consider airbrush to create flawless skin for your big day. Stay away from matte foundation and lean into a dewy appearance for that bridal glow!

>> **Eyebrows:** If we didn't have eyebrows, we would all look strange. The opposite is true if they are over accentuated. Having eyebrows that complement your eyes and not stand out like a sore thumb is key. Less is more on your eyebrows.

>> **Lipstick:** You are about to have the biggest kiss of your life! But what is your fiancé going to look like after your kiss? Whichever color completes your style icon look, consider a smudge proof lipstick. I mean, there may be some kissing on your wedding day, Be prepared with a lipstick that will last all night.

>> **Tanning:** If you want to look sun-kissed for your big day, do that no less than a week before your wedding. If your skin reacts badly to the tanning solution, that will allow enough time for your skin to return to its normal tone. Spray tans are great but test them out a month before your wedding so you know what the end result will be. If you're using self-tanners, start those a month before your wedding to gradually get to your perfect shade of bronze, not orange.

>> **Touchups:** Keep some basic touchup makeup with you on your big day. Have a small bag with your lipstick, powder, mascara, and blush ready in case you need a little touch up along the way.

>> **Makeup trial:** Just as in your hair trial, it's a good idea to have a makeup trial ahead of time so you can see how you'll look before your big day. If you let your fiancé see, they can give you the approval you need to move forward with your bridal makeup. This will also allow you the opportunity to test the sustainability of your wedding makeup.

>> **Take a picture:** It's one thing to see your makeup in person, but taking a picture with good lighting can help you envision what you'll look like in your wedding photos. If your makeup is too light and you look like a ghost in photos, you can adjust that to a warmer tone. Same thing is true if you look like you've been in a tanning bed since the day you were born, you can adjust to a lighter shade. A picture is worth so much when considering your perfect look.

RINGS AND THE ROCK

You already have the engagement ring but there are still two more rings that you need to purchase to exchange during the ceremony and those are your wedding bands.

Your wedding bands are a symbol to everyone that you're married. They are the band that can't be broken. Your engagement ring is worn individually while your wedding bands are something you both wear as a couple. Picking out your wedding bands together is a special part of your wedding planning process.

The first step in picking out the perfect wedding bands is to consider your budget. Wedding bands can be very affordable, but they can also get very expensive quickly. Setting that budget up front will help you stay away from the rings you can't afford. I don't want you to fall in love with a wedding band that is out of budget.

One thing to consider when picking out the perfect wedding bands is your lifestyle, which will help you determine the perfect metal or material. Do you work with your hands a lot? If so, a durable metal such as tungsten or titanium could be the right choice. Another option would be a soft rubber material that is durable. Soft metals such as golds or silvers are great for those who don't work with their hands. Adding gemstones or diamonds is also a great choice!

There are a few ways that you can coordinate your bands with your spouse. One way is through matching your wedding bands. No matter how elaborate your engagement ring is, a simple thin wedding band is always a classic choice. There are several coordinating sets on the market, and this is one approach to make your wedding bands special.

Another way to customize your wedding bands is with personalization. Engraving your initials or a phrase that is special just to the two of you will take your wedding bands to the next level. It's something only you know about. Because the engraving is on the inside, it's like having your own little secret, just for you.

Chapter **10**

What Everyone Else Will Be Wearing

Although the bridal gown is typically a main focus on the big day, it's time to think about what your partner will wear. Your fiancé's attire should complement your attire. If one of you is going for a formal look, you both should be formal. The same goes for a more casual, laid-back look.

In this chapter, I cover some possible choices for your groom/partner. Additionally, I talk you through picking the perfect bridesmaids' and groomsmen's attire, as well as attire options for the rest of your bridal party.

Enjoy this process and avoid drama by addressing the financial commitment early in the process, and by remembering that everyone has their own style, which may or may not match yours. My hope for you is that your bridal party will accept your preferences without drama. Wouldn't that be amazing? I can see it now; you're all going to look flawless.

Duds for Your Dude: The Groom's Attire

It's time to dress up the groom. Although this is often put on the last-minute to-do list, it's important to pick your groom's attire three to six months before your wedding. By then, you'll know your theme and can pick the perfect color and style option for your perfect guy.

To help determine the perfect complement to your attire, I created Table 10-1 for you to reference for suggestions on complements to your dress selection. In case you don't want your groom to know the style of your dress before the wedding, you can use this as a tool to give gentle suggestions on what your groom should wear.

TABLE 10-1 ### Bride's Dress and Groom's Attire

Type of Dress	Coordinating Groom's Attire
Mermaid	White or black tuxedo
A-line	Dark or light suit
Sheath	Dark or light suit
Ball gown	White or black tuxedo
Separates	Colored suit
Strapless	Dark tuxedo or suit
Trumpet	White or black tuxedo
Backless	Black or dark tuxedo
Fit and flare	White or black tuxedo
Slip	Light suit
Sleeveless	Dark suit
Empire	Dark suit

Thinking about the dress code of your event is key to determining the perfect attire for your groom. I created Table 10-2 to show you what the men should wear to fit a particular dress code. Use this table as a guide to help you determine the perfect dress code for your event.

TABLE 10-2   ## Men's Dress Codes and Attire Suggestions

Dress Code	Suggested Attire
White tie	The most formal of all dress codes, with attire that includes a tailcoat, white vest and bow tie, and studs and cuff links for the shirt.
Black tie	A very classic formal attire that includes a tailored black tuxedo with a bow tie or tie.
Formal or black tie optional	An elegant attire that includes a dark suit with a white shirt and tie.
Cocktail	A causal attire that includes a cotton suit or sport coat. Instead of a tie, wear a pocket square.
Semiformal or dressy casual	A less tailored attire that includes a sports jacket with trousers and not tie.
Festive	Throw out the rule book and express your personal style with a combination like a tuxedo jacket, trousers, and tennis shoes.
Casual	This does not mean T-shirt and shorts. This attire includes a blazer with trousers or jeans, casual shoes such as sneakers or boots, and no tie.
Beach destination	For a tropical location, attire can be a short- or long-sleeved shirt with a pair of shorts or khakis. Loafers, flip-flops or barefoot is also appropriate.

Something else to consider is the season in which you're getting married. Table 10-3 can help you pick the groom's attire based on the season. Use this as a reference when picking the perfect look for the big day.

TABLE 10-3   ## Seasons and Groom's Attire Suggestions

Season	Suggested Attire
Winter	White tie or black tie
Spring	Black tie or cocktail attire
Summer	Light colors, black tie, white tie, or cocktail attire
Fall	Dark suit or semiformal

Suit up or suit down?

Deciding how formal your groom should be is a difficult choice guided by many factors. In this section we'll learn about the differences between a tuxedo and a suit, and think through some things to consider when deciding if your groom should be in a tuxedo or a suit.

First, what makes them different? To some, anything above jeans and a T-shirt is a tuxedo. The biggest differences are in the accents. While a suit is generally constructed from one piece of material, a tuxedo often has details such as a satin lapel, decorative buttons, or strips of satin running down the side of the pant leg. The additional accessories also make a difference between the two. A tuxedo will typically include a vest, cummerbund, and bow tie. A suit may or may not include these accessories.

REMEMBER

There are four main factors to consider when picking a suit versus a tuxedo for your groom.

>> **The dress code:** How formal is your wedding? It would be inappropriate for the groom to be the most casually dressed male at the wedding. Think about how formal your want the wedding to be and coordinate the groom's attire with the dress code. He's the one who sets the code for everyone else.

>> **Time of day:** A tuxedo is more appropriate for an evening wedding, while a suit can be for any time of day. If your wedding is in the morning, think about a suit for your groom rather than a tuxedo.

>> **The cost:** A custom-made suit can be a big expense. Consider the financial obligation when choosing the groom's attire. Will the groom wear it after the wedding day? If not, you may want to resource a rented suit or tuxedo to cut down on the cost of the wedding.

>> **The groom's style:** It's important to consider the groom's opinion when picking a suit or a tux. If he feels like a penguin in a tuxedo, then pick a suit. There is nothing worse than feeling uncomfortable in any way on your wedding day. Make sure your groom feels comfortable in his selection. It will make for a much happier day!

Tie, handkerchief, vest?

That is the question. The accessories for your groom's attire will complete the look. There are so many options to choose from, as shown in Table 10-4. Working with a professional men's attire company can help you find the perfect accessory.

TABLE 10-4 **Groom's Accessories Options**

Accessory	Definition
Tie	A narrow long piece of material that is tied in the front.
Bow tie	A necktie tied in a bow or knot with two loops.
Handkerchief or pocket square	A small square piece of fabric worn in the pocket of either a suit or tuxedo.
Cummerbund	A pleated sash worn around the waist.
Shoes	A covering for your feet, that you can use to express your personal style but make sure they're comfortable!
Socks	Fabric worn around your feet. Have fun with picking out your socks. Consider custom-made socks in a pattern of your favorite colors or images of something you love.
Cuff links	A device used for fastening your shirt cuff. These also make a great gift for your groomsmen! Add your personality with custom-made cuff links.
Belt	A strip of leather or material worn around the waist to secure your pants. This is another area where you can add some personal style to your suit or tuxedo.
Suspenders	A pair of straps that go over your shoulders and fasten to the waistline of your trousers. If you're hosting a more casual wedding, consider a clean white shirt, trousers, and suspenders to complete your look.
Boutonniere	A small decorative floral arrangement that is attached to your suit or tuxedo lapel.
Hat	A covering for your head that can allow you to show off your personal modern style or your inner cowboy.
Watch	A small timepiece worn on your wrist. This can be a great gift for any groom who wants a luxury feel for their wedding day attire.
Sentimental item	A family heirloom that can be worn by the groom. Consider wearing a family member's cuff links, tie, bow tie, or pocket square for a special touch to your attire.

Choosing Attire for the Bridal Party

You've picked your squad, and now it's time to figure out what they're going to wear. Shortly after they said yes to being a part of your wedding day support team, they have probably asked, "What should I wear?"

WARNING

Let's discuss the elephant in the room: the bridal party's financial obligation for your wedding day. When someone accepts the job of support team, there is an understanding that they will assume some financial obligation to be involved in your big day. Besides showers, parties, and gifts, when it comes to the attire and wedding day, your bridal party should pay for their own attire, hair and makeup, and travel.

Although it may be uncomfortable, you need to have a conversation with anyone you ask to be in your wedding about managing the financial obligation. You also need to be considerate not to pick the most expensive dress, hair and makeup stylist, and hotel. The chances of someone telling you they can't afford to be in your wedding is slim to none. Even if you don't know, it's important to acknowledge that your people are taking time off work and paying out of their own pockets to be in your wedding.

To think through what the average bridesmaid may spend on your wedding, let's consider the following as a possible example:

Bridal Shower: $100

Bachelorette trip: $300

Hotel: $600

Gas: $200

Wedding gift: $50

Attire: $200

Hair: $75

Makeup: $75

Alterations: $75

That added up to $1,675 for one person to be in your wedding. This may cause financial stress that can be avoided if the lines of communication are left open. If you can help with any of the cost for your bridal party, that is a wonderful gift. If you can't help them financially, my suggestion is to be aware of how much they will be spending with your selections.

In this section, I discuss what your bridesmaids, groomsmen, parents, grandparents, flower girl, ring bearer, attendants, ushers, and officiant should wear on your big day. Together with your attire and your fiancé's attire, you'll have the full picture and theme picked out for your style.

Bridesmaids

The first step in picking the perfect bridesmaid's attire is to keep an open mind. Each of your bridesmaids has a different body. They also have different tastes. As discussed above, they may also have different financial constraints.

HAVE THE MONEY TALK AS SOON AS POSSIBLE

I had a bride one time call me in a panic. The required financial obligations made a bridesmaid withdraw from her wedding. They had been friends since grade school — best friends, in fact. However, the financial stress was too much on her best friend and she had to back out of the wedding. After the initial shock of her friend not being by her side on the wedding day, my client took some time to first see if she could cut down some costs or financially support her friend. Unfortunately, it was just too much for her friend and she couldn't stand by her side on her big day. I was heartbroken for my client because I knew how much she wanted her friend to be a part of her day. But when it all came down to it, she couldn't manage the financial burden.

This is a reminder that it's very important to have those uncomfortable conversations with your bridal party early in the process. If you do this early, you may avoid heartbreak later or, even greater, the loss of a close friendship. Financial stress can cause a lot of tension, and this is one thing that you want to avoid in your wedding planning experience.

REMEMBER

As your friend, I want to let you in on a big secret. You are *not* going to make everyone happy. There, I said it. Now is the time to accept it. While you may love blue, your bridesmaids may hate it. If you pick a particular style or cut, it may not flatter all your bridesmaids' bodies. And you know what, that's okay! Again, you are not going to make everyone happy.

First, I want you to start looking at inspiration photos. There are a million options but within your theme, eventually, you'll start gravitating to a particular color and or style for your bridesmaids. I created Table 10-5 to help you navigate picking the perfect dress, with some things to consider and my tips. Use this as a guide to help you pick the perfect attire for the most important ladies in your life.

Groomsmen

Picking your groomsmen's attire is another piece of the puzzle to becoming style icons. The groomsmen's attire should coordinate with the bride's, groom's, and bridesmaids' attire. This is another opportunity to grab some inspiration online, where you can see many color combinations of bridal parties and themes. Resource those for a visual of what your bridal party photos may look like when everyone is together standing with you at the altar.

TABLE 10-5   **Bridesmaids Attire Suggestions**

Consider	Pro Tip
Color	Bridesmaids' dresses come in a million color options. Based on your theme, you may want to order color samples so that you can pick the perfect color for your squad.
Cost	It's important to consider the financial obligation for your bridesmaids. Most bridesmaid dresses fall in the range of $100–$200. Keeping the cost down will help with the financial burden on your bridesmaids.
Style	Include your bridesmaids with the style selection. Ask them what they're comfortable in. If they don't like strapless, consider sleeves (short or long) as an option. It's important to make sure they feel as comfortable as possible because they will be standing with you in front of a lot of people.
Length	The length should be determined by the dress code set by you and your fiancé. Black tie or white tie: Floor length Formal: Floor length Cocktail: Floor length, tea length, knee length, or midi dress Semiformal: Floor length, tea length, knee length, or midi dress Casual: Sundress or maxi dress Destination: Sundress or maxi dress
Variation	Adding variation is a wonderful way to allow your bridesmaids to display their own personal style! This can be done in a few ways. Color: If you have a general color picked out, consider different shades. Another way to use color is to pick a few colors (2–3) that your bridesmaids will pick from. Just make sure you spread the colors out among your bridesmaids. Style: Allowing your bridesmaids to pick their own style is a great way to add variation. For example, let them pick between halter, strapless, one shoulder, sleeves, or short sleeves. Additionally, let them pick the length that feels the most comfortable.
Picking their own	If you give your bridesmaids the color palette, let them pick their own dress. This can be something from their closet to cut costs, or they can buy a new dress that they love and will wear again.

There are a few initial things to consider when picking out the groomsmen's attire. First, what is the groom wearing? Do you want the groomsmen to match the groom? That's the most popular option, but make theirs slightly different regarding their accessories. Differentiate the two with a different color of tie, bow tie, pocket square, or cummerbund if you select those pieces.

A few more things to consider about the groomsmen's attire is the season, time, and venue for the wedding. If your wedding is in the middle of summer, try to stick with light colors and materials for the men. If you're hosting an evening wedding, consider dark suits or tuxedos. If you're getting married on a beach, consider a more laid-back look with white long-sleeved shirts and khakis.

Once you have narrowed down those elements for your big day, you can focus on the style, color, and accessories. The first task in picking any attire for your groomsmen is to check in with them to see what would be best for them. A custom-made suit, while luxurious, can be very expensive. Take time to think about your groomsmen's lifestyle. Is it practical for you to ask them to invest in something they may never wear again?

REMEMBER

If you're renting suits or tuxedos for your groomsmen, make sure to collect their measurements within three months of your wedding. They can place the order at that time with the suit or tuxedo rental company. There are wonderful online resources that will mail a suit to your groomsmen to try on and make adjustments prior to the big day.

Another resource is a local suit or tuxedo rental store. Whether it's a national chain or a local store, you'll submit your groomsmen's measurements and they will pick up their suits or tuxes a few days prior to or the day before the wedding. It's important that they try them on right away to make sure everything fits just right. If not, the store can make those adjustments at that time.

TIP

Don't forget to make sure you have arranged for all the suits and tuxedos to be returned after the wedding. It's often forgotten, so to avoid extra charges, take care of assigning that detail to one person. If your wedding is on a Saturday, confirm that the suits or tuxedos can be returned on a Sunday before everyone leaves town. Otherwise, you'll need to plan for someone who is local or staying in town until Monday to return them. Your groomsmen are responsible for making sure all the items they rented are in the proper bags that will be returned to the store.

The cost of renting a tux or suit can vary between about $70 and $300 depending on how many pieces you order. If you opt for only pants and a jacket, that will cut down on the cost for your groomsmen. If you choose this route, the groomsmen will provide their own ties, shirts, and shoes. On the higher side, you can get the whole package, which would include a shirt, tie, jacket, pants, shoes, pocket square, cummerbund, suspenders, and even cuff links.

REMEMBER

Avoid matching the groomsmen's attire exactly to the bridesmaids' attire except for black. Their attire is likely to come from two different manufacturers, so it's nearly impossible to get a perfect match. Consider colors that coordinate with each other. If your bridesmaids are in a light color, consider a light color for your groomsmen or a contrasting black or dark navy. If your bridesmaids are in a dark color, consider a darker suit or tuxedo for the groomsmen. Additionally, you can add coordinating accessories like a tie or pocket square that matches the bridesmaids' dresses.

Parents

As a child, you didn't think you would ever need to dress your parents. They dressed you. Well, your wedding is an exception. You parents attire is important because they too are a focus on your big day. The parents walk into the wedding and typically will either give a toast or share a special dance with you at the reception. They will be noticed and need to be considered when picking your bridal party attire.

Mother of the bride

Let's start with the mother of the bride. I know this isn't the case for everyone but typically the mother of the bride has a very important job to do when it comes to your wedding. She has likely been involved in the planning and should be your rock and support on your big day.

Take a day off from planning and focus with her on her attire. This is the time where you get to make her feel special. Go to breakfast or brunch together away from all the planning details and then go shopping. It's important that she feels beautiful too. Her dress should complement the bridal party but not match exactly. Don't forget to consider your dress code, style, and time of year when picking the perfect dress. Pick an outfit that makes her feel beautiful, whether that's a formal gown, maxi dress, or pantsuit. There are no rules here as long as she feels like a style icon as well.

Father of the bride

The father of the bride is also a very important person in your wedding planning journey. He might be walking you down the aisle, paying for your wedding, giving a toast, and sharing a special dance. He will be seen, and it's important to make sure he's dressed to impress!

Just as in picking the men's attire, you need to consider the season, time of wedding, and venue. The father of the bride should coordinate with the groomsmen, but he does not need to wear exactly what they're wearing. If the groomsmen are wearing a tuxedo, the father of the bride could wear a coordinating dark suit.

Mother of the groom

The mother of the groom will likely walk down the aisle and share a special dance with her son. It's a moment all of those who don't have sons wish they could experience. For a long time, the mother of the groom has been his number one female and now she passes the torch of loving her son to another woman.

The mother of the groom's attire should complement the bridal party's attire but not completely match. We don't want any of your parents to stick out in a negative way, so communicate your vision and get involved as much as you can with the dress selection. Allow her the freedom to pick a dress that makes her feel beautiful but nothing that isn't appropriate to the time of year, theme, or style of your wedding.

Father of the groom

The father of the groom's attire is like the father of the bride's attire. They don't need to match each other or the groomsmen but they do need to coordinate with the overall theme and style of the rest of your bridal party. Often the father of the bride and the father of the groom will match the groomsmen's suits or tuxedos, but it's appropriate for them to go their own way as long as they coordinate with everyone else in the bridal party.

Grandparents

Your grandparents are also an important part of your big day. They have watched you grow up into the person you are today. If they're able, they will walk down the aisle during the processional at your wedding.

Your grandparent's attire should coordinate with the theme but not match the colors exactly to your bridesmaids or groomsmen. For both grandmothers and grandfathers, consider the dress code, time of year, and theme of your wedding.

Grandmothers should match that theme from a formal dress to a skirt and blouse. The same is true for a grandfather. He doesn't need to be in a tuxedo, but for a formal event he should wear a dark suit. If the event is less formal, trousers and a sports jacket is appropriate.

TIP

Your grandparents are a great source for marriage wisdom and family heirlooms that can be used at your wedding. Consider asking them for a piece of family heritage such as a vintage brooch for your bouquet or cuff links for the groom to wear. Your grandparents are your oldest relatives, and it's important to make them feel special on your big day. If your grandparents have passed away, consider asking next of kin to represent their legacy that was left behind.

Flower girl and ring bearer

Let's just face the facts, flower girls and ring bearers have a way of stealing the show on your wedding day. They bring so much cuteness to your wedding that's it hard for them not to become the focus of attention. Picking out their attire is just as important as picking out your bridesmaids' and groomsmen's attire.

Your flower girl and ring bearer will walk down the aisle right before the bride. They will be the last thing your guests see just before the bride walks into the ceremony.

Flower girls traditionally wear white or pastel colors that match your theme. Work with their parents, if you aren't their parent, on picking the perfect dress. Also note that some churches or venues don't allow the flower girl to actually throw petals and that's okay. If they don't allow this, you can still have a "flower girl" if there is a younger female who is special to you whom you want to be a part of your wedding. Have her carry a basket of flowers, a miniature bouquet, or a floral head wreath.

The ring bearer tradition dates to antient Egypt, where jewels were carried into weddings on a pillow. It has since been adapted to the custom of having the ring bearer carry the wedding bands tied to a pillow and then handing them off to the groom. But you definitely do not want your ring bearer to carry your actual rings. They can carry fake rings down the aisle to avoid an unfortunate accident. Trust me, I have seen it.

The ring bearer should coordinate with the bridal party, but they do not need to match their suits or tuxes. Although a small suit on the little guy is simply adorable, it's not the only option. They can also wear dress slacks and a light-colored shirt. If you want to get fancy, include suspenders or a bow tie. It really doesn't matter because, in the end, they will steal the cuteness show no matter what they wear!

Attendants

The attendants at your wedding are the first people your guests will see when they arrive at your ceremony. There are female attendants such as a person to pass out programs or attend to the guest book. The male attendants would be your ushers. They will greet the female guests and escort them to their seats. Both should receive either a corsage or a boutonniere because they're part of your bridal party.

Although some clients have opted to match the attendants and ushers to the bridesmaids and groomsmen, I would suggest reaching out to them to coordinate the color and theme. There is no need for them to buy anything new for your wedding as long as they're presentable for your guests. They are the first impression your guests will have of the bridal party you've selected.

Officiant

The officiant may singlehandedly play the most important role on your wedding day. This is the person who will perform your ceremony and make your marriage legal. It's kind of a big job!

Checking in with your officiant on their attire is completely appropriate. For some religious traditions, that attire may already be decided for them. Some ordained ministers are required to wear a robe, and if that is the case, there is no need to let them know your theme and what everyone else is wearing.

A general blanket statement is that those who officiate weddings on a regular basis are used to picking out clothing for ceremonies that is neutral or dark fabric. Their job is not to stand out but to blend into the background.

They will be in your wedding photos forever. Make sure to check in with them and let them know what you would like them to wear to match your season, theme, and style. Do you want them in a suit? Would you prefer a more casual attire? If your officiant is a female, would you want her in a dress that coordinates with your bridesmaids or is a pantsuit appropriate?

WARNING

I am not asking you to tell your officiant what to wear. In fact, don't do that! I am simply suggesting that you mention your theme and style so that they can pick the best option for your big day from their own closet.

4

Ceremony To-Do's

Chapter **11**

Making Your Marriage Legal

Your wedding day is the first day of your life together. But it's important to make sure it's legal! This chapter covers how to pick your officiant, how to obtain a marriage license, how to navigate the legality of a same-sex marriage, and how to change your name if you choose to do so.

REMEMBER

This is an exciting time in your life. Even though the legality of getting married can be time consuming and frustrating, keep a positive perspective. You'll be married, your name will change (if you want), and your new life will begin soon!

WHATEVER YOU DO, DON'T FORGET THE LICENSE!

Before we begin, I want to share an important story about a client to show the importance of taking time to read through the legalities of this chapter so you can officially become spouses. About thirty days before a client's wedding, I talk with them about getting their marriage license. I did that with this client as well, but sometimes life can get so busy that you forget to do something very important!

My client didn't have an officiant, so I had hired one for her. I was setting up the decor in the morning and she was upstairs getting ready in the bridal suite. I checked on her a few times to see if she needed anything.

Around noon, I went up to check on her again. Her wedding was at 4 pm. so we were getting close to the start of photos. This time, I asked for the marriage license so I could have it ready for the officiant when he arrived. I said, "I'm going to go ahead and take the marriage license so I can have it ready for the officiant." As long as I live, I will never forget the look on her face. She said, "I didn't get the marriage license." She had to be joking, I thought. In four hours, we would start her wedding, but there was no license to make it official.

I told her I needed a minute to come up with a solution. I knew there was no way legally that I could fix this. The first thing I did was call the officiant. I explained to him the problem and asked him if he would still perform the ceremony. He could not make their wedding legal that day. To make it legal, the client would have to go to the clerk's office on Monday and get a license. Then they would have to go to the officiant, who would have to talk them through the wedding ceremony again and then fill out the marriage certificate.

That possible solution had one major problem. Their marriage certificate would always have Monday's date and not their Saturday wedding date that we were about to witness, assuming I was able to get the officiant to perform essentially a fake ceremony.

Despite my begging and more begging, the officiant backed out. Now we were about three hours away from the start of the not-so-official wedding ceremony of my nightmares. I told the bride that the officiant had just backed out from performing the ceremony, and out of desperation I asked her if she happened to know anyone who was ordained — perhaps a pastor or judge.

I figured reaching out to someone in her immediate circle would be the best option. Initially, she couldn't think of anyone so I went back downstairs to call everyone I knew in town who could potentially officiate at this wedding. It was an interesting situation.

I had to first find someone in a very short time period. On top of that, I had to convince them to perform a ceremony that they shouldn't by law. It seemed absolutely impossible, and rightfully so. After multiple failed attempts, the bride texted me to come back up to the bridal suite.

She had thought of someone! She reached out on Facebook and they agreed to perform the ceremony. There was one catch, though — she was two and half hours away and we were starting the ceremony in two and three-quarter hours. Talk about cutting it close!

I quickly called the new officiant. She dressed quickly and then hit the road. The plan was to talk her through the ceremony while she was driving to the wedding. I walked her through the entire ceremony and thanked her profusely. She was truly saving this day!.

When she arrived, we quickly reviewed the final details and then off they went down the aisle. I wasn't exactly sure how this was going to go. I had never worked with this officiant and honestly, she had very little information regarding the couple and the ceremony content. Well, she did an amazing job! Truly it was one of the best ceremonies I have experienced. I stood at the back of the room in awe. I couldn't believe this had worked out.

Due to distance and life, the couple couldn't travel to the officiant until a long time after their wedding day. Although the marriage certificate doesn't list their official wedding day, it sure does make for a good story and a lesson that I hope you'll hear. We talk through the specifics of obtaining a marriage license later in this chapter, but let this story be a reminder that it's crucial that you get a marriage license if you want a legal marriage.

Selecting Your Officiant

Selecting the perfect officiant is an important task. They will be in your pictures forever, but beyond that they're performing you wedding ceremony and making it legal. The first step in picking your officiant is to determine what type of ceremony you're having. Is it religious, spiritual, or nonreligious?

If you're hosting a religious ceremony, you may have a pastor at your church, another religious official, or someone from your childhood who would be the perfect fit for you. They have known you for years and you wouldn't want anyone else to perform the ceremony. If you're getting married in a church but don't have a specific officiant picked out, make sure to ask the church if you're required to use one of their pastors to officiate at your wedding.

REMEMBER

Make sure your religious beliefs align with the officiant you choose. It's important to set up a meeting with your potential officiant to go over the content of the ceremony to make sure it's what you want for your religious ceremony. Additionally, certain officiants will require premarital counseling for them to perform your ceremony. Make sure to ask them their requirements for performing your ceremony.

If you're hosting a nonreligious ceremony, consider a family friend who can provide personal stories to enhance your ceremony content. If you don't have a friend or relative who can perform the ceremony, make sure to hire a professional officiant who is used to speaking in public and comfortable with the legalities of making the marriage official. It's important to check with the city or county that you're getting married to confirm if the officiant needs to be an ordained minister or a civil officer.

For example, in my state, a family friend used to be able to perform a ceremony. I have had several clients and even clients I am working with now who want a friend to do their ceremony. However, just recently, our laws have changed and only clergy, politicians, judges, mayors, and ordained ministers can perform wedding ceremonies.

Plan a meeting with your officiant to discuss your ceremony content. If you're hosting a religious ceremony, there will be traditions that your officiant can explain. They can also help you determine if you'll need readings or special song selections. If you are hosting a nonreligious wedding, consider a ceremony that is customized around who you are as a couple and what you individually bring to the marriage. I'll give you some sample ceremonies in Chapter 12.

A PLUG FOR PREMARITAL COUNSELING

If I could, I would gift all my clients premarital counseling. I think it's an invaluable experience to have as a couple. You'll gain knowledge of how to problem-solve as a couple and create your vision of a successful marriage. You'll also navigate past relationships and how they can and will impact your relationship. It's a safe place to let out all the dirty laundry with a neutral person who can help give you the tools you need to succeed in marriage.

Another perk to premarital counseling is that in some states you can receive a discount on your marriage license fees. It can be significant, so make sure to check with the county in which you're getting married so that your premarital counselor can fill out the appropriate paperwork to receive the discount.

Heading to the Courthouse: Marriage License Protocol

As we have discussed, your marriage isn't legal until you obtain a marriage license. But you don't just need to obtain the license; you must also return it by the time period set by your state or county and obtain a marriage certificate for it to be legal. In this section, we'll discuss all the legalities to making your marriage official.

Note: There is a difference between a marriage license and a marriage certificate. A *marriage license* is the document you receive at the clerk's office when you apply to be married. A *marriage certificate* is the official document that you receive after you're married. This is the document that you will need to be able to obtain a new Social Security card or driver's license if you choose to change your name.

REMEMBER

The first step in this process is to reach out to the local clerk's office or town hall in the county where you're getting married. The laws change across the United States and overseas frequently so it's important to confirm the following:

>> **Where do you need to go?** Be sure you know the correct location of where you need to go to obtain a marriage license and whether you need to be there in person or if you can fill out an application online.

>> **How much does it cost?** The cost to obtain a marriage license will vary by state and county. Make sure you know how much your marriage license will cost and if you need cash or a card to handle the payment. Some clerk's offices only accept cash. Confirm the payment amount and type before you go.

>> **Do you have to be a resident?** It's important to make sure you ask if you must reside in a county or state to get married there, especially if you're planning a destination wedding of any kind. Although most states allow anyone to get married, the county could have different policies.

>> **Are you old enough?** If you're under the age of 21, confirm with the county or state how old you need to be to obtain a marriage license. If you're not old enough, there are places that make exceptions with your parents' permission.

>> **When does the marriage license expire?** There are very few states where marriage licenses don't expire. Confirm with your state or county when the marriage licenses expire. For example, if a marriage license expires in 30 days, that means you have 30 days to get married from the time you received your marriage license. So, if you're 60 days out from your wedding, you'll need to wait until 30 days out to obtain a marriage license.

>> **Is there a waiting period?** Some states and counties require a waiting period between the time you obtain a marriage license and when you can get married. Make sure to confirm this, especially if you're traveling to another location for your wedding. If there is a waiting period, you'll need to plan for that when considering your travel timeframe.

>> **Do you need a blood test?** Although blood tests used to be required to get married, they aren't often required anymore. The main reason for blood tests were to confirm that the couple weren't relatives, and the couple didn't have any diseases that could be transmitted. While few states or counties require it, you should confirm that you don't need one.

>> **Do you need a witness?** If your state or county requires witnesses, confirm how many you'll need. The witness will not be with you when you obtain a marriage license. Their job is to witness the wedding ceremony and sign your marriage certificate.

TIP

Check out this book's Cheat Sheet on dummies.com for a handy table to help you navigate the rules and regulations of the state in which you're getting married.

Navigating Same-Sex Legalities

In June 2015, the Supreme Court ruled it unconstitutional for states to ban same-sex marriage. Prior to this ruling, 37 states had legalized same-sex marriage: Alabama, Alaska, Arizona, California, Colorado, Connecticut, Delaware, Florida, Hawaii, Idaho, Illinois, Indiana, Iowa, Kansas, Maine, Maryland, Massachusetts, Minnesota, Montana, Nevada, New Hampshire, New Jersey, New Mexico, New York, North Carolina, Oklahoma, Oregon, Pennsylvania, Rhode Island, South Carolina, Utah, Vermont, Virginia, Washington, West Virginia, Wisconsin, and Wyoming, as well as the District of Columbia.

While it's officially legal to get married to a same-sex partner, just as in heterosexual relationships, it's important to check with your local town hall or county clerk's office to confirm their rules and regulations prior to obtaining a marriage license. The same rules should apply as they do for heterosexual couples. It's also important to confirm that your marriage will be recognized by the state in which you live. If you get married in Hawaii but reside in Tennessee, will you have the legal rights of a heterosexual couple?

For same-sex marriages, I would also seek out same-sex-friendly vendors. Although we have made some progress when it comes to the acceptance of same-sex marriage, I want you to feel accepted with all your vendors. When you can build a relationship with them and feel accepted, you'll have a perfect wedding day.

REMEMBER

Here is some good news: everything in this book is for you too. Just because you're marrying someone of the same sex does not mean that the process to your wedding planning should change in any way. It does not mean that you don't get to plan your perfect day just as you would if you were marrying someone of the opposite sex. Your day is to be celebrated. There may be a few hurdles along the way, which you're no doubt familiar with. Surround yourself with people who love you for you.

Changing Your Name

It's time to start thinking about your new name. Are you going to change your name? Have you been writing your maiden name with someone else's last name ever since you were little? Some have dreamed for a very long time about what their new name will be. For others, the thought of changing their name feels like a loss of some kind.

No matter where you fall on the spectrum it's important to consider whether you're changing your name and how to do it properly after your wedding day. If you do decide to change your name in any way, there are steps you must take to be able to do so. In this section we will discuss the steps to take to make your new name official!

TIP

Before moving forward with anything official, after your wedding you can change your name on social media. You don't need to provide any formal documents to do this. It's the first step in announcing to the world your new name!

To make everything official, you need to change your name in this order:

1. **Get certified or notarized copies of your marriage certificate from the office where you received your marriage license.**

2. **Update your driver's license.**

3. **Update your Social Security card.**

   (Note that items 2 and 3 are in reverse order in some states. Make sure to check you state laws.)

4. **Update your bank accounts, credit cards, and credit union.**

5. **Update your passport.**

After your wedding, you'll have a certain amount of time — typically a few days — to return your marriage license. If you're able, try to physically return your marriage license the next business day after your wedding. It's a quick process, and you won't have to worry about anything getting lost in the mail. They will be able to physically hand you your certified copies of your marriage certificate.

Determining your new name

Before you can change you name, you need to decide what your new name will be. This is an exciting part in the wedding planning process where you get to have fun exploring your options.

The traditional bride will use her first name, middle name, and her groom's last name. This is the one that you have been doodling in your journal since you were a little girl. You finally know what the mystery name is, and now it's your new name!

Another popular option is to combine your last names with a hyphen. This option allows you the ability to recognize both names. Typically, you'll keep your maiden name first and then add a "–" and then your spouse's last name. This is a great option if you don't want to give up your maiden name. Another positive is that if you file joint taxes, you'll be able to use both names on your tax return.

TIP

If either of those options don't work, consider creating your own last name together. You can invent any name you'd like. When you go through what is referred to as a "life change" like marriage, you're allowed to change your name legally. Come up with a new name together that honors your family heritage.

Offices to officially change your name

After you have your certified copies of your marriage certificate, you can officially change your name. There are two bureaucratic offices that you'll need to visit. You'll first need to change your name at the DMV and Social Security office prior to changing your name with financial institutions.

REMEMBER

As noted above, it's important to check with the county that you live in to see if you're supposed to change your driver's license or Social Security card first. Each state has different policies on the order and what is required.

Another important piece to changing your name is that you need to have original documentation and not copies. You may be asked to provide any or all of the following forms of identification. If you don't have the originals, you can request new originals from the institutions.

Certified marriage certificate

Social security card

Birth certificate

Valid driver's license

Passport

Utility bills

Insurance cards

If you're divorced and getting remarried, you'll need your notarized divorce decree from your first marriage.

Let's start with the DMV. The process to change your name on your driver's license is fairly simple, but you'll need to physically visit a local branch and probably deal with long lines. Please check with your local branch about what identification you must bring with you. Another tip is to register to vote while at the DMV with your new name.

In general, you'll need to provide the following:

» Proof of name change: This would be your certified marriage certificate or court documents.

» Social Security card: Depending on your state rules, this may need to be up to date with your new name prior to receiving a driver's license. Some states allow you to change your driver's license first but ask that you change your name with the Social Security office within 30 days or sooner.

» Proof of age: Proof of age can be shown on a current passport or original birth certificate.

» Driver's license: Even though you're trying to get a new driver's license, you'll need your current driver's license as well. Some states will keep and dispose of your old driver's license. Don't get too sentimental; they may take it from you to give you a new one, especially if you moved to a new state.

» Proof of address: Often you are required to prove your address on your driver's license application. This can be done through utility bills or a bill of sale/rental agreement. Typically, you'll need two forms of proof of address.

» Identification: It's not uncommon to be asked to provide multiple forms of identifications. Additional forms could be an insurance card, government ID, or school badge.

When you change your name with the Social Security office, first reach out to your local branch to see if you can schedule an appointment. If appointments are not available, you'll need to mail the necessary documents to the Social Security office.

TIP

I strongly suggest that you mail those items by certified mail, no signature required, or with tracking. This will help prevent your original copies getting lost in the mail. They will mail you back your original copies and your new Social Security card. This process will take 7–10 business days.

When changing your name with the Social Security Administration, you must submit proof of age, identity, U.S. citizenship, and immigration status. Proof of identity includes a valid driver's license, a nondriver identification card, or a U.S. passport. Proof of age includes a hospital birth record, adoption decree, passport, or religious record (establishing your birth date). Evidence of U.S. citizenship includes a birth certificate, passport, Certificate of Naturalization, or Certificate of Citizenship. Evidence of immigration status includes a document issued by the Department of Homeland Security.

The next official document to change is your passport. To do so, you'll need to schedule an appointment with a local passport provider if mailing the documents is not an option. You can typically do so via mail by completing form DS-5504 if you've had the passport for less than one year or the DS-82 if it's been longer. For both, you'll need to send in the required documents: your most recent passport, marriage certificate, and passport photo. Again, regulations are constantly changing, so make sure to call or check online for the most up-to-date information.

While having a new name will be amazing, there are a few steps you need to take that aren't necessarily fun but are required. Once those pieces are completed, you'll officially have a new name. Now that planning the wedding is over, consider changing your name your new project!

Banks, utilities, and more

You have completed the first three institutions that change your name officially and now it's time to change your name with your personal institutions. The first step in doing this is to make a list! Write out all the places that you receive bills or manage bills from.

This list includes all banks, mortgage, rent, car insurance, health insurance, life insurance, credit cards, investment accounts, and more. Additionally, you'll need to change your name with the USPS system.

TIP

Once you have your list in place, the best plan of attack is to call each of those institutions and collect a list of what you need for them to change your name. Most of that can be done electronically, especially if you have relationships with a representative at the business.

When changing your name on your bank account, you'll need to consider if you're combining your bank accounts or if you'll have separate accounts. If you're combining your accounts, you'll need to schedule an in-person appointment with your local branch. They'll be able to tell you what to bring, but one thing you'll need is a certified copy of your marriage certificate. At that time, it's best to order new debit or credit cards as well as checks with your new information.

Speaking of bank accounts, if you're opening a new bank account with your spouse, not only will you need to update your information with your financial institutions, but you'll also need to update your information with any automatic withdraw payments that you have scheduled with financial institutions.

All financial institutions of any kind will need to have proof of your name change. Once you have those items such as a new driver's license, Social Security card, and a passport if needed, a digital copy may be all they need. Therefore, it's important to make a list and start calling each of them to figure out what they need from you to be able to change your name. Once you have that organized, it will be easier to manage.

Chapter **12**

Where the Magic Happens: Planning and Personalizing Your Ceremony

Your ceremony is the most important part of your wedding day. It's the moment you become married. It is a sacred part of the day, regardless of whether you have a religious ceremony or not. Often, clients want to pass over the ceremony part and get straight to the party. I completely understand why you may be in the same boat, but we'll get to the party soon!

You wedding ceremony is the perfect time to incorporate what makes you special as a couple. Regardless of the officiant you picked, you should let your guests know, through their words, what makes your relationship unique. This is the time to share why you're marrying the person you have chosen.

If you think about those who will be with you for your ceremony, some will know only you and others will know only your fiancé. The ceremony allows the guests the opportunity to get to know both of you as individuals and what makes you dynamic as a couple.

In this chapter, I help you create that personalized ceremony. We'll discuss what type of ceremony you want to have. We'll add special touches through stories and your vows. We'll figure out who is walking in with whom. We'll also set the mood with your music selections. Finally, we'll discuss the ceremony must-haves. At the end of this chapter, you'll have a perfect ceremony that is meaningful and celebrates your love for each other. And then we'll start planning the party.

Deciding on Your Ceremony Celebration

Your ceremony celebration is just that, a celebration. Most ceremonies break down into three categories: nondenominational, spiritual, and religious. The first step in planning your ceremony is to determine the type of ceremony you'll have. To help you pick your ceremony type, I'll discuss each of these and provide sample ceremony content.

REMEMBER

If you're using a minister or an officiant, they will have standard ceremony scripts that you may have to follow. This is a wonderful tool to have but make sure you can make it your own. There are religions that don't allow customization in a ceremony, and I completely understand. However, if you can add special touches to your ceremony, I recommend that you do. Even the most rigid formats allow you to at least pick out your scripture readings or song. It may not seem like much, but it is at least something that you picked out as a couple.

Nondenominational

A *nondenominational* ceremony is a religion-based ceremony, but it doesn't acknowledge a particular religion. This type of ceremony would fit those who believe in a higher power but aren't tied to a particular religion. It would also work for couples who have separate religions. There isn't a recognition of a particular type of religion but more an acknowledgment of a higher power.

Here is a sample nondenominational script for your reference.

We have joined together today to celebrate love. We see it in _____ and _____, who stand before us, but we know it in our own hearts as well. This love is powerful enough to untie the strong entangled knot of life. It is a love that is spoken of in all religions, which kindles our souls, and which is our true home, our true meeting place.

_____ and _____ have opened their hearts to one another, and today in just a few moments will share their vows of marriage together. We are deeply grateful to them for opening their hearts to us as well, inviting us to witness and share in this precious moment with them. To this day they have traveled their own journey. Their marriage is being entered into reverently, with the recognition of a true union that has been discovered. For what greater joy is there for two human souls than to join to strengthen each other in all their endeavors, to support each other through all sorrow, and to share with each other in all gladness?

We hope that the words and spirit of our gathering may be filled with a truth that will deepen with the passing years. It is our hope that the meaning of the vows that _____ and _____ are about to share with each other will deepen as well, as they discover the endless possibilities of this life together. This is a love that need not be tarnished by common events, but can flower both in deepest adversity and in greatest joy.

As the years go by, you'll find more and more in one another a loveliness which neither comes nor goes, which neither flowers nor fades, no longer even taking the form of face or hand or words or knowing. Everything in your marriage can partake of this mysterious beauty beyond beauty, until wherever you turn you see reflections of this loveliness.

We ask that the vision you have of one another be always informed by that radiant power which first brought you together. Love is stronger than your conflicts, bigger than life's changes, the miracle always inviting you to learn, to blossom, to expand. It is to love that you must always return.

Reading: True love gives nothing but itself, and takes nothing but from itself, for love is sufficient unto love. Love has no other desire but to fulfill itself, to awake at dawn and give thanks for another day of loving, to rest at noon and meditate love's ecstasy, to return home at eventide with gratitude, then to sleep with a prayer for the beloved in your heart, and a song of praise upon your lips.

Vows: _____, do you take _____ to be your husband, to love him, to cherish him, and to continually bestow upon him your heart's deepest devotion? (I do.) And _____, do you take _____ to be your wife, to love her, to cherish her, and to continually bestow upon her your heart's deepest devotion? (I do.)

Please join hands and face one another, repeating after me: _____, you are my beloved, to love and to cherish, and to have and to hold, for richer, for poorer, for better, for worse, in sickness and in health, in sadness and in joy, to share our lives together, from this day forward. (Both repeat these vows individually).

Rings: May these rings be blessed as a symbol of this affectionate unity. Your two lives are being joined today in one unbroken circle. Wherever you go, may you always return to one another in your togetherness. May you find in one another the love for which all men and women yearn. May you grow in understanding and compassion. May the home you *establish together be such a place of sanctuary that all who are here today and others through the years will find their true friends. May these rings, symbolize the touch of the spirit of love that is in both your hearts. _____, in placing the ring on _____'s left hand, please repeat after me: _____, I give you this ring as a pledge of my love, and as a symbol of our unity.*

(Often there is a unity ceremony, reading, or special song during this time)

Declaration of Marriage: _____ and _____, you have consented together to marriage before this company, pledged your faith, and declared your unity by each giving and receiving a ring, and, as you are now joined together in mutual esteem and devotion, it is my privilege by the power invested in me to pronounce you married. Now you may seal your love with a kiss.

Spiritual

A *spiritual* ceremony is one that is focused on love, inner divinity, and connection to the universe. It is the perfect type of ceremony for those who feel a deep connection with the outdoors. If you're hosting an outdoor wedding, a spiritual wedding may be the right fit for you.

WHO CAN MAKE IT OFFICIAL?

I can't tell you the number of times a client comes to me and wants a family member to perform their ceremony. Unfortunately, it isn't always that simple. It's important to check your state's regulations on who can officiate and make your marriage legal. Where I am from, the officiant, or the one who signs the marriage license, must be an ordained minister or a government official.

I was working with a client who wanted a friend to officiate her ceremony. To be able to make her marriage legal, we hired an ordained officiant to perform the official parts of her marriage ceremony. This way, that person could sign the marriage license and be approved by the county. If she hadn't hired someone to sign the license, her marriage would not have been legal.

Remember: Every state and some counties have different rules when it comes to who can make a marriage legal, so make sure to research that information before you get your heart set on a friend performing all of your ceremony. Although it is extremely sentimental, it may not be official.

Spirituality is a deep personal relationship through life experiences that connects you to something greater than yourself. Spirituality is how you connect to everything around you. Your environment, the people, and your relationship are all connected, leaving you to wonder who you are or what is your purpose in life.

Here is a sample spiritual wedding ceremony script for your reference.

Today is a celebration. A celebration of love, of commitment, of friendship, of family, and of two people who are in it for forever. You're standing in front of a lot of people, holding flowers, and being looked at by pretty much everyone who has meant anything to you. So why do we do it? We have thousands of important moments that happen throughout our lives, but this one is regarded as one so critical, we acknowledge its special status by sharing it with others.

Why this moment? Because despite all our differences, love is what we all share. It's the great unifier — our one universal truth. That no matter who we are, where we've come from, what we believe, we know this one thing: love is what we're doing right. That's why you are both standing here. And that's why you all are here to watch them stand up here. All of us here today have our own love stories. Some are yet unwritten, while others are just getting to the good part. _____ and _____, we're here to hope with you, to support you, to be proud of you, and to remind you that love isn't happily ever after, love is the experience of writing your story.

It's not one moment — not even this moment. It's every moment. Big ones like saying "I love you," moving in together, getting engaged, but mostly a million little ones that come in between the big moments. Falling asleep next to one another, making dinner together, spending holidays with your families, getting a big hug when you get home from work. These everyday moments fuse together into one big experience.

And even though this experience is so incredible, words fail us when we try and explain it. That's just the way it is with love; it's meant to be felt, not described. But trying to describe love is one of our favorite pastimes. We use the words to write stories, and poems, and songs about love. And even though we describe love in different ways and even though love can look different from one person to the next, we all know it when we see it. And we see it here.

Vows: _____, do you choose _____, to be your partner in life and your one true love. Will you cherish your friendship and love them today, tomorrow, and forever? (I will.)

(Repeat)

Exchange of Vows/Rings: The circle has long been a symbol for marriage. These circles are made of precious metal to represent the precious nature of your relationship. Being unbroken circles, each represents unending love. As often as either of you look upon these rings, may you be reminded of this moment and the love you have promised.

Nuptial Blessing: By your free choice you have made a marriage. No matter what the demands on your lives and your time, the meaning of your living is now known through your love. You must nurture each other to fullness and wholeness, renew yourselves in love and laughter, maintain the capacity for wonder, spontaneity, humor, sensitivity, and save time for each other.

Declaration of Marriage: Before this gathering, you have promised each other undying love and have exchanged rings to wear as a sign of everlasting commitment to each other. By the power vested in me, I now pronounce you husband and wife (or married). You may kiss.

Religious

Religious weddings often take place in a church or other religious establishment. Even if they aren't held in an official religious setting, they are officiated by an ordained religious leader. They are focused on the God of your religion. The contain prayer, readings, and symbolism focused on God.

Here is a sample of a Christian nondenominational wedding script for your reference.

Dearly beloved, we meet here today to witness a sacred ceremony in the union of _____ and _____. With great respect, we come together to celebrate the love and devotion shared by these two children of God. We are undoubtedly blessed to be joined today by family and friends. _____ and _____ are honored that you could be here to participate in this important moment in their lives.

As the Bible states in Corinthians, "If I have the gift of prophecy and can fathom all mysteries and all knowledge, and if I have a faith that can move mountains, but if I do not have love, I am nothing." Over the course of their relationship, _____ and _____ have developed a strong bond based on shared values and mutual respect and compassion for one another. With a solid foundation from which to grow, they have made the decision to take the oath of marriage and spend the rest of their lives together.

Let us rejoice in the love on display here today. May we treasure these memories as _____ and _____, under the eyes of God, get set to begin their lives together.

Pastor: *Who gives this bride?*

Bride's companion: *I do.*

Wedding Sermon: *Marriage should be a respected institution, and one deserving of deep reverence. Today we observe the union of _____ and _____ in holy matrimony, a commitment they have chosen to take upon themselves with all the sincerity that it warrants.*

While marriage is a sacred and serious tradition, it is also cause for tremendous joy in your lives. Married life is full of surprises, adventures, and memory-making, all made possible by the enduring power of love. When _____ and _____ finalize this union, they will begin a new life of partnership, one defined by shared desires, goals, and successes.

_____ and _____, as you learn to live together as one, you will face many challenges that can help you grow. I encourage you to spend time doing the things that make life precious — support each other, always make time to laugh together, and never lose appreciation for the love that you share. Remember to cling to the vows that you will make today. Seeking strength from each other, give hope to one another, and let your trials help you grow as one. They say love can build bridges and climb mountains, and they're right.

You will find that as you grow and mature over time, your love for one another will prove to be both fulfilling and empowering. There will be challenges in your life, but the strength of your bond will offer you protection against whatever life puts in front of you. Always make your relationship a priority and continue to care for each other. Through a commitment to love, and with the power of faith, together you will be able to get through any obstacles that come your way.

Consecration: *Under the eyes of God, I solemnly bear witness to these matrimonial proceedings. I will now finalize the sacred covenant you shall both enter on this day. The rite of marriage is an ancient institution, an important ritual that binds two people together for the rest of their days.*

Today, as you form this union, you're choosing to take a vow that is as sacred today as it was to your ancestors. The Bible makes note of the power of partnership in Ecclesiastes. It reminds us that "Two are better than one, because they have a good return for their labor: If either of them falls down, one can help the other up. But pity anyone who falls and has no one to help them up. Also, if two lie down together, they will keep warm. But how can one keep warm alone?"

Vows: *_____ and _____, I now invite you to express your vows to one another. Please face each other as you say these vows before God and in the presence of your family and friends.*

I, _____, take you, _____, to be my lawfully wedded husband. I promise to keep you by my side through the good times and the bad, for richer or poorer, in sickness and in health. I vow to stay true to you, honor you, and love you for the rest of my days, until death do us part.

I, _____, take you, _____, to be my lawfully wedded wife. I promise to keep you by my side through good times and bad, for richer or poorer, in sickness and in health. I vow to stay true to you, honor you, and love you for the rest of my days, until death do us part.

Declaration of Intent: _____ and _____, please join hands. Under the eyes of God, (Groom), do you take (Bride) to be your lawfully wedded wife? Do you promise to support her completely and love her unconditionally, so long as you both shall live?

Groom: *I do.*

Under the eyes of God, _____, do you take _____ to be your lawfully wedded husband? Do you promise to support him completely and love him unconditionally, so long as you both shall live?

Bride: *I do.*

Ring Exchange: It is now time to exchange the rings. The circle formed by each ring is a symbol of your love and eternal commitment to one another. May these rings remind you always of these divine promises you've made to each other today in the company of your family and friends.

_____, please repeat after me as you place the ring on the hand of your loved one. I, _____, give you, _____ this ring as a symbol of my love, commitment, and the eternal vows we have made today to each other. With this ring, I wed.

_____, your turn.

I, _____, give you, _____ this ring as a symbol of my love, commitment, and the eternal vows we have made today to each other. With this ring, I wed.

Pronouncement By the power vested in me, by the state of _____ I pronounce you, _____ and _____ husband and wife.

_____, you may now kiss the bride.

Presentation Ladies and gentlemen, it is with great honor that I present to you, Mr. and Mrs. _____ and _____ (Last

Name)_____!

Designing a Ceremony That Tells Your Love Story

Your ceremony is a time where your loved ones get to witness your commitment to each other. It's also a time where they get to hear about your love story. It is important to write a beautiful love story. In this section, I discuss how you can personalize your story and also provide advice and guidance on the processional and recessional and your vows and ring ceremony.

Personalizing the ceremony script through stories and other details

Although the scripts provided in this chapter could be taken word for word and used in your ceremony, it's important to make them your own. One main way that you can design a meaningful ceremony is to include personal stories in your ceremony script. Doing so allows those guests who don't know your spouse a little insider information about who they are and why you fell in love with them.

TIP

I have an idea for you. Answer the following questions individually, on a sheet of paper or electronically. After you have completed these answers, ask your officiant to use this content as they see fit in your ceremony. Want to make it even more special? Don't show each other your answers. Be surprised on the wedding day with what the other said about you and your relationship.

>> What was your first impression of your fiancé(e)?

>> When did you know that you were in love with your fiancé(e)?

>> Why do you want to marry your fiancé(e)?

>> What do you love about your fiancé(e)?

>> What are some things you wish you could change about your fiancé(e)?

>> What are some things your fiancé(e) does for you that makes you feel loved?

Overview of the ceremony components

While every ceremony may be different, they each include content that is important to understand. In this section, I will explain what each piece is and provide a sample ceremony that can be your guide for setting up your wedding program. You may interchange some of the pieces, but the structure will help you determine your custom ceremony.

The following list covers the typical order of the ceremony, including definitions of each part.

>> **Prelude:** The prelude is the music played while your guests are entering the ceremony. This music begins thirty minutes before your ceremony start time.

>> **Processional:** The processional consists of the entrance of the officiant, grandparents of the couple, parents of the couple, groomsmen, bridesmaids, flower girl and ring bearer, and bride.

>> **Welcome:** The officiant welcomes the guests to witness your wedding ceremony. During this time, the officiant will acknowledge the commitment you're making to each other.

>> **Declaration of Intent:** This is when the officiant asks you if you want to marry each other and where you get to say "I do" or "I will" at your wedding.

>> **Giving of the Bride** This is the official ceremony where the bride's escort gives her away to be married to her fiancé. During this time, the escort will be asked to state that they give the bride to the groom. There is an exchange of handshakes and hugs and then the bride and groom step forward to be married.

>> **Message** During the message the officiant will speak to the couple about marriage expectations and give them words of wisdom or religious content to begin their life together.

>> **Readings** This is where scripture or poems will be read to the couple as a charge to them as a reminder of the sanctity of marriage.

>> **Exchange of Vows** This is where the couple speaks their vow of love and marriage to their spouse. Each will speak or repeat their vows to the other.

>> **Exchange of Rings** This is where the couple will give each other a ring to symbolize their unity to each other.

>> **Declaration of Marriage** This is where the officiant declares the couple married.

>> **Unity Ceremony** Sometimes couples choose to participate in a ceremonial act, such as the lighting of candles to symbolize their unity.

>> **Pronouncement of Marriage** This is where the officiant pronounces the couple married by saying their new name. For example, Mr. and Mrs. _____ and _____ and then their last name.

>> **Kiss** The moment everyone has waited for — this is when the couple seals their love and agreement with a kiss.

>> **Recessional** This is where the bridal party will leave the ceremony.

>> **Postlude** Music that is played while the guests exit the ceremony.

Processing in and skipping out

A wedding ceremony of any kind always includes a processional and a recessional. A *processional* is when your bridal party walks into the ceremony. A *recessional* is when your bridal party walks out of the ceremony. This section covers how to get your bridal party down the aisle and how they can exit your ceremony.

Pairing up the members of your bridal party

The first step in figuring this out is to pair your bridal party in the order that you want them standing. To be able to figure this out, I want you to fill in Table 12-1. We'll use this to determine the order of how your bridal party will enter and exit the ceremony.

TABLE 12-1 ## Bridesmaids and Groomsmen Order

Bridesmaids in order (closest to the bride)	Groomsmen in order (closest to the groom)

Note: The names that you list next to each other will be paired up at the wedding. If you have more bridesmaids than groomsmen or vice versa, the people on the end will pair up with two people. So, at the bottom of the list, you may have one bridesmaid listed to two groomsmen.

Table 12-2 is for you to fill in your parents and grandparents. When you fill in your parents and grandparents, if their spouse is living, you'll list their spouse as their escort. If their spouse is deceased, you'll list their escort. Your officiant does not need an escort, so you can leave that blank.

TABLE 12-2 ## Family Order

Parents of the Bride	Escort
Parents of the Groom	**Escort**
Grandparents of the Bride	**Escort**
Grandparents of the Groom	**Escort**

Note: If you want your dad or multiple parents to walk you down the aisle, you will list him or them in both places. I explain how this will work when we input your names into your ceremony script.

Figuring out the processional order

Now, I have one more question for you to figure out your processional and recessional order. Do you want your groomsmen to walk in with your groom or with your bridesmaids?

If you answered with the groom, your order will be:

Entrance of Officiant

Entrance of Groom with Groomsmen (the groomsmen will come in order closest to the groom)

Entrance of Grandparents of the Groom (with escorts)

Entrance of Grandparents of the Bride (with escorts)

Entrance of Mother of the Groom (with escort)

Entrance of Mother of the Bride (with escort)

Entrance of Bridesmaids (the bridesmaids will enter in reverse order, with the bridesmaid who is standing closest to the bride coming in last)

Entrance of Flower Girl and Ring Bearer

Entrance of Bride (with escort)

If you answered with the bridesmaids, your order will be:

Entrance of Officiant with Groom

Entrance of Grandparents of the Groom (with escorts)

Entrance of Grandparents of the Bride (with escorts)

Entrance of Mother of the Groom (with escort)

Entrance of Mother of the Bride (with escort)

Entrance of Bridesmaids and Groomsmen (in reverse order)

Entrance of Flower Girl and Ring Bearer

Entrance of Bride (with escort)

Recessional: It's all in reverse!

After the ceremony is over, you'll walk out to your forever. Enjoy the first steps together as partners for life. Now, how do you get everyone else out? Here is the order of your recessional.

The Married Couple (YOU!)

The Bridesmaids and Groomsmen (paired and exit in order)

The Flower Girl and Ring Bearer

The Parents of the Bride

The Parents of the Groom

The Grandparents of the Bride

The Grandparents of the Groom

The Officiant

The Guests

Vows and rings

Exchanging your vows and rings at your wedding is the most important part of your ceremony. Your vows are the commitments you make to each other. They are spoken out loud for all to hear. They are only yours, to share with each other.

The same is true for the rings. Your rings symbolize the unbroken commitment that you're making to each other. You wear them for the world to see that you have committed your love to a certain person.

In this section we're going to talk about the vows you'll make to each other and if they are traditional vows or if you'll write your own. I will also share with you some sample ring ceremony commitments. Personalizing your vow and ring content is a perfect way to customize your wedding ceremony.

Opting for traditional vows

I have put together a few traditional vow samples for your consideration, with the most popular at the beginning. Use these as a guide to create your own perfect vows to one another. Say them out loud, individually, to make sure that you're comfortable before you stand in front of a crowd of people.

Here are some samples of traditional vows to consider.

"I, (name), take thee, (name), to be my wedded husband/wife, to have and to hold, from this day forward, for better, for worse, for richer, for poorer, in sickness and in health, to love and to cherish, till death do us part."

"I, (name), take thee, (name), to be my wedded husband/wife, to have and to hold, from this day forward, for better, for worse, for richer, for poorer, in sickness and in health, to love and to cherish, till death do us part, according to God's holy ordinance; I pledge thee my faith [or] pledge myself to you."

"I vow to be your faithful husband/wife, understanding that marriage is a lifelong union, and not to be entered into lightly, for the purpose of mutual fellowship, encouragement, and understanding, for the procreation of children and their physical and spiritual nurture. I hereby give myself to you in this cause with my sacred vow before God."

"I, (name), take thee (name), to be my wedded husband/wife, and I do promise and covenant, before God and these witnesses, to be thy loving and faithful wife/husband; in plenty and in want, in joy and in sorrow, in sickness and in health, as long as we both shall live."

"I, (name), take you, (name), to be my wife/husband and these things I promise you: I will be faithful to you and honest with you; I will respect, trust, help, and care for you; I will share my life with you; I will forgive you as we have been forgiven; and I will try with you better to understand ourselves, the world, and God; through the best and worst of what is to come, and as long as we live."

"I, (name), take you, (name), to be my husband/wife, my partner in life, and my one true love. I will cherish our friendship and love you today, tomorrow, and forever. And I will trust you and honor you, I will laugh with you and cry with you. Through the best and the worst, through the difficult and the easy. Whatever may come I will always be there. As I have given you my hand to hold, so I give you my life to keep."

"I, (name), take you, (name), as you are, loving who you are now and who you are yet to become. I promise to listen to you and learn from you, to support you and accept your support. I will laugh with you, cry with you, grow with you, and create with you. I will love you and have faith in your love for me, through all our years and all that life may bring us."

"I offer myself to you as a partner in life. I vow to love you in sickness and in health. I commit myself to encourage you in good times and in bad. I will cherish and respect you all the days of our life together. Starting anew once again, I give thanks that I have found you. May our marriage be a gift to the world and our families, as your love is a gift to me."

Writing your own vows

There's a growing trend to throw out the prewritten vows and write your own. I love how this adds a special touch to your wedding ceremony. If you're good with words and with expressing your love, go for it!

TIP

Here are my tips to make them perfect!

>> **Talk with each other about what you're going to say.** I had a bride and groom who wrote their own vows. Hers were about five minutes in length and had all the details of their love. People laughed; people cried. They were so touching. The groom's were about five seconds long and basically just said he was going to love her forever.

I and everyone else at the ceremony was grateful that he was going to love her forever, but after his wife just gave a five-minute speech about their love, his felt underwhelming. Make sure to check in with each other so your vows are equally filled with love and devotion to the other.

>> **Consider writing vows together and reciting the same vow.** You're stepping away from the traditional vows, but you're also bringing something very special to your wedding ceremony. It is a commitment that you have decided together.

>> **Write your vows either in a book or a journal that you'll keep in your home.** You can read them whenever you need to throughout your marriage. If you write them in a book, you can hold that, and not a cell phone, during your ceremony to read them. I have seen the cell phones that come out when it's time to say the vows. I am all about giving the client whatever wedding they want, but the cell phone during the vows is not my favorite thing.

Settling on your ring ceremony content

Deciding on your ring ceremony content is like picking your vows. You can write your own if you would like but I also put together a few samples to help guide you in picking your ring ceremony content. Here are some samples for you.

"I give you this ring as a symbol of my love; and with all that I am and all that I have, I honor you, in the name of the Father, and of the Son, and of the Holy Spirit."

"In the name of the Father, the Son, and the Holy Spirit, take and wear this ring as a sign of my love and faithfulness."

"With this ring, I thee wed, and all my worldly goods I thee endow. In sickness and in health, in poverty or in wealth, till death do us part."

UNPLUGGED CEREMONY

We have all seen that photo of the couple walking back down the aisle and all the guests have their phones or large iPads out, capturing the moment but ruining their photo. It's one of my biggest pet peeves. When the couple gets their photos back, that moment is ruined by the aunt standing in the middle of the aisle because she thinks she needs that picture more than you do. Now that everyone has a mobile camera device, it happens all the time. I once watched a client walk back down the aisle and just about every single person sitting on the aisle had their phones out taking a picture of the couple. That is the picture they'll have for the rest of their lives.

A ceremony is a sacred event for the couple and the last thing anyone wants is a cell phone ringing or someone ruining an important moment because they feel like they must capture every moment. Consider an unplugged wedding to help with this nuisance. As your guests arrive to the ceremony, display a sign by your guestbook or where they pick up their programs that says: *Welcome to our Unplugged Ceremony! We invite you to be fully present with us during our ceremony. Please turn off your cell phone and camera. We promise to share all the photos with you that our photographer will capture.*

"This ring is my precious gift to you, as a sign that from this day forward you shall be surrounded and encircled by my love."

"Today I give myself to you and ask for your tomorrows. I promise to love you above all others, to give you my strength and ask yours in return, to stand by you in good times and in bad. I give you all my trust and unconditional love. May this ring be a token of my undying love for you."

"I give you this ring as a symbol of my love and faithfulness. As I place it on your finger, I commit my heart and soul to you. I ask you to wear this ring as a reminder of the vows we have spoken today."

Setting the Mood with Music

Music has a way of moving people to tears. Adding it to your wedding ceremony will create a sacred experience for all to be a part of. But where do you start? How do you know when and where you'll need music for your wedding ceremony? Well, I'm here to help you figure out this important detail for your big day.

In this section, we'll discuss what types of musicians you'll use and I'll give you song selection ideas for each part of your ceremony where music is appropriate.

Selecting the musicians

Selecting the right musician for your wedding may seem like a daunting task. Let's first start with determining what type of music you want. Do you want traditional or contemporary music?

Traditional music is a list of the most popular composers such as Bach, Wagner, Handel, or Beethoven. If I just spoke in a foreign language to you, you may be a more contemporary music enthusiast.

If you're a transitional music lover, you can't go wrong with a string quartet, string trio, harpist, pianist, or organ for your wedding. If you love the traditional feel for your ceremony but aren't getting married in a church or a place suitable for string musicians, your DJ could also play whatever music you would like.

A contemporary feel can often be played by live musicians such as a guitarist or pianist. String musicians and live musicians may be slightly limited by their repertoire or your contemporary selections, so you may want to stick with the DJ for your ceremony music. A DJ can essentially play whatever song you would like.

Selecting specific songs

When you select your songs for your ceremony, you're setting the tone through lyrics or instrumental music to express your love for each other. Although some songs may seem like epic love songs, they're actually breakup songs. Make sure to listen to the lyrics of your song selections so that you don't have a breakup song playing at your wedding.

In this section, I'll walk you through how many songs you'll need to pick out for your wedding to give to your musicians. I will also share with you some of my favorite traditional and contemporary music selections.

Prelude

Your prelude music needs to be 30 minutes of music. As I said before, this music sets the tone for your wedding ceremony while your guests are entering the ceremony.

TIP

Here is a list of some of my favorites:

"Somewhere Over the Rainbow," from *The Wizard of Oz*

"Make You Feel My Love," by Bob Dylan

"You Are the Sunshine of My Life," by Stevie Wonder

"What a Wonderful World," by Louis Armstrong

"Water Music: Hornpipe," by George Frideric Handel

"A Thousand Years," by Christina Perri

Main title from *The Notebook,* by Aaron Zigman

"Come Away With Me," by Norah Jones

"At Last," by Etta James

"Can't Help Falling in Love With You," by Elvis Presley

"Chasing Cars," by Snow Patrol

"Here Comes the Sun," by The Beatles

"I'm Yours," by Jason Mraz

"Make You Feel My Love," by Adele

"Marry You," by Bruno Mars

"This Will Be (An Everlasting Love)," by Natalie Cole

"Yellow," by Coldplay

Processional

Your processional is when your bridal party is walking into the ceremony. You'll need two or three songs during this section, depending on how large your bridal party will be. You'll need a song selection for:

Entrance of the Officiant and Family

Entrance of the Bridesmaids and Groomsmen, and Flower Girl and Ring Bearer

Entrance of the Bride

TIP

Here is a list of some of my favorites, to hopefully inspire you to pick your favorites:

"Bridal Chorus," by Richard Wagner

"Canon in D," by Johann Pachelbel

"Highland Cathedral," Traditional Scottish

"Water Music: Hornpipe," by George Frideric Handel

"Jesu, Joy of Man's Desiring" by Johann Sebastian Bach

"La Rejouissance (Music for the Royal Fireworks)," by Handel

"Ode to Joy," by Ludwig van Beethoven

"Rondeau," by Jean-Joseph Mouret

"Simple Gifts," Traditional

"I Will," by The Beatles

"Be Thou My Vision (Slane)," Traditional

"How Great Thou Art," Traditional

"Oceans (Where My Feet May Fail)," by Hillsong United

Special Music

Adding special music to your ceremony is a wonderful way to personalize your day. If you know someone close to you who is a wonderful musician or singer, asking them to be a part of your wedding to sing or perform a special song will add a lovely touch to your day.

You can use a special song anywhere in the ceremony, or as part of your unity ceremony. I have seen some amazing artists perform a song during a client's wedding and they are always crowd pleasers. My favorite is the father of the bride who performed "How Great Thou Art." He could have been a professional opera singer. Another time, a client's friend from college sang "The Prayer." She tore the roof off that church!

Adding those unique moments through a special song is just one more way to make your day unforgettable. Think through a list of your talented friends and add a special song to your ceremony.

Recessional

The recessional music is what's played while you and your bridal party leave the ceremony. This song should be upbeat and fun! After all, you just got married and now it's time to party!

The recessional is a great time to play a fun song that means something to you as a couple. It can be related to the ceremony and your marriage, but it can also be a song that is special to you as a couple. Planning many of our weddings in Tennessee, "Rocky Top" is a fan favorite.

TIP

Here is a list of some of my favorites.

"Wedding March," by Felix Mendelssohn

"Ode to Joy," by Ludwig van Beethoven

"Water Music: Allegro Maestoso," by George Frideric Handel

"Brandenburg Concerto No. 1: Allegro," by Johann Sebastian Bach

"Coronation March," by Sir William Walton

"Hallelujah Chorus," by George Frideric Handel

"Water Music: Hornpipe," by George Frideric Handel

"Spring, Allegro," by Antonio Vivaldi

"Toccata," by Charles-Marie Widor

"Trumpet Tune and Bell Symphony," by Henry Purcell

"Wedding Song," by Noel Paul Stookey

"Largo," from *Xerxes,* by George Frideric Handel

"One Hand, One Heart," from *West Side Story,* by Leonard Bernstein

"On Wings of Song," by Felix Mendelssohn

"Badinerie," by Johann Sebastian Bach

"Rondeau," by Jean-Joseph Mouret

"Sonata in G Major," by Giuseppe Tartini

"Triumphal March," by Edvard Grieg

"Eine Kleine Nachtmusik and Posthorn Serenade," by Mozart

"You Are the Best Thing," by Ray LaMontagne

"This Will Be (An Everlasting Love)," by Natalie Cole

"All You Need Is Love," by The Beatles

"On Top of the World," by Imagine Dragons

"Signed, Sealed, Delivered (I'm Yours)," by Stevie Wonder

Postlude

The postlude is the music that plays when your guests leave the ceremony. Start setting the tone with your postlude music. Pick a selection of upbeat music for your guests to dance their way out of the ceremony and into the reception, to get them excited to celebrate and ready to party all night long at your reception.

Additional Ceremony Must-Haves

Now that you have your ceremony style, content, and songs picked out, it's time to think about the additional must-haves for your wedding ceremony. In this section, I discuss those items that you should have at your ceremony.

BEING READY FOR ANYTHING WITH A WEDDING DAY EMERGENCY KIT

Putting together a wedding day emergency kit will save you on your wedding day. You should have this with you all day just in case you need anything. I can't tell you how many times people ask me for these items at a wedding. I keep a big "supply box" with me at all times to make sure I can pull that rabbit out of the hat.

Here is what you should pack in your emergency kit.

- Tweezers
- Tissues
- Breath mints
- Toothbrush, floss, and mouthwash
- Feminine products
- Lotion
- Lip balm
- Q-tips
- Deodorant
- Perfume
- Razor
- Ibuprofen
- Pepto Bismol
- Allergy medicine
- Band-Aids
- Rubbing alcohol
- Cotton balls
- Superglue
- Tape
- Scissors
- Mirror
- Eye drops

- Phone charger
- Extension cord
- Bluetooth speaker
- Cash
- Pen and paper
- Wipes
- Hand sanitizer
- Lighter
- Batteries
- Sewing kit
- Safety pins
- Extra jewelry
- Earring backs
- Tide To Go pens
- Dryer sheets
- Armpit pads
- Lint roller
- Flip-flops
- Sunglasses
- Steamer/iron
- Hair ties
- Bobby pins

- Brush or comb
- Clear nail polish
- Nail polish remover
- Nail polish
- Eyelash glue
- Baby powder
- Sunscreen
- Bug spray
- Umbrella

Guestbook

Your guestbook is a lasting keepsake of the guests who were with you on your wedding day that you can always look back to. Never will those people be in the same place at the same time again. It is a wonderful way to freeze time and take it with you into your marriage.

Pick a guest book that reflects you as a couple. What do you love to do? What is your favorite date night? Turn those things that you love into your guest book. If you love science, name a star for your wedding, and print a poster that shows the star you named and have your guests sign that.

Assign someone to making sure the guestbook arrives at the ceremony and is removed from the ceremony five to ten minutes before the ceremony begins. The long lines will begin to form, and your wedding will be late if you leave it for people to sign. The guestbook can travel with you to the reception for your guests to continue to sign.

REMEMBER

And don't forget the pens! Make sure to purchase pens that are smear proof.

Gifts

Even if you didn't want your guests to buy you gifts, they will. You'll need to have a spot designated for gifts. Provide a card box for your guests to leave their cards. Again, assign someone to make sure the guests know where to put their gifts and cards at the ceremony.

The card box will travel with you to the reception. Tell one person to be responsible for this. That way you'll avoid the wrong person picking up your cards. During dinner, have that person collect all the cards and place them in your personal bag.

I had a father of the bride call me at 3 am after a wedding because he couldn't find the cards. He was in charge of collecting the cards for the bride but neglected to do that. He was in a complete panic, asking if I saw the cards or if I had picked them up. I explained to him that I did not see the cards at the end of the night. He didn't want to tell the bride and groom he didn't have the cards, so we searched and searched until we found them. After hours of checking the surveillance footage at the venue, we saw that the maid of honor had picked up all the cards.

Your cards will have cash in them — cash you will want. It's important to make sure those are protected and taking the steps to communicate who is picking those up at the end of the night will help you avoid misplacing any of them.

Programs

Programs are the script of your wedding ceremony for your guests to follow. Those should be at the ceremony and include the order of service, song selections, and your bridal party information. Additionally, if your reception is held at another location, you should include the reception information, such as start time and location.

It's important to make sure someone has the responsibility of distributing the programs to your guests. They don't need to give one to every guest; giving one to each couple is appropriate and will save you some money on printing costs. For 200 guests, ordering 100–125 programs will be enough.

If you're getting married in the summer, consider printing your programs on a fan. In that case, order one for every guest so that they can stay cool during your ceremony. Your program will be a part of your keepsakes forever. Personalize them with a message to your guests thanking them for being a part of your big day.

5

Let's Party

» **Deciding on your timeline of events**

» **Choosing the traditions to have at your reception**

Chapter **13**

Celebrating After the Ceremony: The Reception

The ceremony is over — congratulations, you are officially married! I am so happy for you! Now we get to celebrate. The reception is a favorite part of the day for so many. When the formal ceremonies are over, you get to socialize and party with some of your favorite people. Everyone is happy to have witnessed your love and commitment to each other, and now they get to experience it firsthand through dinner and dancing.

Most of my stories come from the reception. Receptions and the guests who attend have provided me with an abundant amount of content. People do funny things, and then we add alcohol into the mix and the stories start flowing. I love what I do and the stories that I have witnessed through the years. Now is the time to share some of them to help you have the most amazing day.

In this chapter, you'll find out how to set the tone of your reception and then walk through all the pieces of the reception to determine which ones will be a part of your day. I also share with you my sample timeline of events to help you create your own. Remember, I'm here to share my experience with producing an event that flows and everyone enjoys. Your job is to take that knowledge and make it your own. So let's get this party started!

Setting the Tone

What do you think of when you picture walking into your reception? What does the room feel like, what music is playing, what flowers are on the table, and who are the people with you? There are so many ways you can set the tone of your event, from the flowers to the music.

Music

Let's start with the music. Are you booking a DJ or a band for your reception? A DJ can provide a limitless number of music selections. A band can provide you with a particular genre that you love. While there are benefits to each, whomever you choose should be able to give you the reception that you envision.

I created Table 13-1 to help you choose your songs for the reception. In Chapter 15, I'll help you with specific song selections, and this table will give you a place where, when you do pick your songs, you can make note of your choices. In the first column, I listed the times during your reception that you may need a special song selection. In the second column, you can write in the song that you picked.

TABLE 13-1   **Reception Song Selections**

Event	Song Title and Artist
Bridal Party Introductions	
Cake Cutting	
First Dance	
Father-Daughter Dance	
Mother-Son Dance	
Bouquet Toss	
Garter Toss	
Last Dance	

Flowers and decor

Another way to set the tone of your event is through the flowers and decor. What will your guests experience at dinner? Will you set the table with china, glassware, and silverware? Will there be candlelight? What will the floral centerpieces look like?

TIP

When designing your floral centerpieces, make sure the centerpieces aren't obstructing your guests' view across the table. If you want tall centerpieces, consider a thin vase where your guests are still able to see across the table while also enjoying the flowers.

Refer to Chapter 8 for details on adding special touches with flowers.

Other details

Another way to set the tone is to remember that it's all in the details. From your place cards to the menus and custom signs, every piece should work together to create the ambiance of your reception. What will your guests experience? Will you book a photobooth or maybe a live event painter to capture your event? Will you hand out glowsticks on the dance floor and keep your guests dancing all night long? Every piece of the puzzle reflects who you are as a couple, and the pieces collectively work together to set your reception tone.

I once worked with a bride who provided every guest a handwritten personal note thanking them for being at her wedding. This was a wonderful detail, and the guests felt loved and appreciated. The outside of their personalized note had their name and table number, so we were able use those notes in two ways. Another bride had a friend who made pottery and made china for her to use at her wedding. It was a beautiful, unique touch to the overall feel of her reception decor.

Examining the Elements of a Typical Reception

When you're planning your reception, you have several elements to consider. Do you need a cocktail hour? Will you do a bridal party introduction? Will someone give a welcome and possibly a prayer before dinner? Will you do specialty dances? Will there be toasts? Will you cut your cake? Will you do a bouquet toss or garter toss? Will you plan a formal exit? In this section, you take a look at some elements to consider when planning your perfect reception.

REMEMBER

I'm certain that you're going to plan an amazing night that your guests will remember forever. I wish I could be there with you to celebrate your love! Remember to have fun planning your party. It's about the two of you, and everything you do will reflect your relationship. Share that with your guests, and you will have an amazing night filled with memories that will last forever.

Cocktail hour

The cocktail hour (or mocktail hour if you aren't serving alcohol) is used as a buffer between the ceremony and reception. It serves several purposes. The cocktail hour is typically built into the schedule as a transition period from your ceremony to your reception. If you are not seeing each other before your ceremony, this time will be used to take your combined family photos, bridal party photos, and couple photos.

TIP

I would suggest doing that in the order listed. Start with the largest number of people and continue moving down to the smallest number of people. Once the family and bridal party are done with photos, they can leave for the cocktail hour or reception.

If you are doing a first look before your wedding, you will be able to take the majority of your photos before your wedding begins. When your ceremony is over, everyone in the bridal party can head to the cocktail hour or reception. If you're done with your photos, you can attend your cocktail hour or take a few minutes with your spouse to have some appetizers and a beverage in a secluded location. This will give you a minute to breathe and just have time for the two of you to enjoy the calm before the party begins. It also allows you a minute to freshen up for your reception.

The cocktail hour for your guests is the perfect time for them to grab a beverage and possibly an appetizer if you choose to serve those at your reception. It is also the perfect time for them to leave their gifts or cards, pick up their table assignments, or sign your guest book.

WARNING

We have all heard the stories about how guests were left to fend for themselves between the ceremony and reception. "The bride and groom were gone for hours!" No one wants or enjoys that at a wedding. They want to get the party started. The transition between ceremony and reception is an important time and can be used quickly and efficiently so that your guests aren't left to wait for hours.

I have a few tips to help you keep the cocktail hour at an hour and not two hours.

> » **Make photo lists.** Make three lists of photos that need to be taken with your family and give that list to your photographer. You do not need to include your bridal party unless they are family. Your photographer will know they will be taking photos of the bridal party. The lists help speed the photos along and allow you the peace of mind knowing that you didn't forget anyone. These are the lists you need to provide:

> Bride with . . .

> Groom with . . .

> Bride and Groom with . . .

The "Bride with" list is just for the bride alone. Who does she need to have a picture with by herself?

Bride with Mom

Bride with Dad

Bride with Mom and Dad

Bride with Siblings

Bride with Grandparents

Bride with Immediate Family

The "Groom with" list is just for the groom alone. Who does he need to have a picture with by himself?

Groom with Mom

Groom with Dad

Groom with Mom and Dad

Groom with Siblings

Groom with Grandparents

Groom with Immediate Family

The "Bride and Groom with" list is for the two of you together. This list is often a larger combined list. Consider the pictures that you would want to put up in your home. Would you put a picture up of the two of you with one of your parents or both parents? Again, start with the largest group of people when you create the lists. Immediate family are your parents and siblings, while extended family is your immediate family with grandparents, aunts, uncles, and cousins.

Bride and Groom with both extended families

Bride and Groom with Bride's extended family

Bride and Groom with Bride's immediate family

Bride and Groom with Bride's parents

Bride and Groom with all parents

Bride and Groom with Groom's extended family

Bride and Groom with Groom's immediate family

Bride and Groom with Groom's parents

>> **Communicate.** Make sure to communicate with those family members who will be in photos after the ceremony. Delays always occur if they do not know they are supposed to stay for photos and then other family members are running around trying to find them.

>> **Stay in place.** Photos go so much faster if everyone who is supposed to be in the photos stays in place until they are done with photos. It's easy to lose track of people if they run off and grab a drink or say hi to a guest they haven't seen in a while. Make sure everyone stays in place until they're done with photos.

>> **Read the list.** If you have a list for your photographer, have them call out the names on the list of the people who need to be in the photos. If your photographer is unable to do that, assign that task to someone. This will speed up your photos tremendously.

REMEMBER

The cocktail hour shouldn't be longer than an hour, and implementing these tips will help that time go efficiently so that you can officially begin the reception with happy guests.

Bridal party introductions

If you are introducing your bridal party, make sure to give a list of their names to the emcee or DJ. You can omit their last names and just use their first names. Last names can be harder to pronounce, so omitting them avoids an upset bridal party member. Line them up in reverse order, with the maid of honor and best man introduced last, just before the bride and groom.

It is also common to introduce your parents before the bridesmaids and grooms-men. This isn't a requirement, but it is a nice gesture so that all the guests know who the VIPs of the night are. Additionally, you can consider introducing your flower girls and ring bearer during this time as well.

Now it's time to be introduced into your reception. It's also important to list how you would like to be introduced. Here are some common options to consider:

Mr. & Mrs. [Groom's first name] and [Bride's first name and new last name]

Mr. & Mrs. [Groom's first and last name]

Mr. & Mrs. [Groom's last name]

The [new last name]

[Groom's first name] and [Bride's first name]

TIP

Pick an upbeat song for your bridal party introductions. This is the first official event that starts your party. Have fun with it and encourage your bridal party to show off their personalities when they get introduced.

Welcome

The welcome to your reception is typically given by the host or someone special in your life. It's often the time where the father of the bride gets his time to shine and thank everyone for being a part of his daughter's big day.

During the welcome is a perfect time to thank the guests who have traveled a long distance to be with you. If you aren't using a wedding planner, you might consider giving a quick rundown of the night. Here is an example for you to consider:

> "Welcome to [bride and groom's names] big day. It has been a wonderful day and we are honored that you are all here with us today. *(If Dad wants to say a few words, now is the time)*. We are about to start dinner where the staff will release the tables. After dinner, we will cut the cake, toast the couple, and dance until 10 pm."

TIP

If you don't have a displayed timeline of events at your reception, the welcome is the perfect time to inform your guests of the events for the evening. A general description of the night will provide them with as much information as they need. It is also important to let them know how long the event will go so that they can make transportation arrangements or generally know how long you're staying.

Dinner

Determining how you will serve dinner is an important part of your reception planning. Will you have a buffet or plated seated? They are different, and it's important that you understand the difference between the two.

Opting for a buffet style

For a *buffet*, your dinner is set up on display for your guests to get on their own. This can be stations or a preselected meal. Stations are what I call small vignettes of food. You could do a meat station, a veggie/salad station, or a carbohydrate station. Each station stands alone and represents a particular type of food.

Stations can also be set up for your guests to create their own, such as a pasta station or a potato station. The pasta or potatoes would be available and cooked and then your guests add all their toppings for a customized experience.

For a traditional buffet, your guests will choose from a selection of food in one line. Buffets typically contain a salad, bread, meat selections, and a few side options. If you can have your caterer set up your buffet line where your guests can get their food from both sides, this will speed up the time it takes for everyone to get through the buffet line.

Going more formal with plated seating

A plated seated meal is where your guests select a main option on their RSVP card. All of your guests will remain seated at their table and the waitstaff will deliver their meal to them that they preselected. A plated seated meal usually begins with a preset salad selection and then dinner service following.

Another form of plated seated is offering a family-style meal. This is where dishes are brought to the guests' tables for them to pass. If you're doing this style of dinner service, make sure to confirm with your caterer the amount of serving pieces that you will need. This style often requires additional rental items to serve your guests properly.

TIP

Whichever you decide, you should be served first, followed by your bridal party, your immediate family, and then the guests. Take this time to eat. If you are served first, you will get to eat at your wedding. It is important that you do, so make this a priority. Yes, guests will come up to you and say hello while you are trying to enjoy your dinner. However, eating first helps minimize my biggest pet peeve. (There's always that person!)

Cake cutting

Cutting your cake is a wedding reception staple. It might even be the main event for some of your guests. In over 600 weddings that I've attended, there hasn't been a couple yet who didn't cut some sort of dessert or cake at their reception. There are elements that you may choose to not include in your reception, but cutting the cake is one of those must-do moments. Some guests will leave after you cut your cake. I can't explain it, but, trust me, it happens all the time.

The tradition once began with the groom breaking bread and sharing it with the guests as a symbol of prosperity. I don't know about you, but I am glad it has evolved to cake or sweets.

When the time has come to cut your cake, you will cut a piece from the bottom layer — the layer closest to the table. A popular tradition is to save the top layer or smallest layer for your one-year anniversary. If you cut into that layer, the cake will dry out by the time you take it out of your freezer after a year, so make sure to cut the bottom layer.

After you cut your cake, you will serve it to each other. I know, I know, to each their own on this one, but feeding each other cake is supposed to be a moment that shows your guests how you value each other. Yes, it is popular to smash cake in the other person's face, but just hear my little voice telling you to honor your spouse and avoid that temptation. If you don't hear what I'm saying, make sure to have some napkins nearby to clean out the cake from inside your nose.

After you're finished serving or smashing each other with cake, you'll share in a ceremonial drink together. Whichever beverage you choose, you'll hook opposite arms and drink from your own glass. It's the ultimate cheers to each other!

TIP

Position your cake in a location where your guests can see it without having to get up from their table. Yes, they can absolutely come stand by you and see the cake cutting and most will. But if some guests are still finishing up their dinner, they won't have to get up to see the cake cutting if it takes place where everyone can see.

Toasts

Toasts are a very special part of any wedding reception. It is a time where your loved ones get to tell you all kinds of wonderful things about you and your fiancé. Who doesn't love to hear all the good things? Or maybe that gives you major anxiety about what stories may be shared that you don't want grandma to know.

Toasts at your reception should be a short list. Most often, they are left for the maid/matron of honor and the best man. The rehearsal dinner is where everyone in your wedding party can toast you and your fiancé. If you leave an open microphone at your wedding reception, you may find you lost an hour of the dancing or party due to all the toasts.

TIP

When you're planning that timeframe, reserve 5–10 minutes per person and let them know their allotted time so they don't take up too much time. I once had a maid of honor speak for 45 minutes at a reception. She basically shared every moment the bride and she had since they were babies. Toasts should be the CliffsNotes version of your life, not the whole novel.

REMEMBER

Make sure you pick the right people to give a toast. Confirm that they are comfortable speaking in public. We don't need anyone having a panic attack at your wedding reception. Trust me, it has happened.

I once had a best man who during his toast professed his love for the bride and said that he should be her best man for life. He used his toast as an opportunity to potentially win her over two hours after she married his best friend. Let's just say that didn't go over well for anyone involved. He was escorted out of the wedding reception. It was epic.

WARNING

My last piece of advice about toasts is to make sure that they are supportive of your relationship and marriage. The toast at your wedding reception should be a celebration of the two of you. It should highlight who you are as individuals and as a couple. Be careful who you give a microphone to at your wedding reception. I highly suggest avoiding those awkward moments along the way.

Special dances

Special dances at the reception are always, well, special. These moments have evolved into viral social media sensations. From choreographed dances to emotional moments, the special dances are always a crowd favorite, no matter how elaborate you get with the choreography.

These special dances officially open the dance floor. You may choose to do your special dances at the beginning of your reception or after dinner to open the dance floor. Either way, it's time to brush up on your dancing skills and have fun picking the perfect song for your special dances.

First dance

The first dance is appropriately named because it should be the first official dance before your guests hit the dance floor. It is the dance you will share with your spouse. Your guests will celebrate your love as they watch you dance for the first time together as a married couple.

If you are someone who has two left feet, dance lessons always make for amazing date nights! It also gives you the confidence you need to tear up the dance floor. If you are naturally gifted in dance, do make sure to at least practice before your reception. Put on your song and practice in your living room. It is one thing to dance with a bunch of people at an event, but when it is just the two of you on the dance floor, what will that look like?

Speaking of your song, selecting your first dance song is the perfect way to express your love for each other. This song will always be a special one for the two of you to share during your life together. Think about whether there is a song that you both feel describes your love for each other.

TIP

If you are stuck on picking the perfect song, consider having a custom song created for your first dance. Several online companies offer the opportunity to have a musician write and perform a custom song that will last a lifetime. This is another way that you can share your love story with your guests.

Regardless of what fits you best, make this moment special. It is only for the two of you, to mark the start of the rest of your life together. I encourage you to play that song often in your home to bring you back to one of the happiest days in your marriage. It is always good to remind each other of the commitment you made, and replaying your first dance will always take you back to a special time in your life together.

Parent dances

Parent dances symbolize your love up until this moment in life when you begin a new life with your spouse. They are an iconic part of a wedding reception. There are often tears along the way and memories made for a lifetime. Traditionally, the bride will dance with her father and the groom will dance with his mother.

REMEMBER

When it comes to these traditions, be patient with your parents' emotions. Being a mother of all girls, when I observe the groom-mother dance I often think about the fact that I will never experience that in my life. I also know from being a parent that when the time comes that my daughters get married, they will love another and not just their mom and dad. Although this is an amazing thing for them, a little piece of a parent's heart can hurt even through the joy.

Sharing a special dance with your parents is a perfect way to celebrate the love they have given you through your life. It can also bring pain to those whose parents have passed away. If that is your story, please know that I am sorry this happened to you in your life. But there is still an opportunity for you to share this moment with someone special.

If your parents have passed away, consider asking a close relative, family friend, or your spouse's parent to dance with you. In doing this, you are still honoring those who have loved you in your life. You can still have this special moment and honor those who have gone before you.

Like the first dance, picking your song for these dances is a perfect way to express the love that you have for each other and your relationship. My dad and I always sang a certain song together when I was young. We never knew the actual words and would sing the same line repeatedly. We would laugh the whole time and so when I picked our song, I knew it had to be that one because it brought me back to a happy childhood memory that I shared with only my dad.

TIP

Take time to think about a special moment that you have shared with your parent and customize this moment at your wedding reception to reflect your love for each other. It may have been your first love and it is nice to honor that on your big day.

A TOUCHING MOMENT VERSUS A CRINGEY ONE

I had a client who had a tradition in her family where they would dance to this song when she was a little girl. It would always end up with the entire family dancing in the living room. For their first dance, she and her dad took to the dance floor alone and began the song. By the middle of the song, her mother and siblings joined them on the dance floor. This was very special to their family. It took them back to a time when they were children and the only thing that mattered was dancing together as a family in the living room.

On the flip side, I once had a groom and mother who danced together as if they were the bride and groom. They must have had a special relationship, and it left everyone with their jaws open while they observed. Talk about uncomfortable. Keep it tasteful and pick an appropriate song that is appropriate for a parent relationship.

Dance, dance, dance

After the special dances are complete, it's time to officially open the dance floor to your guests. The first song should be an upbeat one that gets your guests to the dance floor. It's officially time to celebrate, so pick a fun song that will appeal to all age ranges and people who like different genres.

Make sure you have a safe, appropriately sized dance floor. I have cleaned up my fair share of drinks that have spilled on the dance floor and someone on your team may have as well. It's likely to happen, so be prepared to ensure everyone's safety while dancing all night long.

I once had a guest who slipped on a spilled beverage and blew out her knee. There she was, lying on the dance floor while all the guests were dancing around her. I was told to call the ambulance. I went to check on the poor woman who fell and then stepped out of the room to make the call. When they arrived, they came into the reception with a stretcher, checked her vitals, and got her loaded onto the stretcher and into the ambulance, while the guests kept right on dancing. I have never seen anything like it in my career. As they were carrying her out, the guests cheered, and the party continued into the wee hours of the night. The moral of the story is that beverages will spill, so be prepared to keep everyone safe.

WARNING

Additionally, make sure your dance floor is on appropriate flooring. Grass or gravel is not a good option when it comes to dancing. There are divots and unseen holes that can cause an accident. You don't want anyone to hurt themselves at your wedding, so consider the dance floor when you are planning your wedding reception.

TIP

If possible, position the dance floor close to the bar and restrooms. I cannot tell you how many times a bridal couple needed a drink or to use the bathroom and then they were gone for thirty minutes. If you want to dance all night long, this will help you do so. As soon as you leave the dance floor, your guests will stop you and talk to you. It will take you a long time to make it back to the dance floor. Shorten that timeframe by locating the dance floor close to the bar and restroom facilities.

Bouquet toss

The bouquet toss is a longstanding tradition in wedding receptions. The tradition has evolved through the years, but it is designed for the single women to gather on the dance floor and try to catch the bride's bouquet. The original tradition held that the person who caught the bouquet would have good luck to have something from the bride. This concept evolved into the idea that the woman who caught the bouquet would be the next person to get married.

When considering the bouquet toss, think about your guest list. Will there be several nonmarried women at your wedding reception? If so, this can be a fun activity. If not, it can often end up being an uncomfortable moment as the emcee is left to beg for women to come out to the dance floor.

TIP

Getting your bouquet back from the person who caught it may cause a few issues. So if you want to keep your bouquet, make sure to order a tossing bouquet from your florist. If you don't want to pay for that extra bouquet, use one of your bridesmaids' bouquets as the tossing bouquet.

You guessed it: I have a lot of stories about the bouquet toss. I once witnessed a grown woman take out an unsuspecting child while trying to catch the bouquet. The child won. I have seen women get into a fight trying to pry the bouquet out of the other women's hands. I have also witnessed someone who caught the bouquet get tackled by another woman who thought *she* should have caught the bouquet. I have also seen a bride take out a large chandelier while throwing the bouquet.

The bouquet toss is always entertaining. Pick a fun song that will fit all that entertainment and be prepared to see the competitive side of those you love come out for all to see!

Garter toss

In the tradition of the bouquet toss, the garter toss is meant to give the single men good luck because they caught something from the bride. I would say about half of my clients do the garter toss. Traditionally, the groom will remove the garter from the bride's leg and toss it to the single men.

Oh, the stories I could tell you. I once had a groom ask me to put a beer under the bride's dress. When he went for the garter, he pulled out a beer and chugged it on the dance floor. The crowd went wild! Another groom got lost under the dress for a few minutes. I thought I was going to have to call in the rescue squad.

Just like the bouquet toss, consider your guests. Will there be enough single non-married men at your wedding reception to join you on the dance floor? If not, you may decide to skip this one and keep dancing the night away.

WARNING

Some love this activity while others find it inappropriate. It has provided me with a lot of laughs through the years. If you do decide to make it a part of your wedding reception, consider all the eyes on this and keep it tasteful. Trust me, they are watching and taking it all in!

Late night

Late-night snacks or activities are always a crowd pleaser at wedding receptions. This is a perfect time to incorporate a photobooth close to the dance floor. I have also seen aerial performers or a special band or performer. Impersonators have made a few appearances through the years as well. I even had a mascot from a local team show up and entertain the crowd.

TIP

Having a late-night activity will add a unique touch to your big day that won't be forgotten. Since most dance floors are open for two hours, a late-night snack can help soak up some of those alcoholic beverages before your guests leave for the evening. Past clients' choices have included pizza, french fries, food trucks, and doughnuts. If this is an option for you, I highly recommend it. Your guests will go running towards the late-night snack. I once had a bride who ordered a popular hamburger food truck. I am certain those guests are still talking about the amazing cheeseburgers they got when they left the reception.

Changing your clothing may be something you have considered. Often, couples will want to change into something more comfortable during their reception. Do that after all the formal activities are finished. That way you will have photos in your attire for the entire night.

Another popular late-night activity is for only the couple. When the guests head outside for the grand exit, the couple shares a private dance together on the dance floor to end the evening. It is a special private moment that only the two of you experience to end your perfect day.

Exit

All good things must come to an end. It's time to plan your exit. It's my least favorite part of a client's wedding day when I have to say goodbye. We have planned their big day together for quite some time, and now it's over. But you know me, I always try and see the silver lining, which is that now your life together will begin!

When planning your exit, make sure to confirm with your venue what they allow. Although sparklers are fun, your venue may have a policy against them. If you are serving your guests alcohol, you may want to avoid them altogether and use bubbles, glowsticks, or something that won't hurt you or your guests.

TIP

Incorporating a vintage car or a vehicle that is special to you as a couple is a wonderful way to personalize your exit. Make sure your bags are loaded into your getaway car prior to the exit. When you line up for the ceremony, pack up your bags and show those to the person who will be putting them into your car.

TIP

Arrange with your caterer to provide a to-go box for just the two of you. When you get to the hotel or wherever you're staying on your wedding night, it may be late, and you might be hungry. Having a snack ready to go will make your night together more enjoyable.

Making the Most of Your Time with a Reception Timeline

It's time to work on your specific timeline for your reception. Most receptions average four hours. The question is, how will you make the most of those four hours? In this section, you design your wedding reception timeline.

TIP

When I sit down with a client during their schedule-of-events meeting, I ask them a few questions that help me determine their schedule.

Is the reception being held at the same location as the ceremony?

If not, how far away is the reception?

Do you need to take photos after the ceremony?

Do you want a cocktail hour?

Do you want sunset photos?

What time do you need to leave the venue?

What time would you like to leave the venue?

Do you want a bridal party introduction?

Is there someone who wants to give a welcome?

Do you want to eat dinner with your guests?

Do you want a cake cutting?

Will the best man and maid/matron of honor give a speech?

Are you doing a first dance?

Are you doing a father-daughter dance?

Are you doing a mother-son dance?

Do you want to do the bouquet toss?

Do you want to do the garter toss?

Do you want to do a formal send-off?

After those questions are answered, we determine how much time we need for each element. I created Table 13-2 to help you determine how long you will need for each piece. Use this as a tool to help determine how much time you need to factor when creating your reception schedule.

Now that you have a general amount of time you need to add into your schedule, I wanted to give you a sample timeline of events from a past client's wedding reception. In this case the ceremony was held at the same location as the reception. If you host your reception at another location, you need to factor the time in transit and then add 15 minutes. The 15 minutes is for guests who linger after your ceremony or before your reception. Table 13-3 is a sample timeline of events for you to use to help create your own. Keep in mind that some items will overlap, as you can see in the table. This means a few things are happening at the same time. I have also noted when you need to include additional information for your vendors and emcee.

TABLE 13-2   **How to Determine Your Reception Timeline**

Event	How much time?
Transport to reception	Transit time plus 15 minutes
Photos after the ceremony	30–45 minutes
Cocktail hour	45–60 minutes
Moving guests into the reception	15 minutes
Bridal party introductions	5 minutes
Dinner	1 hour
Cake cutting	5 minutes
First dance	3–5 minutes
Father-daughter dance	3–5 minutes
Mother-son dance	3–5 minutes
Bouquet toss	5 minutes
Garter toss	5 minutes
Dancing	2 hours
Last dance	5 minutes
Exit	15 minutes

TABLE 13-3   **Sample Reception Schedule**

Time	Event
5:30 pm	Ceremony ends
	Combined family photos
	(Include the list for your photographer)
	Guests head to cocktail hour
6:15 pm	Move guests from the cocktail hour to the reception
6:25 pm	Line up the bridal party
6:30 pm	Bridal party introductions *(Include the list for your emcee to announce)*
6:35 pm	Welcome and prayer *(Include who will do this)*
6:40 pm	Dinner begins

(continued)

TABLE 13-3 *(continued)*

Time	Event
7:30 pm	Cake cutting *(Include the song title and artist's name)*
7:35 pm	Toasts *(Include who will be giving the toasts)*
7:45 pm	First dance *(Include the song title and artist's name)*
7:50 pm	Father-daughter dance *(Include the song title and artist's name)*
7:55 pm	Mother-son dance *(Include the song title and artist's name)*
8:00 pm	Open the dance floor
9:00 pm	Bouquet toss *(Include the song title and artist's name)*
9:05 pm	Garter toss *(Include the song title and artist's name)*
9:45 pm	Last dance *(Include the song title and artist's name)*
9:50 pm	Line up guests for send-off
10:00 pm	End

Chapter 14

What's on the Menu?

ave you ever met someone who gets hangry? Let me tell you, guests get hangry if they wait too long to eat. It is important to consider their needs when it comes to food on your big day. Selecting your reception meal can feel overwhelming because there are so many options. What type of caterer will you pick? How will you serve your guests, and what's on the menu for food and beverages? There are so many options, and, in this chapter, I share tips on picking the perfect caterer, the types of dinner service, food selection, dessert, and what to drink.

Selecting the Caterer

Selecting a caterer is an important piece to a smooth wedding day. A caterer will help you select the perfect meal within your budget, offer menu suggestions, and take care of setting up, maintaining, and cleaning up at the end of your reception.

REMEMBER

Catering can consume a large part of your budget quickly. Trust me, I understand. Even if you do a local restaurant drop-off, it is very important that you have the appropriate staff to set up the food, maintain the food, and tear down and clean up. Invest in the staff you need to make sure your meal is perfect.

When you think about your catering budget, I want you to imagine you're treating your friends to dinner. How much per person would you spend if you went out to eat? Now, added to that is the staff that will set up, maintain, and tear down your meal.

There are several types of caterers to choose from, including a local restaurant, a catering service, or a food truck company. The following sections discuss these different options to help you determine what's best for you.

Local restaurant

A local restaurant can be very cost effective to fit your budget. Choose one of your favorites because, remember, I want you to pick food that you like. To save money, you can do a drop-off, which means they bring the food but they don't set it up, maintain it, or tear it down. If you go this route to save money, make sure to hire either a staffing company to take care of the service aspect, or designate a friend or family member to handle the setup, maintaining, and tearing down.

TIP

One thing to remember if you do a food drop-off is that the food should not be left out longer than two and half hours. This will avoid upset stomachs from spoiled food. Additionally, because you don't know all the ingredients the company used to prepare your meal, make sure to properly store leftovers in the refrigerator — better safe than sorry!

Catering company

The next possibility is hiring a catering company for your reception meal. A caterer is the most expensive option, but you'll have nothing to worry about. You will sit down with them and do a tasting to make sure you like the food you picked for your reception. They can offer suggestions that will give you a wonderful meal within your budget.

A catering company is a full-service provider of your food and beverage needs. They can handle everything for your reception food, desserts, beverages, alcoholic beverages, bartenders, and servers. Some caterers even offer linens and dinnerware. If that is the case, they can take care of setting up your guest table settings. Yes, it is the most expensive option, but you'll have nothing to worry about when it comes to planning the perfect meal for your guests to enjoy.

Food truck

The final option is a food truck. Food trucks are cost effective and offer a unique guest experience. Your guests will order their food directly from the truck. You can't get much fresher than that! Pick your favorite festival foods and enjoy a not-so-conventional way to serve your guests some of your favorites.

When my husband and I were married, everyone expected a plated seated meal because I'm a wedding planner. But I wasn't planning the wedding for a client, and we aren't a fancy restaurant-type of couple. Instead, we did food trucks of burgers and tacos. We love simple foods, so we picked something that we would love to eat and then spiced it up a bit. I planned it around what my husband and I loved to do together and eat on a date night, and our guests commented on how much they loved the food. In the end, our favorite foods were enjoyed by all, even us!

TIP

One tip I have for food trucks is to do a minimal selection of food options for your guests, rather than offer the entire food truck selection. Pick a few items for your guests to choose from and stick with that. This will avoid longer than normal food lines. Giving them the entire regular menu to choose from will slow down the service. Keeping the menu simple will allow for a fast and efficient dinner service.

Picking Your Preferred Type of Dinner Service

There are three main ways to serve your guests: plated seated, buffet, and stations. They're all very different from each other and make a difference when it comes to your catering bill. The following sections provide more details on each option so that you can select the one that makes the most sense for you and your budget.

Plated seated

A plated seated meal is the most elegant — and expensive — way to serve your guests. A plated seated meal is when your guests select their entrée ahead of time through their RSVP and are served their meal by the waitstaff. For this type of dinner service, you'll need to assign seats at the tables for each guest. You'll also need to inform your caterer of how many guests have chosen each entrée type.

When your guests submit their entrée selections you'll need to input them into a database that will be shared with your caterer. Reference Chapter 7 on more information on how to collect and track your RSVP's. Table 14-1 is an example of how the entrée selections should be entered into a database. You do not need to worry about sorting this list in a certain way at this step.

The first column should list how you would like your guests' name to appear on the place card. It's important to make sure you include all the appropriate punctuation. For example, if you say "Mr. Guest Name" make sure to include the (.) Whatever you type will be what you print on the place cards. Since the guests are selecting their entrée, you'll print one card per guest.

The next column is the table number that you assign to your guests. Make sure you spell out "Table" and the number so that it will print onto the place card. When you have your final RSVPs, draw a diagram of your tables in your reception space. Number the tables and then assign the guests to a table. A 60-inch (5-foot) table can seat eight to ten people. A 72-inch (6-foot) table can seat 10 to 12 people. A 96-inch (8-foot) table can seat eight to ten people, with a guest on each end of the table. If you have 100 guests, you'll need approximately ten tables.

The third column is the entrée selection, where you'll list the "meat" category, such as beef, chicken, fish, or vegetarian. This will be a key part of a successful dinner service. The place cards get the guest to their assigned table but also let the caterer know what they ordered so that they know what to serve them.

TABLE 14-1

Plated Seated Place Cards

Guest Name	Table Number	Entrée Selection
Mr. Guest Name	Table Five	Beef
Mrs. Guest Name	Table Five	Chicken
Miss Guest Name	Table One	Vegetarian
Mr. Guest Name	Table One	Beef
Mrs. Guest Name	Table Four	Beef
Miss Guest Name	Table Four	Chicken

After you have entered all the guests' table numbers and entrée selections, you can data-sort them to be able to determine how many of each meat variation you'll need to order through the caterer. It is easiest to sort them by table number, starting with one and then by entrée selection. This will be the best way for you to add up the entrée selections. You'll need to give the caterer a list that includes the number of guests at each table and their entrée selections. Table 14-2 is an example of what you'll need to provide to the caterer.

The information includes the table number and how many guests per table. In the example, there are eight guests at Table 1. Next, you'll list how many of each entrée type at that table. In this example, table one has four beef, three chicken and one vegetarian. Keep a running total at the bottom so that you can check your work to make sure it is accurate.

This example has a total of ten tables and 90 guests. As recorded, 39 have chosen beef, 38 have chosen chicken, and 13 have chosen vegetarian. Those numbers add up to 90, so I know it is accurate. You don't want to pay for one more guest than you have to, so this is an important step to ensure you aren't overpaying.

TABLE 14-2   ## Plated Seated Guest List for Caterer

Table #	Guests	Beef	Chicken	Veg
1	8	4	3	1
2	10	5	3	2
3	8	3	5	0
4	8	4	4	0
5	10	3	3	4
6	10	0	8	2
7	10	5	3	2
8	10	5	3	0
9	8	8	0	0
10	8	2	6	0
Total	90	39	38	13

Buffet

A buffet-style dinner service is where all the food is set up on a buffet line. Your guests will walk up to the buffet, get the food they would like, and sit down to eat their food. Serving dinner in this way is the most cost-effective approach. There is no need to assign your guests to a specific table. If you would like to, you can, but it doesn't affect the dinner service and the caterer does not need to know where your guests are seated.

TIP

When selecting the perfect buffet, it is best to offer a salad, one or two meats, and two or three sides. This will offer enough selection for any vegetarians attending your reception. It will also allow for a meal that will fill up your guests without breaking your budget.

BUFFET MADNESS

When working for a client, I will often release the tables to avoid long lines. I have so many stories of wacky things guests have said and done, but here are just a couple for your enjoyment.

You know that feeling that someone is watching you? I was releasing tables and had this overwhelming feeling that I was being watched. Now, I know I'm being watched when I'm releasing tables. It's the only time I'm noticed at a wedding. At some point, I locked eyes with this guy. I thought, okay, well that's why I had that feeling. He was going to win the staring contest. Without saying any words, he was saying, release our table next.

As I moved closer and closer to his table, the stares seemed to pierce through me like an arrow. I was starting to get a little uncomfortable at this point because I was raised that it is rude to stare at someone. Pretty soon, he called me over to him. Oh no, what in the world was he going to say to me? Quickly he tried to hand me a hundred-dollar bill if I released his table next.

I explained to him that I couldn't accept his offer and that my job was to release the tables in a certain order. I also explained that it was almost his turn. Let's just say he wasn't happy with me. He got up and walked his grumpy self to the buffet. The thing is, he was going to do what he was going to do and he didn't care what I had to say about it. While watching him walk up to the buffet I thought, I totally should have taken the money.

Another fun fact that happens to guests while waiting for the buffet line is that they somehow develop illnesses that require them to eat immediately. It never fails — someone will come up to me when they see it is going to be a few minutes before I release their table. They usually approach me in a panic saying they must eat immediately. If they don't, they will likely pass out.

Here's the thing. If you're attending a wedding or leaving your home for any reason and you have a condition where you must eat immediately, take some snacks with you. Of course, I let them go immediately to the buffet, but every time, I have a slight moment of doubt that they were telling me the truth. All I know is that if I had to eat at certain times, I would have the best snacks stashed in my purse just in case.

For a buffet style, have your caterer or DJ release tables so that there isn't a long line at the buffet. Make sure they release you and your spouse first or have the caterer bring you your meal, then the bridal party, the parents, and the guests.

Stations

Stations are what I call the "vignettes" of the dinner service styles. When you set up your dinner service in a stations style, each setup stands on its own. For example, you can have a potato station that includes sweet potatoes and russet potatoes with a selection of toppings. Your guests will pick out the type of potato and then put on their specific toppings to customize their meal.

Adding stations to your wedding is a unique way to display your food and your personality when it comes to your menu. If you and your fiancé love to travel, you can have an Italian station, a Southern comfort food station, and an authentic Mexican station. It's an amazing way to let your guests know a little about what you as a couple love to eat without committing to a traditional meat and three options on a buffet line.

REMEMBER

I recommend setting up your stations all in one area so that guests can easily see all the food available. If you set them up away from each other, here is what will happen. Guest A will go to one station while Guest B will go to another station. When they both return to the table, they will see there is more food available. While at the station, they may feel like that is the only food you're providing and load up their plate with one item. This will throw off your numbers and there is a higher chance that you'll run out of food.

TIP

Putting all the stations in one area can also save you money because you can rent or purchase regular-sized dinner plates rather than the small plates caterers often suggest for a station setup. Say you have four stations and 100 guests. You'll only need to order 100 dinner plates instead of 400 smaller plates. And if you set up the stations in a buffet-style line, you also save your guests time because they only need to wait in one line instead of four different ones.

Another tip to successful stations setup is to avoid items such as omelets that have to be cooked onsite. The eggs must be cooked and prepared as your guests order their selection. This will take a very long time for your guests to get through the dinner line. For a pasta station, have your caterer set up chaffing dishes of pre-cooked pasta and sauce and toppings choices rather than cooking the pasta onsite. We want to get to the party, not have guests waste too much time waiting in line!

Avoid the temptation to go overboard with too many stations or too many choices. Overcomplicating your food selection will slow down the dinner lines and drive up your costs.

Thinking about What You Want to Eat

Picking your meal can feel overwhelming because, let's face it, there are so many options. But which one is right for you? What do you like to eat? When you go out on a date night, where do you go? What do you order?

One of my least favorite things to do is to figure out what's for dinner for my family. Around 2 pm each day, I start thinking what in the world am I going to make for dinner? I'm not a person who enjoys cooking in the kitchen for hours, so often it is a very simple meal. The same is true if we're planning on going out to eat for dinner. We often get in the car and just drive around to find a place rather than picking out the restaurant before we leave the house. Trying to commit to one place is difficult. What if I make the wrong choice? What ends up happening is we go to the same place we always go.

If you struggle with this like I do, I want you to make a list of your top five favorite foods. What is your go-to? What are the items you pick when you don't know what to eat on a Friday night? In Table 14-3, write in your top five meals to help you narrow down what you'll serve at your reception.

TABLE 14-3

Top 5 Meals You Love

Number	Meal Selections
1	
2	
3	
4	
5	

Now that you have your favorites in that list, you can start to create your meal. As this point in the process, you do not need to consider food allergies. When your RSVPs come in, reach out to your caterer and let them know if there are vegetarians or food allergies. They will be able to accommodate those guests with a separate meal or designate which items you have selected that they can eat.

Give your top five selections to your caterers. The selections may be all over the board, but they will be able to take your top five favorite foods and create a customized menu that you'll love. I'm going to use my top five favorite foods as an example: pizza, salad, chicken Parmesan, cheeseburgers, and chicken piccata.

The caterer can take my top five and create a dinner selection like this example.

Appetizers

Mini Cheeseburger Sliders

Mini Hot Chicken Bite Sliders

Salad

Spring Mix Salad with Granny Smith Apples and
Sweet Pecans with a Strawberry Vinaigrette

Entrée

Chicken Parmesan

Chicken Piccata

Sides

Angel Hair Pasta

Penne Pasta

Asparagus

Brussel Sprouts

Late-Night Snack

Pepperoni Pizza

Yes, I had two chicken dishes and yes, that is okay. Do you know why it is okay? Because those are my favorites. Always remember to think about what you love. If you do that, you'll create a custom menu that everyone will enjoy. It will reflect a few of your favorite things as a couple.

The following sections cover what you need to serve for appetizers, cocktail hour, dinner, and desserts. Everything works together to create the perfect meal for your perfect day and my hope is that after you read this section, you'll be able to lock in dinner selections that you and your guests will enjoy.

Appetizers and cocktails

Appetizers and cocktails are the first piece to a perfect dinner. It's the smaller amount of food that your guests receive before dinner begins. There are several things to consider when planning your appetizers and cocktails.

First, do you need them? The only time when you don't have to serve them would be if you're doing a first look and going straight into your reception from your ceremony. If that is the case, you can skip this step and focus on the dinner selection. However, the cocktail hour also serves as a buffer between the ceremony and reception. If you didn't get all the pictures you needed, this is a perfect time to do those. If you just want a minute to yourself before you go into the reception, this time allows you a much-needed break with your new spouse.

When selecting your appetizers, consider easy items for your guests to eat. Often, they're standing at this time, and offering items that are messy or hard to eat can be challenging. Additionally, consider if your guests can eat them from a napkin or if you need to order additional plates for the cocktail hour. When trying foods at your catering appointment, think about if you could eat them in one or two bites while standing and holding a drink.

REMEMBER

The appetizers can be simple. They are not meant to fill up your guests but rather to give them a little something to keep them from getting hangry. It is a small amount of food before the main meal. Picking two to three appetizers is plenty. This is not the main meal, so save your money and apply that toward the dinner.

Appetizers can be served in two ways, passed or stations. Passed means the catering staff walks around and serves the appetizers on platters to your guests. This is my preference because while your guests are standing with their beverages, they can grab a quick appetizer from the waitstaff. Stations are when the appetizers are displayed on a table. Your guests will walk up to the table and pick what they would like to eat. For this setup, you'll need to order smaller plates that are displayed on the appetizer table for your guests to pick up and get their food.

TIP

If you're hosting your cocktail hour in a separate area of your main reception bar, consider a smaller selection of beverages at the cocktail hour. For example, just offer beer and wine or just a signature drink that the bartender can pre-pour or premake to cut down on the lines. Signature drinks are a great way to incorporate your personality, and serving them only at the cocktail hour will also cut down on the bar costs.

What's for dinner?

As discussed above, picking the perfect dinner should reflect what you love to eat. If you receive your food first, you will eat. I know you have probably always heard that couples don't eat at their wedding. This can be true for many reasons but there are also ways to avoid not eating the food that you paid for.

One thing to consider is whether you're going to let your guests eat before you arrive at the reception or if they will wait to be served until you get there. If you let them eat before you arrive, schedule a time where the two of you will eat in a separate area. This way, you can guarantee that you eat and when you enter the reception, you can go ahead and get into the scheduled activities of the night.

If you have them wait, coordinate with the catering company for them to bring you your meal first. Even if your guests are going through the buffet line, they can bring food for you to your table. You will have guests stop by and say hello, but for the most part they will be focusing on getting food for themselves and leave you to eat in peace. Once you're done eating, you can get up and mingle around the room to each table and say hello to your guests while they're finishing dinner service.

TIP

Everything works together for your big day, so when you're picking your meal, consider color. Is everything fried and brown or is there a good mix of color on the plate? I am all about fried food (I live in the South), but it doesn't look pretty on the plate. Consider the presentation of the food when planning the perfect dinner for your guests. It seems small but it will make a difference in your guest experience. Remember, I told you to pick foods that you love. If you love chicken tenders, I am in support of you having chicken tenders at your wedding. However, a caterer can help enhance them and make those tenders fancy for your big day!

How sweet it is

Serving cake to your guests is a quintessential part of your reception. We have all seen the pictures of the couple serving each other cake. We have also seen the pictures of them smashing cake in their faces. Regardless of what is right for you, serving something sweet is what some guests came to your wedding to experience. You will have the traditional guests who attend the ceremony, eat their dinner, have their dessert, and then leave. It happens every time I produce a wedding. To some, dessert is the final activity that they need to witness. After they have enjoyed the dessert, they leave.

In this section we will discuss the bride's cake, groom's cake, and a dessert bar option for your big day. Choosing the perfect option for you is the icing on the cake!

WHAT IF I DON'T LIKE SWEETS?

It is possible that you are not a sweets person. That's okay too! I once had a bride who had a wedding piñata because they don't eat sweets. When the time came for them to cut their cake, a piñata came down from the ceiling of the tent and both the bride and groom put on the blindfold and took a shot at the piñata. After several attempts, pre-wrapped cake pops fell to the floor and the guests scurried around to grab as many cake pops as they could.

I love this story because it shows their style. They didn't love cake or desserts, so they wanted to make it a fun and memorable moment at their wedding. They did just that and it's something their guests will never forget. I won't forget it either because no other couple has requested that at their wedding.

Bride's cake

The bride's cake is a staple in wedding traditions. What will it look like? What flavor will you pick? Where will it be displayed for all to see? It is the main event when it comes to picking your desserts.

If you're planning on serving your guests cake, the bulk of those servings will likely come from the bride's cake. As we discuss additional dessert options, it is important to consider all the desserts that you'll offer when picking the size of your cake. For example, if you're serving a groom's cake, your bride's cake won't need to be as big. Together they will serve your guests.

If you're only serving a bride's cake and you have 100 guests, your baker will help you determine how many tiers and the size you'll need to be able to serve a piece of cake to your guests. In this scenario, you'll need a bride's cake big enough to serve 100 guests. If you have a groom's cake that serves 50 people, you'll need a bride's cake that serves 75 people.

If you aren't into cake but want the traditional cake cutting, consider ordering a small cake and offering a dessert bar. This way you can have a ceremonial cake cutting but won't be locked into eating cake at your wedding. You can offer small desserts and give your guests a variety of options to choose from.

REMEMBER

An important piece of the bride's cake is the anniversary layer. This is the smallest part of the cake. If you're planning on saving the top of your cake for your first anniversary, you'll remove this number of servings from the total count of servings. If you're keeping this portion of the cake, you will not cut the top. You'll cut the bottom of the cake during your cake-cutting ceremony. For example, if you have 100 guests and you plan to keep the top and it serves 25 people, you'll need to order a cake that serves 125 people.

It's important to consider the atmosphere of your reception when you select your cake. If you're getting married outside, schedule the delivery for as close to the start of the ceremony as possible. Cakes do not hold up in heat and if your cake sits outside for a long period of time, you'll have the leaning tower of cake by the time you cut it. Trust me, I have seen it — it isn't pretty and it's not what I want to happen on your wedding day. Work with a reputable baker who understands how to construct a cake that won't fall over or melt into itself from the time they drop it off to the time you cut it. A cake should have support rods inside that keep the cake from falling over or sliding into a pile of crumbs.

After you know how many servings you'll need for your guests, an important piece of the budget is the design. Buttercream cakes are less expensive than an elaborate fondant cake. (A fondant cake is covered in fondant to create a smooth finish. They are often elaborately designed.)

THE LEANING TOWER OF CAKE

I had a bride who hired her own baker. It was a company that I hadn't worked with, but their online presence was strong. My client held her reception at one of the most prestigious venues in Nashville. Everything about the building was spectacular. The placement of the wedding cake in the reception space was nothing short of spectacular as well. The cake table had its spot in the middle of the room with a spotlight on it. It sat at the bottom of the stairs as the guests entered the reception hall. Let's just say, no one missed it.

A few minutes before we let the guests into the room, one of the waitstaff came to me in a panic. There was something wrong with the cake. I quickly ran down the grand staircase to look. Half of the four-tiered cake was leaning to the left. When I say leaning, I mean it was almost about to fall off the table.

I had about five minutes before the guests entered the room, so in a quick second I grabbed the two layers and put them on a tray and gave it to the waitstaff to cut in the kitchen for the guests to eat later in the evening. I immediately grabbed as many leftover flowers as I could and filled that cake with flowers to hide as much as possible.

The cake wasn't built properly and so it became the leaning tower of cake! I will never forget the look on the bride's face. I'm certain the cake was her favorite part of the planning process. She couldn't wait to see the cake. Of course, it was the only thing that went wrong that day. While we did our very best to cover the cake, it obviously wasn't what she envisioned. Avoid this happening to you by hiring a baker who knows how to properly construct a wedding cake.

When you schedule your tasting with your potential baker, make sure to take with you any design inspiration that you have. They will be able to look at your theme and help you design a cake that fits within your budget. They can also help you determine if you want flowers added to your cake. A simple design with flowers added is cost effective and a beautiful option to consider that is budget friendly.

When you have locked in your design, you get to pick your flavors. I work with bakers who offer an assortment of interesting flavors and those who have simple flavors with fillings added between the layers of cake. Pick a flavor that you love. Flavors and fillings have come a long way since the traditional white cake that everyone selected. Nowadays you get to select a flavor that reflects your personality.

REMEMBER

There are two important things to consider when picking your wedding cake.

>> **How will it be displayed?** Bakers can provide pedestals to rent, or you can rent one through your decorator. Don't forget to consider what your cake will sit on. If you don't, it will just sit on the table where it is being displayed without a pedestal or cake stand.

>> **Who is going to cut the cake?** Most often it would be your caterer, so it is important to discuss this with them during your catering meetings. They will need to be prepared with the appropriate utensils to cut and serve the cake. If you aren't using a caterer, make sure to designate someone to cut the cake. The last thing you want is for your cake not to get cut because that wasn't discussed. You paid a lot for that cake, so make sure it is cut and served for your guests to enjoy.

Groom's cake

While the groom's cake isn't always a part of our clients' wedding receptions, it is an option for your big day. The groom's cake shows off the groom's personality. It can be displayed with the bride's cake or on its own at the wedding reception.

Groom's cake themes represent something that the groom loves. It can be a favorite sports team, hobby, or interest. For example, if the groom loves basketball, it could be a cake in the design of a basketball. Or maybe he loves golf, so it could be a set of golf clubs made from cake.

Groom's cakes can be served at either the rehearsal dinner or the wedding. It is your preference. If the groom's parents are hosting the rehearsal dinner, you can display the groom's cake at that event. Some families prefer to display the groom's cake at the reception, especially if it is a custom-designed cake with an elaborate theme.

Originally, the groom's cake was offered to guests as a second flavor option. Today, it is used to highlight the groom's personality and interests. It is a present from the bride to the groom. Some couples have even seen it as a war of cakes between the bride and groom. Whichever way you look at it, it is not a requirement when it comes to picking the dessert for your reception. If you have the budget, I love incorporating something special for the groom at your wedding. If you don't have the budget, serving the bride's cake to your guests is sufficient.

Dessert buffet

A popular option if you don't love cake is a dessert buffet. This is a selection of small desserts that are served to your guests at the reception. They can be a variety of cookies, miniature cakes, miniature pies, or dessert shooters. We have also seen ice cream bars, chocolate fountains, and candy buffets.

For those who choose this option, they typically will order a small cake just for the couple to be displayed on the dessert bar. This will still allow you to cut a ceremonial cake at your wedding. If that isn't important to you, skip the small cake and enjoy a sample of dessert options.

Dessert bars are a great way to incorporate your theme and make it unique. You can use a specialty linen with a design in your theme and pick desserts within a specific color palate. Regardless of the design, make it easy for your guests to access quickly. They can pick up a dessert as they would like throughout the evening.

TIP

Dessert bars can also be utilized as your wedding favor. You can include boxes or bags for your guests to take their dessert with them at the end of the night. Additionally, you can prepackage desserts such as cookies or candies with a custom label and utilize those on your guest tables as their favor and eliminate the dessert table all together.

Either way, dessert bars are a fun way to add your personality and flare to your reception. If you have a family cookie recipe, bake those for your guests to enjoy. Include the recipe if you want to share the family secret so that your guests can enjoy that after your wedding is over. Every time they bake those cookies, they'll remember your special day.

Let's Drink to That

Determining the beverages at your wedding may be a touchy subject. One family may love to party while the other thinks drinking alcohol is forbidden. Can you relate? It is often a topic of discussion with my clients. What is the happy medium between providing an appropriate amount of alcohol and hosting a free-for-all that ends up with guests unable to walk at the end of the night?

There is a balance to being responsible when selecting what you will serve at your wedding. How much is too much? What is too little? Let's face it, alcohol is expensive. If I go out to dinner and get alcohol, my bill is significantly higher than if I didn't. The same thing is true for weddings. It can eat up your budget if you aren't careful.

In this section, we are going to discuss the types of bars to offer, how to be efficient in the service of the bar, selecting your beverages, and offering liquor or not at your wedding reception.

Cash bar versus hosted bar

The first step in determining your beverages is whether you're offering a cash bar or a hosted bar. A cash bar is where your guests pay for their drinks. The alcohol is supplied by either your venue or a bartending service and your guests pay them directly for their drinks. While this is a way to save money for your big day, for some this is not an option because they don't want their guests to pull out their wallets and pay for their beverages. But if it isn't in the budget to provide alcohol, guests can pay for their own.

REMEMBER

If you're offering a cash bar at your wedding, make sure to notify your guests. You can simply say that you aren't providing alcohol but that they can purchase it at the event. This will give them the information they need to make sure they have their wallets with them at your wedding.

A hosted bar is when you pay for all the alcohol for your guests. An open bar has no limitations. This is beer, wine, and liquor. This is the most expensive option for several reasons. Typically, hosting liquor requires additional insurance and there are also expenses to making sure you have the appropriate mixers and supplies for liquor drinks.

TIP

The more common route is to supply beer and wine for your guests. If you can have a host bar at your wedding, this is the most cost-effective way to do so. I would suggest picking three wine selections and three beer options. There are several online tools that can help you determine how much alcohol you'll need to purchase.

The first step is to evaluate your guest list. How many are drinkers? Are they heavy or moderate drinkers? Often when someone attends a wedding and they don't normally drink a lot of alcohol, they can't stop going to the bar. There is something about offering free alcohol that turns a moderate drinker into a heavy drinker.

The average would be to factor three drinks per person. So, if you have 100 drinkers, you'll need 300 beverages. Those can generally be split 50-50 between beer and wine. However, if you know you have more wine drinkers than beer drinkers or vice versa, consider a 60-40 spilt.

You can also combine a cash bar with a hosted bar. If you host the beer and wine, you can have your guests pay for liquor if they want that. In doing this, you allow those who drink liquor the ability to purchase it, but you aren't paying for the additional expenses that come with serving liquor.

WARNING

Alcohol doesn't always bring out the best in people, especially at an emotional event. You have the power to control that by determining how much is too much. Sometimes you can have too much of a good thing. I don't want that happening to you.

CAUTIONARY TALES FROM THE BAR

Liquor has a way of causing problems at weddings. It's just a fact. At weddings where liquor is offered, there are always those guests who consume too much and typically cause a scene. I have seen it time and time again where someone has simply had too much to drink. I had a guest lock himself in a portable toilet. While using the facility, he overflowed the toilet and somehow managed to lock himself in while the toilet was overflowing. When we finally convinced him to simply unlock the door, he came out soaking wet and looked as if he had just seen a ghost.

Another guest passed out while the father of the bride was giving a speech. Right in the middle of his emotional speech, this woman stood up out of her chair, walked toward the father of the bride, and passed out right in front of him.

Another guest ended up in an area of the venue he wasn't supposed to be. He wasn't found until the next day. He didn't know how he got there or why his friends would just leave him there. After trying to figure out who he was, we were able to get him a ride home to where he belonged.

I have also seen the ugly, angry side of liquor. I have watched guests break into a fist fight on the dance floor. Another guest decided to punch the wall in anger, breaking through a glass door. Battered and cut, he somehow believed that he didn't need help and left the reception without seeking medical attention.

Tending bar: Leave it to the professionals

Most venues will require a certified and insured bartender to serve your alcohol. I highly recommend this even if your venue doesn't require it. A bartender can handle everything that you need to successfully supply alcohol to your guests.

The bartender will take care of setting up, maintaining, serving, and tearing down your bar. They can also supply all the cups, ice, napkins, and mixers you need to make it a success. I understand that you may not be required to have a bartender, but hiring one is worth the investment for your protection.

If a guest drinks too much, drives at the end of the night, and something horrible happens, that could potentially fall on you legally. A bartender holds what is called *liquor liability.* Just as if you went to a restaurant, a bartender is ultimately responsible to make sure that no one is overserved.

The bartender has the duty to cut someone off from the bar if they have had too much to drink. This means you don't have to have the uncomfortable conversation with one of your friends that they need to take a break from the bar. It is the bartender's responsibility to have that conversation with your guests.

This also means that they hold the power when it comes to your bar. If they want to check IDs, they can. If they feel like someone has had too much to drink, they will cut them off or make them take a break before their next drink. This can come as a shock to couples because they're hosting the bar and feel like their guests should be served as much as they want. Again, this falls under responsible drinking and that is the bartender's job to monitor for everyone's safety.

Avoiding a traffic jam

No one loves a traffic jam, especially at the bar. The last thing you want at your wedding is long lines at the bar. There are several things you can do to avoid this, so in this section we'll discuss some tips and tricks to avoid long lines at the bar.

If you're hosting your ceremony and reception at the same location, the main time where the bar will be crowded is immediately following the ceremony. This is the only time at your wedding that all the guests will go to the bar at the same time. As the night goes on, the number of people at the bar at one time will decrease.

First tip is to hire enough bartenders for your wedding reception. It isn't important to focus on how many physical bars you have. Most important is the number of bartenders. You can have one bar with the appropriate number of bartenders. If you do this, you'll cut down on the bar cost with multiple bar setup fees and supplies.

WHEN "OVERSERVED" GETS OUT OF HAND

I had a bartender come over to me during an event and let me know that someone had too much to drink, and they were making the guest take a break. First, let me paint the picture. I was nine months pregnant. As I waddled over to the bar, there was a crowd of angry guests, all men, who were upset that their friend had to take a break from drinking for 30 minutes.

They were in my face because I was "the boss" and were so upset that I knew it was going to get ugly. In my head, I kept thinking, how am I going to protect this baby that I may or may not deliver at this wedding if things go south. I had to get the groom involved because the angry guests were his college buddies.

I explained to the groom that they needed to calm down because the security guard had the right to shut down the reception at any point if he felt it was getting out of control. I didn't want that to happen, so I told him to take his friends to the dance floor, away from the bar, to divert the situation that was quickly escalating.

As he left to go to the dance floor, his friends followed him a few steps and then immediately started yelling at the bartender and me again. They wouldn't stop. When someone has had too much to drink, they lose the ability to reason. You cannot get them to calm down and they become highly emotional.

They started picking up the bottles of liquor on the bar and drinking them straight from the bottle. Soon 10 people turned into 20 people and then 30 people who were angry that one guy needed to take a 30-minute break from the bar. There was one female in this group of guys. She was the ringleader and was in my face screaming about the situation.

Well, what do you think happened next? The security guard shut down their wedding two hours earlier than we anticipated. Just like that, the party was over. The music was turned off and the guests were escorted out of the building. This was, of course, the last thing I wanted for the bride and groom but unfortunately, the liquor won.

Consider a bartending service even if you aren't required to have one to avoid overserving. Yes, we had a bartender, but that bartender knew only the amount of alcohol that he served the guests. We don't know what that person had prior to the event. When the situation became obvious to the bartender, he asked him to take a break from the bar. What happened after that was out of his control.

You should hire one bartender for every 50–75 guests. For example, if you have 100 guests you should hire two bartenders. If you have 200 guests, you should hire three-four bartenders. This will allow an efficient bar service and avoid the traffic jams. You could even hire the max suggested from the start of cocktail hour until the end of dinner and then cut that in half. As the night goes on, you won't need as many bartenders because guests will leave, and they won't be at the bar at the same time.

Another tip is to have your bartenders pre-pour what they can prior to the start of the cocktail hour. It will be important to your guests to get a drink. If they're wine drinkers, they can head to the bar and pick up a pre-poured wine glass quickly. This will significantly cut down on the lines because they don't have to wait for a beverage.

After the initial rush at the bar, the lines will normalize because the guests will go to the bar at different times throughout the night. Until that time, utilizing these tips will eliminate the long lines at the bar.

Bar aesthetics

Often forgotten but nevertheless important is what your bar will look like. As I said earlier, it is more important to have the correct number of bartenders rather than bars. Focus on one bar and don't forget to decorate it in style.

The bottles of alcohol will adorn the bar and do add to the decor, but what else can you add? Reusing the flowers from your ceremony is a great way to spruce up your bar and there isn't an additional cost to do that. If your budget allows, create a custom floral centerpiece for the bar. That can flank the bar on each side, sit in the center of the bar, or drape on the front of the bar.

Every bar needs a bar sign so that your guests don't have to ask the bartender what they have available to serve. This will also help with long lines. Imagine if every guest went to the bar and said, "What is available?" The bartender would have to tell them a list of options. If you repeat that 200 times, you'll have a very long line at the bar. Displaying the beverage selections where the guests can read them while they wait and decide on their choice before they order will cut down the long lines.

When picking the perfect place for your bar, consider where the guests will be. Your bar should be placed close to the dance floor. If it is too far from where the action will be, it will take too long for the guests to go to the bar and get back on the dance floor.

TIP

Adding custom napkins, cups, or koozies is a way to give your bar a personalized flare. Those items can also be utilized as your wedding favors. Additionally, ordering these custom items will eliminate this expense through the bartender. Yes, you can use their standard cups and napkins but personalizing the guest experience is a wonderful way to add your special touch to the bar.

Selecting wine and beer

The number one requested bar selection is wine and beer for your guests. It is important to consider which types you should have for a well-balanced bar that will appeal to your guests.

You should pick three-four wine options. Consider the time of year when choosing your wine. If you're hosting a summer wedding, pick lighter, more refreshing wine. A winter wedding should have richer wines.

It is always good to select a white wine variation and a red wine variation. For example, you could select pinot grigio, chardonnay, cabernet, and merlot. This will provide enough variation for those who don't drink a particular type. I'm a white wine drinker, but I don't like chardonnay.

A question that often comes up regarding wine is whether to offer champagne. Gone are the days where everyone received champagne for the toast. While I do believe that having champagne as a potential wine option is a good idea, your guests can drink what they have during the toasts. I do love a champagne toast, but it is a place where you can save some money on your alcohol without affecting the experience in a negative way.

Just as in the food selection, pick alcohol that you enjoy drinking. Depending on if you provide the alcohol and can keep it after the wedding, you don't want a bunch of alcohol left over that you won't drink or add to your collection to enjoy.

The same is true for selecting your beers. It is best to select three-four options. Always have domestics on hand but it is also fun to add a seasonal or high-gravity beer to the mix. Offer a light beer and a dark beer for variety. This will allow you to appease beer drinkers on all levels.

Specialty drinks

A perfect way to incorporate a little bit of liquor in your drink mix is to offer a specialty drink for your guests to enjoy. A specialty drink or signature drink is one that you design expressly for your event. This is a great time to incorporate your favorite elements into one special drink.

Specialty drinks are the perfect addition to the cocktail hour. While you can offer them the entire night, adding them into the cocktail hour mix is the perfect amount of time. If each of you want to pick a specialty drink, you can customize them with unique names.

I love rosé and so I would offer Sarah's Frozé as my specialty drink. I have also had clients name their specialty drink after their pets. Display a picture of your pet on the bar for your guests to see, along with a list of the ingredients in the specialty drink.

When considering specialty drinks, design one that can be premade and distributed easily and efficiently to your guests. If your drink must be individually prepared, this can add significant time to your bar line. Consider a premixed drink in a canister that can be poured quickly for your guests to enjoy.

Liquor

If you decide to serve liquor at your wedding, a full bar would include vodka, rum, gin, scotch, bourbon, whiskey, and tequila. If you don't need all those selections, pick two or three to offer. This will appease those who want liquor at your wedding without breaking the budget and going overboard.

When considering liquor, it is also important to remember the garnishes and mixers to add to the drink. They're often forgotten, and I don't want that happening to you. For garnishes, consider including limes, lemons, oranges, cherries, and olives. For the mixers, consider including tonic water, club soda, soft drinks, grenadine, sour mix, lime juice, pineapple juice, orange juice, and cranberry juice.

If you would like to have liquor at your wedding, talk to your bartender about the best options for your selection. This will allow your guests to customize the drinks that they enjoy. Leave this to the professionals who can offer their advice on popular selections for your bar.

music

Chapter **15**

Enjoying Your Party

t's officially time to enjoy your party. While there are certainly pieces of your big day that you'll enjoy, after all the "official" ceremonial parts are completed you get to relax and simply have fun. That's right, you heard it from me. You will enjoy your day and now it's time to discuss the parts that you may enjoy the most.

This chapter covers selecting the perfect music for your reception. I also present some pros and cons of picking a DJ over a band or vice versa. And because all good things must come to an end, I also discuss your grand exit and booking the honeymoon suite.

Selecting the Perfect Entertainment

Think about the weddings that you've attended in the past. Did you notice the music? What was playing during the cocktail hour, dinner, and dancing? Which weddings do you remember being the most fun? Did they have a DJ or a band? Were the guests on the dance floor or sitting at their tables talking during the reception?

Now, think about your wedding. What do you want when it comes to entertainment? Do you want the dance floor packed all night or are you more of a sit-and-observe kind of person? Regardless of what fits your needs, selecting the perfect entertainment for your wedding reception is a big part of the planning process.

When that dance floor opens and you get to just enjoy the rest of your night and cut a rug with some of your favorite people, memories will be made.

The first step in picking the perfect music is locking in a particular style. What type of music do you enjoy? Are you looking forward to dancing the night away, or do you have two left feet and you would much rather chat with your guests during your reception? Table 15-1 is a list of styles and which music type would fit that best.

TABLE 15-1   ## Music Styles and Types

Music Style	Music Type
Traditional	Live performers, string quartet, choir, bagpipes
Sophisticated	Piano with sax or violin, classical musicians, jazz band, swing band
Formal	Solo guitar, duo guitar, jazz band, big band, string musicians, classical singer
Background Music	Small jazz ensemble, harpist, pianist, guitarist, duo of piano and guitar, vocalist and piano, vocalist and guitar, string musicians, indie music
Dance	Rock band, top 40 band, pop cover band, '80s band, '70s band, soul music, jive music, tribute music, funk band, saxophone, trumpet

The next step in picking the perfect music selection for your wedding is to consider the audience. Who are you inviting and what type of music do they like? If there is a mixed crowd, consider a mix of music that will appeal to everyone in attendance. In Table 15-2, I listed the age ranges and the music type that is appropriate for that range.

TABLE 15-2   ## Music Styles by Age Range

Guest Age Range	Music Type
All Ages	Cover bands, pop, rock, swing music, R&B, soul, tribute bands
30–50	Swing music, jazz bands, acoustic bands, tribute bands, pop cover band, soul and R&B, Latin
50+	Rock 'n' roll bands, tribute bands, light pop cover bands, classical ensembles, big band, symphony, jazz band

It's important to make sure that your music selections will appease all age ranges at your wedding reception. This will help keep the dance floor filled all night long. You can even use the different music selections during dinner or cocktail hour.

Cocktail hour music

The cocktail hour is the first time the guests will be able to mix and mingle with the other guests. It's important to make sure the music during this time is lower in volume. If you hire a DJ, ask them to play a mellower selection of songs during this time.

If you can join your guests for the cocktail hour, you'll want to be able to hear what everyone is saying. Keeping the music light and at a lower volume will allow guests to hear others around them.

TIP

The cocktail hour is also a perfect time to highlight a particular type of music that you enjoy. If you like to listen to bluegrass music, bring in a small bluegrass quartet. If you love jazz, consider hiring a jazz pianist. If there's something that you want to highlight in your culture and heritage, the cocktail hour is the perfect time to do that.

Dinner music

Dinner music is like cocktail hour music. While the guests are trying to speak to each other, it's best to keep the music at a lower volume so they can have conversations. Additionally, with each step you are setting the tone or vibe of the party that you'll soon have.

It's best to save the popular dance music songs for the dance floor. During dinner is a great time to introduce different genres for a mix that covers all ages in attendance. The classic love songs are always popular because everyone seems to love them, they're typically more mellow, and they're well known to everyone.

TIP

Create a playlist and give that to the DJ or research your band's playlist and pick songs that you love. Think about songs that bring positive memories for you and your fiancé. Are there special songs you listened to while you were dating? Are there particular songs that take you back to a special memory that you have only with each other? Set up a playlist that reflects who you are as a couple. Remember to keep it light, because at this point in the event, it's still just background music.

Dancing music

It is officially time to turn up the volume and let the official party begin! It's important to make a list of your favorite dance songs and give that to your DJ, or pick songs from the band's list that you love. Select songs that bring joy and are fun to dance to.

WARNING

Don't pick songs that talk about breaking up. There's a very popular song often played at weddings, but the song is about the couple breaking up. It always makes me laugh whenever it's played. I see the couple so happy and just giggle inside thinking about what the song means.

REMEMBER

More importantly, make a list of those songs that you do *not* want played at your wedding. The last thing you want to happen is for a song to be played that takes you back to a past relationship. Or maybe you just can't stand line dances and don't want them to play those songs where everyone is on the dance floor doing the same dance. Either way, it's an important part of creating the perfect set list for your dance party.

Try to focus on 90 % upbeat songs and 10 % slow songs. Some people won't even come out to the dance floor until a slow song is played. I understand you may want to dance your shoes off all night but taking a small amount of time to slow it down a bit includes those who want to dance with their partner at your wedding.

Pick a playlist that includes the hits. Stay away from songs that no one knows; otherwise you'll clear a dance floor fast and they'll scatter like ants. Having a mix of songs that everyone will know and love will keep your guests on the dance floor all night long.

REMEMBER

Make sure to check in with your venue to confirm that there aren't any noise restrictions, and if there are, discuss that with your DJ or band. I'm always the one who walks over to the DJ to ask them to turn down the music a bit. For the moment, they may, and then quickly the music is up past the venue requirements again. Having music playing too loudly can cause a lot of problems for a venue. I have seen police show up and shut down a reception due to the music being too loud for the area. It's an important issue to confirm with your venue.

Booking a band

There really isn't anything better than live music. We're especially aware of this in Nashville, Tennessee, where live music runs through our blood. There is live music playing in every establishment and we love it that way. If you're anything like us, you may already know that you want a band at your wedding reception.

Let's discuss some pros and cons to booking a band. I always like to start with the cons and finish with the pros.

Some cons to booking a band:

>> Bands can be significantly more expensive than a DJ so, simply put, the budget may not allow it.

>> Bands may also have a limited repertoire of songs they can play. They may not know your favorite songs, so prior to booking a band you should look at their set list.

>> Bands take up more space than a DJ, which may present a problem in a small venue. When considering a band, make sure you know what space the band requires and that you have that available at your venue.

Here are some pros to booking a band:

>> As we said above, there really isn't anything better than live music. Being able to have that personal interaction with live musicians is always a favorite way to celebrate for couples everywhere.

>> The sound quality you get from a band is a big pro! Live bands offer a sound that is different than a DJ.

>> Live bands can adapt on the spot to the party atmosphere. They can also keep their versions of a song clean for the little ears that may be attending your wedding.

Spinning with a DJ

There are also pros and cons to booking a DJ for your wedding reception.

Consider these possible cons:

>> The biggest con is if your personalities don't mesh. It is important to make sure that you like the DJ's personality. After all, they're the ringmaster for the night and if their personality and DJ style annoy you, you will not be happy with the overall feel of your reception.

>> Another con is the DJ who takes over the schedule. If your DJ announces the cake cutting and the photographer isn't there, you have missed those pictures. Make sure to communicate the schedule, but also be sure that the DJ is communicating with whomever is in charge for the night.

And now for some pros:

» You'll have an almost limitless amount of music available to play at your wedding reception. If you give the DJ a list prior to your wedding, they can download essentially whatever song you'd like. You have more control over the playlist if you work with a DJ.

» If you book a DJ, you won't have to worry about the music stopping. Bands typically require breaks. While they can often play music while they're taking a break, a DJ stays the entire time to make sure the party is still going strong. You won't have to worry about when you need to schedule those breaks at your reception, and you can focus on building your stamina to dance all night long.

» DJs also don't take up as much room as a band and require less equipment and a shorter sound check. This is important if your venue doesn't have a lot of space or power to accommodate a band. A DJ will take up about a 10-by-10-foot space and require less power than a band. Prior to booking a band or DJ for your wedding reception, make sure to check in with your venue on their power supply to make certain it will be adequate for the music you're planning.

Your Grand Exit

Sad to say, all good things must come to an end. Consider how you will leave your reception in style. Think about all the months of planning that you have been through. Think about how everything about your process has gotten you to this moment right here. And now it's time to leave and begin your life with your spouse.

That sounds exciting, doesn't it? Devising your grand exit is an important part in your planning process. Gone are the days of simply throwing rice at a couple as they left their reception. Now grand exits often include sparklers, releasing butterflies, bubbles, glowsticks, fireworks, releasing lanterns, and so much more. But what is right for you?

First, let's think about the logistics. Do you need a send-off? Are you staying at your venue and don't feel like you need to do a send-off? Or maybe you're hosting a backyard wedding and find it silly for your guests to send you off just to walk into your home. But what if you do want one? One idea may be to have everyone circle around you for one final dance. Or, you can give everyone a final hug and send them on their way.

In this section, we'll discuss all the parts to a perfect send-off, which includes the last dance, party favors, exiting, the getaway vehicle, and the honeymoon suite. After reading this section, my hope is that you'll be able to pick the perfect way to leave your big day.

Last dance

I love the last dance. It's the final song that's played at the reception prior to your exit. Most of the time, everyone is on the dance floor one final time to celebrate your marriage before you head off to your forever. The last dance is special, and you should spend some time picking the perfect song that reflects your relationship and celebrates your day one final time.

The last dance is typically upbeat in nature. It is a final time to gather on the dance floor with those you love. It's time to raise a glass one last time to the fact that everyone on the dance floor will never be in the same place at the same time ever again. Just think about that for a minute and let that sink in. Now pick an amazing song that will commemorate that statement.

TIP

One new trend that is becoming more and more popular is a last dance with just the couple. I truly love this moment. After the guests have left the reception space, the couple will have one final dance together. This is typically done when the guests are waiting outside for your send-off. However, I have also seen it done with the guests in the room if you aren't doing a formal send-off. There are several benefits to doing this.

>> You can control the crowd and get them outside faster. This helps when it comes to venue time limits. If your venue says that you need to be out at 10 pm, I would schedule the exit of the guests for 9:45 pm. That would leave enough time for you to have a final dance together at 9:55 pm.

>> It's a special moment that only the two of you get to share. The entire day has been shared with your loved ones. This one is only for you. Take the time to stop and take in your perfect day. You will only get this day one time in your life. Sharing a final dance together is a wonderful final way to celebrate your day.

Party favors

Party favors are used to thank your guests for coming to your wedding. I know, you may be thinking, "I'm already paying for everything for them to be there." While this is an accurate statement, a favor is designed to be a tangible item that your guests can take with them to remember your day.

THE MAGIC OF THE LAST DANCE

I remember a particular wedding where the bride and groom shared a last dance together. We lined up all the guests for the sparkler exit outside. Once the guests left the room, the bride and groom shared a special last dance together. I will never forget it. We planned their wedding for almost a year, and everything came down to this final moment and it was very special.

This couple wasn't the most affectionate couple I have ever worked with. They didn't have a big dance party. They weren't big on dancing. Well, at least the groom wasn't big on dancing. The song was a surprise for the bride. The groom had picked a song that talked about how, for her, he would dance with her all night.

Let's just say there were a lot of tears shed during that moment. It was one of those times that helps me remember, on my most frustrating days, why I do what I do. Wedding planning is hard. I once read that it was listed as one of the top five most stressful jobs, right up there with brain surgeon and fire fighter. My body on Sundays hurts in places I never knew could hurt. It is a hard job. But why do I continue to do it? It's for those last dance moments. When the father of the bride comes up to me at the end of the night and thanks me for all that I did, it's worth it. When I see the joy on others' faces and know that I made a difference in their day, every ache in my body has purpose.

The options seem limitless when it comes to party favors. Most importantly, you want to pick something that your guests will appreciate and use after your wedding. As a planner, I know that party favors are those things that we pack up at the end of night. It never fails that there are often a lot left over at the end of the night. This only leaves the client wondering what to do with all the leftovers the next morning.

TIP

When ordering your party favors, you don't need one for every guest. This will cut down on the number you have left over at the end of the night. When you think about your guest list and your party favors, remember that most of your guests will be couples. Do they need two of your party favors, or one for their household? They might need two based on what you pick, but often one per household is sufficient.

Some of my favorite party favors are those the guests can use at the event. Items such as koozies or novelties for the dance floor like glowsticks or light-up glasses are the perfect way to see your money well spent.

TIP

Another popular favor is a photobooth. This is where your guests will take a picture of themselves and have either a digital or a printed image from your event. Often photobooth companies can create a custom book for you at your event with printed images. When they put the image into the book, your guests will leave you a message. This is also a great guest book option for your wedding. You will leave with a unique guest book and the guests will leave with a memory frozen in time.

Edible treats are also a great option when picking your wedding favor. Consider giving your guests a late-night prepackaged snack. This gives them something to enjoy after your wedding is over, such as popcorn or cookies. It will be a few hours from the time they had dinner, so offering a late-night treat is a popular option. The guests love them and appreciate them.

WARNING

As much as you may want to put your monogram and name on your favors, depending on the favor you select, you may want to omit the customization. If you're giving them a favor that they'll use on a regular basis, such as essential oils, hot sauce, coffee, or soap, it may be best to leave the monogram off your favor.

Favors are not mandatory but are greatly appreciated by your guests. You have invested a lot for them to be there and that can be enough if the budget doesn't allow for additional trinkets that may get thrown in the trash. That is why, if you do decide to offer a favor, it's important that you spend time thinking about a particular gift for your guests to enjoy at your wedding and for time to come.

Exit celebration

There is a reason why this section is called exit celebration. True, we don't want to leave the best day ever behind, but we can also celebrate. What are we celebrating? First, that you are married. Next, that you and your spouse found each other along life's journey. Finally, that you have planned and executed this amazing day with your favorite people. And it was a success! That is all to be celebrated.

The two times that you will potentially plan an exit celebration is at the end of the ceremony and at the end of the reception. There are several scenarios that will determine if you plan an exit or not. Let me just say this: you can plan both exits if you want them. This is your day and if you want both, plan both and celebrate twice. However, most who are hosting a ceremony and reception at the same location only plan an exit at the end of the evening. Since everyone is in one place, there is no need to do an exit to the ceremony.

Additionally, you may not want a formal exit to your reception. Maybe you're getting married at the same place as your reception — for example, your home or a home-share location. If that is the case, I understand why you may not want a formal exit. My husband and I were married at our home and to us it felt strange to do a formal exit and then walk into our home. Obviously, if this is your situation, you're the only one who can make this decision.

If you're planning a wedding where the ceremony and reception are held at separate locations, you can celebrate both. In this scenario, after the ceremony, all the guests will line up outside and you'll exit through the guests. Typically, there will be a getaway vehicle. This can be a rented vintage car, a limo, or even a personal vehicle. You and your new spouse will leave the ceremony and meet your guests at the reception.

If your ceremony and reception are held at separate locations, it's appropriate to skip the formal exit at the church and allow your guests to head to the reception location immediately following the ceremony. In this scenario, the bridal party and family will remain at the ceremony while the guests head to the reception location. This is a perfect time to take your formal family photos if you didn't do a first look prior to your ceremony. Remember to create a list so that the photos don't take a long time and the guests are left to wait for you for an extended period to arrive at the reception.

The most popular formal exit celebration is at the end of your reception. This is where all the guests line up and send you off in style to your forever. It is the perfect time to say your final goodbyes before you head off to the honeymoon suite and or your honeymoon.

Often clients will use sparklers, glowsticks, pompoms, or bubbles for this exit. If you pick sparklers, make sure to check with your venue that they're allowed. Pick something fun for your guests to cheer you onto your forever as you leave your reception.

Prior to the exit celebration, make sure to say goodbye to your family before you go. Remember that scene in *Father of the Bride* where the bride and her father never got to connect before she leaves the reception? He says, "She was gone." She ends up calling him and thanking him for the amazing day just before she leaves for the honeymoon. In the hustle and bustle of the day, make sure to say goodbye to the special people in your life before you formally leave.

A popular trend is to do a "fake" send-off at your reception. The reason why a couple may plan a fake send-off is because the photographer is only booked for a certain time period, and they want to capture those photos. Let me speak to you professionally and as your friend. I am not a supporter of a fake send-off. First, you must stop your reception and party and get everyone outside. What if everyone is enjoying themselves? You must stop the fun to be able to pull this off. Then, when the guests come back in, you'll lose a lot of them. That will be the time when they'll just leave. I know you may need to do this for your event and so I wanted to share with you what I don't like about it so that you can be prepared.

If you do plan a fake exit, make sure to have someone announce that this is only for pictures and that the party will continue until a certain time. It is important to make sure the guests know that the party isn't over, and you plan on heading back inside to continue the night. You don't want to plan this and then lose half of your guests. You paid a lot of money to have them there the entire night. Maximize that by avoiding a fake exit if possible.

Getaway vehicle

One piece of your planning process to consider is how you will leave your reception. Will you drive yourself in your own vehicle? Will you hire a transportation company to provide a limo or a vintage car? Where are you going on the night of your wedding?

If you need a ride after your wedding, I highly suggest booking a getaway vehicle. If you're planning on drinking on your wedding night, it's best to be safe and have someone transport you to your hotel. Booking a getaway car is also an asset when it comes to your photos.

Most of my clients will book a vintage car. The guests always enjoy seeing vintages cars at the end of the night. However, I understand that this may not be in your budget. An alternative is to book a limo or a higher-end rideshare at the end of the night to get you to where you need to go.

TIP

Another popular option is to resource your family. Think about who you know and if anyone has either a nice car or a vintage car. Ask them if they would be willing to drive you from the reception to where you're staying on the night of your wedding. You would be surprised by how many people in your circle would love to help you make it a dream day however they can. This will save you money from renting one and you'll be able to enjoy your party without wondering how you'll get from one location to the next.

Be prepared that some fun decorations may be added to your car. Bridal party members often enjoy making this as outrageous as possible, and I love getting to watch them decorate your car. As obnoxious as the decorations may be, it shows they love you and it feels good to be loved.

Honeymoon suite

The honeymoon suite is where you'll spend your first night together as a married couple. It is important to consider where that will be. Will you be staying at your home or at another location? After all the planning is done, this is your oasis for a little R & R. I give you permission to splurge! You deserve it and this is a special night, so you should be in a special place to celebrate.

When you book your reception location, go ahead and start researching and booking your honeymoon suite. A honeymoon suite is typically a hotel room that is higher end than your standard hotel room. Hotels have a limited availability on their higher-end rooms, so make sure to book this as soon as possible. That way you can ensure that you'll have a nicer room than the standard room to spend your first night together as a married couple.

TIP

Instead of booking online, call the hotel where you want to stay. Explain that it will be your wedding night so that they can help you book the perfect room. Additionally, they'll add this information to your reservation. While it isn't guaranteed, hotels typically decorate your room before arrival or leave a bottle of champagne and chocolates for you to enjoy. If they don't know it's your honeymoon suite, they may not treat you like the celebrities that you are!

REMEMBER

Prior to leaving your reception, make sure you have assigned one person to get your bags into the getaway car. The last thing you want after a long day is to be without your flip-flops and toothbrush. Pack a bag with what you'll need for that night and bring that with you to the reception.

TIP

Typically, at weddings, that person assigned to put the bags into the getaway vehicle is me. I also include a to-go box of food and cake for them to enjoy that evening. If you don't have a planner, ask the caterer to box up some food for you to take with you to the hotel. After a long day, you'll likely arrive at the hotel after their kitchen is closed. You may be hungry, so be prepared by having this added to your belongings at the end of the night.

Additionally, depending on your travel plans the next day, make sure to assign someone to pick up your dress and/or tux from the hotel the next day. If you're heading to the airport the next morning, you won't know what to do with your clothes from the night before. You can leave them at the front desk for someone to pick up. That way, they can return the tux if needed to the rental company without additional charges on your account.

My last tip on booking a honeymoon suite would be to book a location away from everyone else. If your guests are staying at a particular hotel, consider one down the road a bit. This is your time and booking a honeymoon suite at the same location as your guests may not give you the peace you would like on that night. Either way, make it a special place to spend your first night together as a married couple.

6

Wedding Weekend Events

Chapter **16**

Practice Makes Perfect

After you've done the hard work and planned the perfect day, it's time to put the plan on paper and distribute it to the key people who need to know. It's true: practice does make perfect. This may be my favorite chapter to write and one of the most important for you to read.

In this chapter, I walk you through your master plan for your wedding weekend and discuss who needs to receive the plan for a successful event. Additionally, I cover everything you need to know to practice with your bridal party for your big day and enjoy your rehearsal dinner. And finally, I have suggestions for who you need to thank and give gifts to for being a part of your big day.

The day before your wedding day is almost as important as the wedding day itself. After reading this chapter, you'll be prepared to practice for your perfect day.

REMEMBER

Drawing Up the Master Plan for the Weekend

My favorite part of planning a wedding is in the details. There is no such thing as too much information when it comes to creating your details document. I always tell my clients that the details document is like the Bible. If it isn't in there, it isn't truth.

If it's important that your aunt cuts the cake, that needs to be listed. If you want to do a first look with your father, that needs to be listed. If you want your maid of honor to do a toast, that needs to be listed. Creating your details document is a vital piece of the puzzle when it comes to planning a perfect event.

In this section, I provide a sample details document that I use for every event. This tool will help you create your own. It's the roadmap for your day, and including as much information as you can will help you have the stress-free day of your dreams. It will take you time to put this information together, but it will be worth it at the end of the day.

TIP

As we work through your detailed schedule of events, I will go through each piece and let you know what needs to be included along the way. A final sample of the detailed schedule of events from a past client's wedding can be found at www. sarahlizabeth.com/planningaweddingfordummies. This way you can see what each piece looks like together as a whole.

Vendor contact information

It's important to include each vendor's company name, contact name, email, and phone number. This will ensure your team's information will be listed in one place where vendors can retrieve other vendors' information if needed.

TIP

Start your details document with your wedding date and your last names. As much as you may feel that the vendors are doing only your wedding, they may have a wedding every weekend. Including the date will make sure they arrive on the right day.

01.01.0000 Vendor	(Last Name) / (Last Name) Wedding Details Company Name, Contact Name, Email, Phone
Wedding Planner	
Ceremony Venue (also include physical address)	
Reception Venue (also include physical address)	
Photographer	
Videographer	
Caterer	
Bartender	

| 01.01.0000 | (Last Name) / (Last Name) Wedding Details |
Vendor	Company Name, Contact Name, Email, Phone
Baker	
Ceremony Music	
Reception Music	
Transportation	

Bridal party contact information

The next information that you'll include in your details document is the bridal party information. While this may not seem important to include, if I was on your team, I would want to know the names of your parents. The DJ will also need to know the names of your bridal party in order to announce them. I can't tell you how many times vendors reach out to me and let me know that they appreciate having the bridal party names before the event. Include your squad in this order.

Bridal Party	Name
Bride (include email & phone)	
Groom (include email & phone)	
Maid of Honor	
Best Man	
Bridesmaids	
Groomsmen	
Flower Girl	
Ring Bearer	
Parents of the Bride	
Parents of the Groom	
Bride's Grandparents	
Groom's Grandparents	
Attendants	

Bridal Party	Name
Ushers	
Officiant	
(company name, contact name, email, & phone)	

Timeline of day-before-the-wedding events

For my clients I include the schedule for the day before the event as well. You may need to send this to a vendor working with you on your rehearsal, for example, or your church or venue coordinator. They need to know when to open the doors so you can rehearse your big day. Table 16-1 is an example of a schedule for the day before your wedding.

TABLE 16-1   **Day Before Wedding Day Schedule Sample**

Time	Event	Special Notes
4:30 pm	Rehearsal begins	Include the address
5:30 pm	Rehearsal ends	
	Transport to rehearsal dinner	
6:00 pm	Rehearsal dinner begins	Include the address
	Cocktails	
6:30 pm	Dinner begins	
7:30 pm	Toasts	
9:00 pm	End	

Timeline of the big day (with a first look)

Table 16-2 is an example schedule of the day if you decide to do a first look. (A first look is when the couple sees each other before the start of the wedding.) The first column is the time. The second column is the description of the event. The final column lists special notes about what you need to include with the information from the second column.

Note: This sample schedule assumes a ceremony and reception held at the same location. If you're hosting a ceremony and reception at different locations, you'll need to add in the time in transit from the ceremony to the reception.

TABLE 16-2   ## Wedding Day Schedule Sample, with First Look

Time	Event	Special Notes
9:00 am	Bride & bridesmaids hair & makeup begins	Include the location & the hair & makeup schedule
	Reception venue opens, vendor load-in/setup	Include the vendors' setup times
2:00 pm	First look	Include the location
2:15 pm	Couple photos	
2:45 pm	Bridesmaids & groomsmen photos	
3:30 pm	Family photos	Include the following lists: Bride with . . . Groom with . . . Bride & groom with . . .
4:00 pm	Prelude music	Include a list of 5-6 songs you would like played during the prelude music
4:30 pm	Ceremony begins	
	Entrance of officiant & groom	*List song title*
	Entrance of bride's grandparents	Include escorts' names, if needed
	Entrance of groom's grandparents	Include escorts' names, if needed
	Entrance of groom's mother	Include escort's name
	Entrance of bride's mother	Include escort's name
	Entrance of bridesmaids & groomsmen	List song title & the order of the bridesmaids & groomsmen
	Entrance of flower girl/ring bearer	
	Entrance of the bride	List song title & escorts name if needed

(continued)

TABLE 16-2 *(continued)*

Time	Event	Special Notes
4:40 pm	Ceremony	Input your ceremony order & include any song selections
	Welcome	
	Giving of the bride	
	Declaration of intent	
	Message	
	Exchange of vows	
	Exchange of rings	
	Unity ceremony	
	Declaration of marriage	
	Kiss	
	Pronouncement of marriage	
4:55 pm	Recessional	List song title
5:00 pm	Cocktail hour	Include the location
5:45 pm	Move guests to reception	
6:00 pm	Bridal party intros	Include the bridal party member names & how you want to be officially introduced for the first time
6:08 pm	Welcome/Prayer	List who will give a welcome and/or prayer
6:15 pm	Dinner begins	
7:00 pm	Cake cutting	List song title
7:10 pm	Toasts	List who will give toasts (maid of honor/best man)
7:30 pm	First dance	List song title
7:35 pm	Father-daughter dance	List song title
7:40 pm	Mother-son dance	List song title
7:45 pm	Dance floor opens	
8:30 pm	Bouquet toss	List song title
8:35 pm	Garter toss	List song title
9:45 pm	Last song	List song title
9:50 pm	Line guests up for exit	List location
9:55 pm	Grand exit	

Time	Event	Special Notes
10:00 pm	End	
TBD	Vendors end	List time by which the vendors must be out of the venue so they know how long they have to tear down

Timeline of the big day (no first look)

I created Table 16-3 as an example if you're not planning a first look before the start of the ceremony. This is a consolidated example for your reference. Use all the details from Table 16-2 but revise the timeline to the schedule seen here to accommodate the additional time needed so that you don't see each other before the wedding and only when you walk down the aisle.

TABLE 16-3   **Wedding Day Schedule Sample, No First Look**

Time	Event	Special Notes
9:00 am	Bride & bridesmaids hair & makeup begins	Include the location & the hair & makeup schedule.
	Reception venue opens, vendor load-in/ setup	Include the vendors' setup times
1:00 pm	Bride gets dress on	
1:20 pm	Bridal photos	
1:40 pm	Bride with bridesmaids photos	
2:00 pm	Bride with family photos	Include the following photo list: Bride with . . .
2:30 pm	Groom's photos	
2:45 pm	Groom with groomsmen photos	
3:15 pm	Groom with family photos	Include the following photo list: Groom with . . .
4:00 pm	Prelude music, all photos conclude	
4:30 pm	Ceremony begins	
5:00 pm	Cocktail hour	
	Combined family photos	Include the following photo list: Bride & groom with. . .
6:00 pm	Reception begins	

Flowers and decor

Your flowers and decor are an important part of your day and I want you to include them in your details document for the vendors to see. One of the main reasons to include them is so that all the vendors can see your theme.

It's important the caterer knows what your flowers and decor will look like so they know how to decorate the buffet. Additionally, while the attire of your vendors will likely be basic event black, if you have an accent color, they may send their staff dressed to match your details.

The flower and decor section of your detailed schedule of events should include the following:

» Bride's bouquet

» Bridesmaids' bouquets, and how many

» Boutonnieres, and how many

» Corsages, and how many

» Flower girl/Ring bearer

» Ceremony decor: altar and aisle

» Cocktail hour decor

» Reception decor: guest table decor, lighting, draping, room accents

Floor plan

You should also include a floor plan such as the one shown in Figure 16-1 so vendors can see the venue layout and where they'll set up in the room. Doing this will eliminate a lot of questions from your vendors on the day of the event. If you're planning your own wedding, they'll have a lot of questions for you, so including this will let you enjoy your day without filtering vendor questions.

Guest list

There is one additional piece of information that I add to every event details document and that is the guest list. It's important to include this so the vendors have a copy to be able to assist your guests when needed. There are many moving pieces when it comes to any wedding day, and informing your vendors who is attending will give them the information they may need in case a guest has a question.

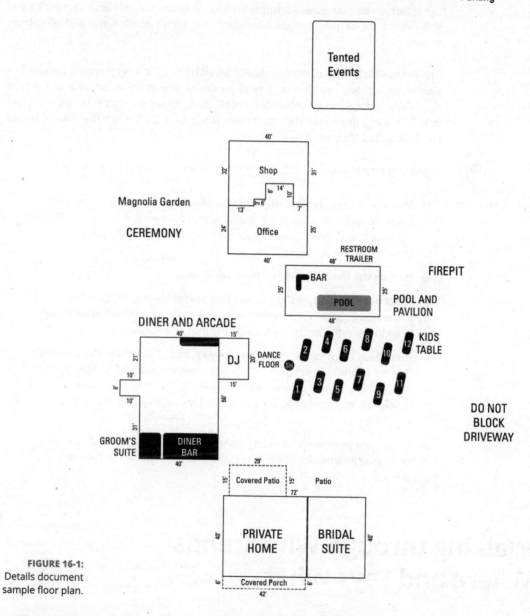

FIGURE 16-1:
Details document sample floor plan.

Distributing Your Master Plan

Now that you have the details of your day in one pretty package, it's time to discuss who should receive all the information. Some people just don't need to have all the information, such as the bridal party or family and friends. Be selective in the information you give. Giving too much information to those closest to you will cause a lot of questions and opinions that aren't needed and will add stress to your plate.

The detailed schedule of events should be distributed to every vendor involved in your wedding. For my clients, I send an email to every vendor with the details document by two weeks before the event. This allows enough time for the vendors to ask any questions they may have, but it isn't too far out that they'll forget the details that they need to know.

REMEMBER

When you're crafting that email to your vendors, include the following:

>> **Make sure they confirm that they received the email.** A few days later, follow up with a phone call to those vendors who have not confirmed. There is a chance that they are busy, but your email may also be stuck in their spam folder.

>> **Include the load-in time and load-out times.**

>> **Make sure they know the venue's policies for loading in.** Can they pull up to the venue, unload and then move their vehicles prior to the event? They'll need to know this to ensure a successful load in and load out.

>> **Give them the onsite contact for the day.** If you have a wedding planner, that will be their information. If you don't, assign one person to filter phone calls and talk to your vendors when they arrive. This is not a job that you need to take on. You need to be present and enjoy your day. Give that job to someone else.

>> **Make sure they don't have any questions.** Let them know that after they review the information to let you or your planner know if they have any questions.

Walking through Who Stands Where and Says What

This is one of my favorite parts with my clients. I feel like I have said that a million times through this book. Can you tell I love weddings and the process of planning weddings? It's officially time to plan where everyone is going to stand during your ceremony. In this section we'll also discuss the best way to practice during your rehearsal and at what points people will give special toasts during your wedding weekend.

Getting everyone in order at the rehearsal

Let's start with the order. In Chapter 2, you have an opportunity to enter your bridal party names and order. (If you haven't already done that, do that first, in Table 2-2.) They have officially been partnered together and now we need to practice how they'll get to their spots.

When I start a rehearsal for a client, I begin with the bridesmaids and groomsmen standing at the altar in the correct order. The reason I do this is so that they can see when they walk down the aisle the spot where they are going.

The bride's side is on the left and the groom's side is on the right. I created Figure 16-2 as an illustration so that you can see the order of your bridal party. Use this as a tool to place your squad in the correct space. The maid of honor and best man should stand the closest to the couple. Your parents and grandparents should be seated in the front row of your ceremony on either side.

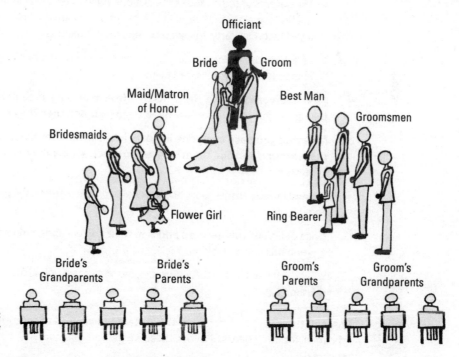

FIGURE 16-2: Bridal party order.

You'll want to make sure there are seats reserved for your parents they when enter in the processional, so the ushers should not seat any guests in the front row. Make sure to inform your ushers or leave a sign on the front row of your ceremony chairs that is marked "Reserved." This will ensure that the parents and grandparents will have seats and that guests will not sit in those seats when they arrive at the ceremony.

When you're rehearsing your big day, follow this order.

1. **Start with the bridal party in their order at the altar.**

2. **Talk through the content of the ceremony with your officiant and bridal party.**

   You do not need to practice your vows. There's a superstition that it's bad luck to say your vows during your rehearsal.

3. **Practice the exit.**

   Make sure the bridal party does not exit until you're out of the ceremony location. This will avoid them being in your pictures walking down the aisle. As soon as you leave, they can begin their exit:

   - The bridal party will leave in pairs, beginning with your maid of honor and best man, followed by your bridesmaids and groomsmen.

   - The parents of the bride are the last ones who enter the wedding before the bridesmaids, but during the recessional they are the first ones to leave after the bridal party, followed by the groom's parents.

   - After the parents leave, the grandparents are next. The bride's grandparents will leave first, followed by the groom's parents.

4. **After everyone has left, the officiant often makes an announcement telling the guests where they need to go next and then they exit.**

5. **Now that you have everyone lined up in the back after the exit, turn them around and line them back up to practice how they'll enter the ceremony.**

   This will include all members of the bridal party, the parents, the grandparents, and the officiant.

6. **Once everyone has entered and is in their correct spot, check to see if anyone has any questions.**

   You do not need to run through your ceremony again unless there are specific questions.

REMEMBER

Through the years, this has been the system I have used to coordinate an efficient rehearsal for my clients. Follow these steps and you too will have a successful rehearsal.

Who's giving a toast?

There will be several moments throughout your day when a special person in your life will give a toast. I put together a list of who needs to publicly give a toast for your big day. I understand this may not fit you exactly, but use it as a tool to determine who'll be needing the microphone.

- **»** **Rehearsal Dinner Welcome:** If one family is hosting the rehearsal dinner — traditionally the groom's family — the head of the family will give a welcome to the guests and toast the couple before the dinner begins.

- **»** **Rehearsal Dinner:** The rehearsal dinner is where most of your bridal party and family will give you a toast. There is no need to create a formal list for this event. Simply open the floor to whoever would like to toast you before the big day.

- **»** **Reception Welcome:** If one family is hosting the reception — traditionally the bride's family — the head of the family (father of the bride) will give a welcome to the guests and toast the couple before the dinner begins. Additionally, they may say a prayer over dinner at this time.

- **»** **Reception Toast:** The reception toasts are meant for the maid of honor and best man. This is the moment where they get to share meaningful words about your relationship with them up until this point. Keep this list small because you want to get to the party. I have seen toasts at receptions go on for way too long and then the couple misses out on a longer time to dance and enjoy their reception.

Informing Your Bridal Party

I had a bride reach out to me saying she was overwhelmed with her bridal party. This is a common trend with most of my brides. They get frustrated with their bridal party and all the questions they ask. Her bridal party wanted to know when they needed to be with her so that they could schedule their own activities around the weekend events. This bride felt that they should just be present with her and not run around the city checking out the attractions nearby.

I could write a book all about what not to do if you're asked to be in the bridal party. The bridal party often has a way of stressing out the couple. It happens almost every time I work with a client. But let's discuss why they stress them out.

First, they're excited to be in your wedding. If they aren't, they shouldn't be in your wedding. With excitement comes a lot of questions. They want to know everything about your day and what they need to do because they're excited. However, you don't want to be asked if you have a cake cutter or if you have a guest book. Why do they need to know that? But they do need to know what their responsibilities are for the weekend.

TIP

Distributing a condensed schedule to your bridal party will help you in the end. They'll know when they need to be where, and will hopefully limit the questions that can often leave brides stressed. Keep the details for those who need to know and give a condensed version to your bridal party.

This condensed timeline would include a list of the activities for the weekend and the times that they need to be there. It's also important to include the addresses for each location. Additionally, if you hire a wedding planner, include their contact information so that they can help filter all the bridal party questions.

If you're hosting your event in a destination city where the members of the bridal party haven't been, chances are they may want to explore the city during their down time. The information that you give your bridal party should include the planned group activities for the weekend. If they have this information, they'll be able to arrange their social calendar around your planned activities. Let's just be clear here: it is not your responsibility to organize their social calendar outside of the events you have planned for the weekend.

REMEMBER

One thing to remember is that they are your special people. There is a reason why you want them in your wedding. They are excited and everyone handles stress differently. Informing them two weeks before your big day about what's going to happen when and where they need to be will help eliminate the stress that bridal party members often cause for the couple.

Enjoying Yourself at the Rehearsal Dinner

The rehearsal dinner is held immediately following the rehearsal, with your bridal party and close family. Rehearsal dinners began when weddings started becoming larger events. At one point in time, weddings were small events. Now that weddings are typically large events, a rehearsal dinner is hosted with a smaller, more intimate guest list.

WARNING

Your rehearsal dinner should not cost as much as your wedding. It's easy for them to get out of control when it comes to your wallet and so in this section, we'll discuss who you should invite, how to pick the perfect location, choosing your food and beverages, and who should give a toast. Additionally, we will discuss who you'll give a gift to at the rehearsal dinner and what you'll do when the rehearsal dinner is over to prepare for the big day.

Picking the guest list

The rehearsal dinner guest list should include your bridesmaids with partners/spouses, groomsmen with partners/spouses, flower girl/ring bearer with parents, officiant with parent/spouse, parents, grandparents, and your other immediate family, meaning your siblings. If your loved ones have children, you will need to determine if you are allowing them to bring them.

Depending on the size of the group, my clients will invite VIPs in their life or extended family — aunts, uncles, and cousins. VIPs are those people who aren't biological family but should be because of who they are in your life. If you have a large family, I suggest keeping the guest list down to just your immediate family. This will help avoid spending a fortune on your rehearsal dinner and wedding.

REMEMBER

By design, the rehearsal dinner is an intimate group of people. There will be toasts and love shared for you by those in attendance, so keeping it smaller is always best. It's appropriate to mail separate invitations to those who are attending the rehearsal dinner. You'll also collect RSVPs from your guests to ensure you have an appropriate space to accommodate the event.

While it can be a challenge to guess your guests' response to the wedding, you'll have a better idea of the total number of guests for the rehearsal dinner because those are your bridal party and family. They'll already be with you at the rehearsal, so you'll be able to figure out an approximate guest count for this event ahead of time.

TIP

A trend in the wedding industry is to host a "post-toast" event. This occurs immediately following the rehearsal dinner, to give guests who have traveled a long distance to be at your wedding the opportunity to grab a drink and say hello before the wedding day. It's a wonderful cocktail reception where you'll get to mix and mingle with your wedding reception guests before the big day. Consider hosting an event like this instead of having them all attend your rehearsal dinner. This way you'll get to see them, and your pocketbook will thank you.

Scouting out the perfect location

When you have your guest list in place, it's time to pick the perfect location. You'll want to create a short list of options. Limit the list to an area that is close to either the ceremony location or where you plan to end up at the end of the night.

Since the traditional guest list at a rehearsal dinner is smaller than the wedding guest list, it opens unique venues that wouldn't be able to accommodate a large group. Consider booking a small room at your favorite restaurant. Give your guests a sense of what you would enjoy on a date night.

Rehearsal dinner locations can be unique, such as a local brewery, winery, or bowling alley. I had a client rent out a movie theatre that served food, and at the end of the rehearsal dinner they watched a slideshow on the big screen together. It's the perfect event for setting the tone of the following day.

TIP

Since rehearsal dinner locations are typically smaller, consider a location that doesn't needs a lot of "dressing up" with florals and decor. If you're looking to save some money, consider using only candles or your floral arrangement that will be used on your wedding day. Although I am a florist, I advise keeping the decor simple and save the money on the floral and decor budget.

I have often had clients use the venue where they are getting married for their rehearsal dinner as well. A popular trend is booking a home-share location for a wedding. If you do this, you'll already be at the venue for the weekend, so it makes logistical sense to use the property. The rentals are already delivered the day before the event, so you can maximize the budget by using the same location.

The same is true for a backyard wedding. Consider booking your vendors for the weekend rather than one day. Booking a vendor for multiple days may save you money overall. Most of our team will offer a discount on the rehearsal dinner if the client is booking them for the wedding. Either way, picking the perfect locations gives you another opportunity to show your guests who you are as a couple.

Choosing the food and beverage

Selecting the food for your rehearsal dinner is the perfect way to incorporate your personal tastes into your wedding weekend. There aren't any hard rules when picking your food. Since the guest list is typically smaller, you can create a unique experience for your guests to enjoy.

The rehearsal dinner food can reflect your heritage or what you like to do on your dates. Bring in foods that celebrate your family heritage. If you're from the South, host a BBQ or low-country boil. If you frequent food truck festivals, create a mini food truck festival for your guests. If you love the local pizza place, have them cater your rehearsal dinner.

REMEMBER

Rehearsal dinners are less formal than the wedding, so it's the perfect opportunity to go outside of a normal meal of meat and three sides and give your guests a fun experience. Don't forget to bring in a sweet treat for your guests to enjoy. Bake your favorite cookies or a family recipe dessert and serve that to your guests. It will be personal and appreciated for all to enjoy.

Rehearsal dinners are also the perfect event to feature a signature drink. If you love mimosas or margaritas, offer a mimosa bar or a margarita bar. If you love old-fashioneds, serve those to your guests. If you have a favorite IPA, select that as the beer choice. If you have a favorite wine, use that for the wine selection. Again, use this opportunity to share your favorite things with your guests.

Because a large majority of the toasts will occur at your rehearsal dinner, it's appropriate to offer champagne. While the guests can use the beverages that they are drinking, it's also nice to offer champagne for your guests to enjoy after dinner and during the toast.

Regardless of whether you offer alcohol to your guests at any event, don't forget the nonalcoholic beverage. I would suggest a minimum of water, sweet tea, and unsweetened tea with sweeteners available. Additionally, you can offer sodas, but that is not needed unless you love it! Offering tea and water is appropriate. The beverage focus is often on the alcohol, but don't overlook additional options for your guests to enjoy in case someone doesn't drink alcohol.

Toasts

I personally love the toast time during a rehearsal dinner. Allowing your guests to make a toast at your rehearsal dinner is always a special time for clients. It's the time where those you love get to share a few stories and memories and tell everyone in the room why they are so happy to be a part of your day.

It's the moment where you get to feel celebrated and loved by those around you. Logistically, this will happen after dinner, during dessert. It's best for a parent or family member to start off the toast. This will help get the ball rolling without you having to stand up and ask people to toast you.

After the parent welcomes everyone and gives you all a toast, they can simply open the floor to anyone who wants to give you a toast. I have seen this go either way — everyone wants to give a toast, or no one does. The majority will give a toast, but it's okay if some do not. They may not feel comfortable speaking in public, so give them the freedom to just sit and listen to everyone else around you.

After everyone has finished toasting you, it's your turn! Make sure to take the time to thank everyone for being a part of your wedding day. Remember, they have traveled and spent money to be with you and they should be thanked. Even if some of them have gotten on your last nerve, thank them.

I have often seen couples toast each other at their rehearsal dinner. I mean, after all, it's all about the two of you and the rehearsal dinner is an appropriate place to share your thoughts about what the next day holds. I understand that this may not be something you're comfortable with, but if you are, it's the perfect time to share with your fiancé how grateful you are to soon be their spouse.

Gifts for your bridal party

Giving gifts at your rehearsal dinner is an important part of the rehearsal dinner experience. It allows you the opportunity to give a gift in a more intimate setting, making the giving more personal. It gives you the opportunity to sincerely thank those who are with you for your big day.

In this section, we'll discuss some of the groups you should consider when thinking through your gift giving. Gifts are never expected but always appreciated. Take time to think through gifts that have meaning for each group discussed here.

Couples exchange

First and foremost, give each other a wedding gift. Depending on the gift you give each other, you may or may not want to give it to your fiancé in a public setting. You also may not be able to give it to them at your rehearsal dinner due to the size of the item you pick.

I once had a bride give her groom photos from a boudoir session. Obviously, this isn't a public-setting kind of gift. They exchanged gifts at the first look. I gave him the book and he turned as red as a tomato. I have had couples purchase large gifts for their soon-to-be spouse and so they printed a picture of the gift and gave that at the rehearsal dinner.

Additionally, I have given gifts to clients on their wedding day while they were in different locations. The only downside to this is that you don't get to see their reaction to the gift. Consider exchanging gifts in person when you can be together so that you can both be a part of the gift-giving experience.

TIP

If you want to give a gift before the wedding but don't want to see each other, have the best man or maid of honor deliver the gift and make sure the videographer and photographer capture the moment so you can see it later.

Another gift giving option is to buy something for each other on your honeymoon or a gift you will use in your home. You can commemorate an amazing honeymoon location by buying something specific to that location that will be displayed in your home.

Bridesmaids' and groomsmen's gifts

The rehearsal dinner is the perfect place to give your bridesmaids and groomsmen a little something special. A trend in both groups is to give them something they can wear on the wedding day.

For example, gift your bridesmaids a robe for when you're all getting ready, or a necklace or earrings that you want them to wear on the wedding day. For the groomsmen, consider custom cufflinks or a tie. This is a great way to be resourceful. Give a gift and make it practical for them to wear on your wedding day.

Another popular option is to personalize items with the monogram or name of the bridesmaids/groomsmen to whom you are giving a gift. Customizing tumblers, wine glasses, beer mugs, wallets, purses, or beach bags are great options. Give them something that they can use again after your wedding is over. Every time they use it, they'll remember the memories from your big day and your friendship.

Parent present

Honoring your parents with a gift at the rehearsal dinner is a special moment. You are about to leave your family and create a new family. Spend time thinking of memorable gifts that honor the life you had with them prior to meeting your fiancé.

Consider framing a sketch of your childhood home. Imprint your favorite childhood recipe on a hand towel. Make a memory book of your childhood. Either way, it's important to acknowledge your parents in a special and memorable way.

REMEMBER

Take the time to consider a gift that will honor your upbringing. Trust me, your parents will appreciate it more than you know. You are now off to begin a new life, but they stay behind and take on the role of a spectator. Giving them something that they can hold onto and cherish will be the best way to honor them.

Love for the littles

Even if they're young, they are still a mighty part of your wedding day. I was a flower girl once in my life. I am still very close to the couple. We're all grown up now but let me just tell you, I will never forget being a part of their wedding day.

Adolescent years are the formidable years. Your flower girl and ring bearer will remember being a part of your wedding for the rest of their life. They will likely remember more details than you do one day. It's important to honor those little ones that you have picked to be a part of your day.

It's always a popular choice to gift them something that they could wear on your wedding day. However, depending on how old they are, give them a gift based on something that they love. You can also use this gift as a source of entertainment for them.

We gave our ring bearer a set of miniature toy dinosaurs. He loved dinosaurs and couldn't believe the new collection he had. But you know what else? That four-year-old was entertained at our rehearsal dinner and our wedding. After seeing that I told myself that I would encourage all my clients to do the same. He wasn't up running around sticking his hands on everything around him. Instead, he was sitting at the table, playing with his new friends.

Late-night celebration

Celebrating after the rehearsal dinner is over is the definition of walking a fine line. You want to hang out with people who have traveled to be with you, but you also don't want to feel bad the next day. I am a supporter of spending a little time with those you love after the rehearsal dinner is over, but everything in moderation — remember that tomorrow is a big day.

As I mentioned earlier in the chapter, the post-toast is gaining popularity. This is where you invite out-of-town guests to join you for a drink. Note that I said *a* drink. This isn't designed to be an all-night party. Trust me, you do not want to feel bad at your wedding.

HOT MESS TRAIN

I would love to share with you a story from a past client. We still laugh about it to this day, but on her wedding weekend we weren't laughing. When I arrived at the rehearsal, the bride had partied a little too hard that morning and afternoon. I was told by her friends and family that she was in the restroom and wouldn't be coming out. Additionally, the groom was missing. He was out with his groomsmen, and no one knew how to get ahold of him. So we didn't rehearse.

I informed the bridal party what time I needed the bride and groom to arrive at the venue the next day and they assured me they would have them there on time. I left hoping both were going to be okay.

The morning came and our staff was the first to arrive. We were busy setting up when all of a sudden I heard a voice at the end of the hallway yell, "Hot mess train is here!" It was the bride. Honestly, I was grateful to see her standing up. I got her settled in the bridal suite and continued the event setup.

I checked on her frequently and as much as she wanted to feel better, she seemed to be feeling worse. It was horrible. We propped her up on the couch halfway laying down and sitting up and the hair and makeup team worked to get her put together while she took a nap. About midday, I realized she wasn't going to be better without some help that I couldn't provide her.

I called a local mobile IV company and they arrived at the venue a few hours before the start of the wedding to administer an IV. She needed fluids and I knew that was the only thing that would help her. Once she received the fluids, she started to perk back up but, honestly, she felt crummy the entire day.

The last thing you want is to be a hot mess train on your wedding day. Enjoy your weekend in moderation so that you can feel good and remember your wedding day.

TIP

Set a time when you want to make sure you're in bed. Tell that time to someone close to you and make sure they hold you to that. It's easy to get going and then before you know it, you've gone too hard. I do not want that happening to you. Instead of focusing on the late-night celebration, focus on spending time with those you love, and then go to bed.

Rest and Recover for the Big Day

The night before your wedding is a big night. You have planned this day for a long time and soon it will be here. It's exciting and it may feel like Christmas Eve. There's a chance you may not sleep well the night before your wedding. But I want you to do your best to rest and recover for the big day that you're about to experience.

Before you go to bed, make sure you have everything laid out for the next day. If you go to bed with a lot of tasks to do when you wake up, you may not get much sleep because you'll be up thinking about all the things that need to get done.

Go ahead and pack the bag that you'll take with you to the ceremony and reception. Lay out your attire and accessories so that you aren't scrabbling the next day to find the pieces you need. Additionally, if you're going on a honeymoon, make sure you have those bags packed as well.

TIP

Whatever you can do prior to your head hitting the pillow the night before your wedding, do it. This will help your mind rest with anticipation rather than anxiety over the next day. While the excitement can seem a bit overwhelming, it's important to try and get the best night's sleep possible.

When I got married, one of my bridesmaids and I had a grownup sleepover. We did face masks, soaked our feet, had some wine, and pampered ourselves a little bit. It was so much fun without having too much fun. We just enjoyed being together and sharing funny stories from the past. I don't often pamper myself and she was persistent that we were going to do something relaxing before I went to bed. I am so glad I surrounded myself with a squad who knew exactly what I needed.

REMEMBER

Take time for you, to rest and recover. Your best day is about to be here.

Chapter **17**

Pre- and Post-Wedding Events

The wedding day is your main event — it's the one single day you have been planning this entire journey — but there are also events throughout your wedding weekend that you may want to consider. When I was getting married, I didn't want any attention on me. Remember, my job is to move all the pieces of a client's day but not be seen. It was an interesting position to transition into the role of a bride. I struggled with hosting additional events prior to or throughout the weekend.

Getting married is one of those big life moments. Even if you're hesitant like I was to participate in all the pre- and post-wedding events, I challenge you to jump all in! In this chapter, we'll discuss several bridal party activities such as showers, a bridesmaids' lunch, and groomsmen hangouts. Additionally, we'll talk about a very important piece of the wedding weekend: bidding farewell to your loved ones who were with you on your wedding day.

Bridal Party Activities

You have picked the perfect squad to be a part of your big day. The bridal party should include your close friends and family that have been with you through this journey in life. They're what we call "your people." It's important to take time to celebrate with them the biggest commitment you will make up until this point in life.

REMEMBER

While most of the bridal party activities are hosted by other people, you need to be in the know. There will be questions and we want to make sure the parties are all a success. Knowing the details of the showers, lunches, and hangouts will help you answer the questions you'll receive from the host so you can communicate what you want.

Getting showered

Let's start with the showers. A shower is held before your wedding day. It's a time to gather with your loved ones before the big day and get "showered" with gifts. Who doesn't love the sound of that?

Your shower (or showers) should be held approximately two months to two weeks before your event. Showers are hosted by your maid of honor, bridesmaids, or close friends. A parent doesn't typically host a shower because it's seen as the family asking for gifts.

So much love, so many showers!

Showers are a great way to celebrate with your "groups" of friends prior to the big day. Take some time to think through how many "groups" you have in your life to determine how many showers you'd like. Let me give you some examples.

>> **Co-workers:** Are you close with your co-workers, and they want to throw you a shower? You could have a shower at work, or in a location where you can do a fun activity together such as taking a painting or pottery class. While you like the people you work with, you may not be extremely close to them. Hosting a shower with an activity involved will allow you the opportunity to celebrate but avoid uncomfortable conversations. You do have to see these people every day, so keep it light and have fun.

>> **Bridesmaids:** Celebrating with your bridesmaids is the number one shower to participate in when preparing for your wedding. If you don't do any other shower, have a bridesmaid's shower. The bridesmaids agreed to stand with you on your biggest day. Plan a shower with them to celebrate your soon-to-be marriage.

>> **Religious organization:** If you're very connected at a religious organization, having a shower with those who participate in the same organization is a great option for a shower. These people may not be close enough to you to attend your wedding or maybe you have to limit your numbers at the wedding, so being able to celebrate with this group of people allows them to shower you even if they're unable to attend the wedding for whatever reason.

>> **Close friends:** Having a shower surrounded by those you love the most is a perfect group to celebrate with. This group may also be combined with the bridesmaids. It's extremely common to have a smaller bridal party. That doesn't mean that you don't have other close friends, but they may not be your bridesmaids. Consider planning a shower with those who are closest to you prior to your big day.

>> **Family:** Your family are people who have loved you and known you the longest compared to any other group. They want to celebrate you, and planning a family shower is a great way to honor your soon to be new life and family. In this group, a family member can be a host because everyone is family. If you have a large family, a shower is a great way to bring them all together. Consider a couple's shower to bring both families together before the big day.

>> **In-law family:** If your future in-laws want to host a shower, this is the perfect opportunity to meet the other side of the family. I am certain they want to meet you too and planning a shower that can bring them together is the perfect way to meet everyone who will soon be your family.

>> **Geographic:** If you grew up or lived in a particular area, consider bringing your friends in that area together again through a shower. They may or may not be able to attend your wedding, but they still want to celebrate you. Plan a weekend away and reconnect with those you love in a particular area.

Ironing out the specifics

Since showers happen before your wedding, it's important to make sure your registry is up to date. A shower is designed to give the couple gifts for their home. Nowadays, couples are more established before marriage. However, adding items to your home that you both like is a great way to blend the items you had prior to meeting each other.

For each shower, make sure to give your guest list to the host so that they can send out invitations. Those need to be sent out four weeks before your shower and should include your name, date, time, location, registry, and RSVP information. The invitation should also include the host's name and contact information.

Planning gifts, games, and other important details

Speaking of the details, showers are typically hosted at the host's home, neighborhood clubhouse, winery, or small restaurant. Showers can also be a brunch setting or an afternoon soiree, but no matter the location, they're generally held during the day. Most showers are two hours in length, which allows enough time for catching up with those you love, enjoying some food, and opening gifts.

REMEMBER

Make sure someone is keeping a good record of the gifts you receive and who gave it. This way, you can personalize your thank-you notes — for example, "Thank you, (guest's name), for the throw blanket. I am certain we'll use it often in our home." Guests want to know that you remember what they got you and that you liked the gift, and also that you will use it. When you write your thank-you notes, make sure to list the specific item and how you plan to use it in your home. That will make them feel that the money they spent is of value to you.

TIP

Showers are the perfect event to incorporate a theme. You or the host may choose a bridal shower theme but if you're planning several showers, consider separating those into categories relating to what you need. One shower could be all about cooking supplies, and another could be for home accessories. This way, each shower will have a particular registry based on your theme.

If you've ever attended a bridal shower, you know there are always games. Incorporating games into your shower is the perfect ice breaker. There is a chance that everyone in attendance won't know each other. They may not even know your soon-to-be spouse. Selecting games about you as a couple gives your guests the opportunity to learn a little more about your fiancé and your relationship. Games also produce laughter, and laughter is a good thing. Everyone will enjoy a few moments away from their busy lives to celebrate you and laugh.

Bridesmaids' lunch

A bridesmaids' lunch is when the bride treats her bridesmaids to brunch, lunch, or dinner. It's a special time for you to celebrate your bridesmaids and thank them in an intimate setting for being a part of your day.

I hear it all the time from my brides: "My bridesmaids are driving me crazy!" I haven't yet figured out why this happens to brides. The only explanation I have is that big life moments can cause stress. People handle stress in all sorts of ways, and sometimes it isn't handled well. You may be laughing right now because the last thing you want to do is celebrate someone who has been on your last nerve. Trust me, this is completely normal. My hope is that your bridesmaids haven't created unnecessary drama for you. Even if they have, the bridesmaids' lunch is the time to simply celebrate your friendship and move into your forever with those you love by your side.

While the bridesmaids' lunch is typically just the bridesmaids, often mothers, sisters, or grandmothers may also attend. You can decide if you want to include only your bridesmaids or extend the invite to the other close women in your life.

TIP

This event can take on several different forms. If you don't want to host a lunch, you could do an activity with your bridesmaids. Maybe you all get manicures and pedicures the day before your wedding. You could also spend time together at a winery or attend a community event together. The main purpose is to spend time with those women you love the most.

REMEMBER

Make sure those you're inviting know that no gifts are expected at this event. If you want to give them a small gift, you can, but covering the bill for this event is a gift. Personalized notes are also a special way to give them something without breaking the bank.

If the setting allows, toasting your bridesmaids is always a special touch for the bridesmaids' lunch. Remember, they're toasting and celebrating you and have been for as long as you have been planning your wedding. Now is the time to let them know how much they mean to you and switch the focus to honoring them.

TIP

Your bridesmaids may all live in different locations, and it could be away from your wedding location. Hosting a bridesmaids' event during the few days prior to your event will be the best opportunity to gather with those you love the most. They're already coming to town and will all be in one location. Hosting this event a few days before your wedding gives you the best opportunity to have everyone together in one location.

Groomsmen bro time

At one point, weddings were a morning affair with a light punch and mints reception after the wedding. Now weddings are typically hosted in the late afternoon or evening, leaving us with one important question: "What do the groom and groomsmen do in the morning?"

It's a very important question, and in this section we're going to discuss a few options to keep the guys from getting into trouble before the wedding (see the nearby sidebar).

Like the bridesmaids' lunch, the groomsmen hang time is when the groom treats his groomsmen to something special on the morning of the wedding day. I have had clients golf, exercise, go to a barber for a haircut and shave, play cards, or play basketball.

SOMETIMES IT'S JUST TOO MUCH

One of my grooms planned a morning with his groomsmen that was a little too much. They spent the morning bonding over alcohol. The wedding wasn't until five o'clock that afternoon. We were busy getting the decor set up in the morning. The bride was getting dressed and taking her bridal photos and the bridesmaids' photos.

At some point, she mentioned to me that she hadn't heard from her groom in quite some time. She was texting with him in the morning and then she didn't hear anything from him after noon. She was concerned, but I tried to assure her that he was probably busy getting ready and enjoying his time with his groomsmen. Well, that was the understatement of the year.

When it was time for the groom to arrive, he wasn't there. We tried calling him several times but there was no answer. We also called his groomsmen, but still no answer. I thought maybe I was experiencing a runaway groom. I had never experienced that before, so this was going to be a first for me.

Finally, he showed up! He was an hour late, but he had arrived. I went to meet him at his car to explain we were now running behind and he needed to walk with purpose so we could get all the pictures taken in time. Let's just say that he wasn't walking anywhere fast or with intent. His groomsmen had to carry him into the church because he couldn't walk.

I knew we had a little situation on our hands. My brother was the photographer for this wedding, and I quickly went over to him and said, "The groom can't stand up." We tried to take his photos with him standing but quickly determined that wasn't going to happen.

First, he was wearing sunglasses. He insisted on keeping them on. Next, he couldn't stand up. So all his photos show him sitting down with sunglasses on. We positioned his groomsmen around him and started taking photos. I'm not sure those photos will ever be displayed in their home.

We had about an hour before the wedding was going to start, so I got him some water and crackers and told him to have those to try and get him to sober up so he could walk down the aisle. He did make it down the aisle but has no memory of the wedding day.

Brunch the Day After Your Wedding

At the end of your reception, you will quickly say goodbye to those you love. It may feel like a whirlwind and like you didn't get the opportunity to truly say goodbye. My clients often plan a brunch the morning after their wedding to be able to truly say thank you to their guests before they leave for their honeymoon. While it isn't a requirement, a day-after brunch is a nice way to spend a few more moments with those you love.

The brunch should be held late enough for your guests to get some rest after your wedding but not too late where it will interfere with their travel plans home. I would suggest 9 or 10 am for the post-wedding event. While it's generally called a brunch, it doesn't have to be traditional brunch food, although this is the most common. You could host a BBQ, a picnic, or high tea as opposed to serving brunch food.

The post-wedding brunch is generally hosted by the family. However, you can host this event if you'd like. It's a good idea to split the cost between the two families. Or one family can pay for the wedding, and the other family can pay for the rehearsal dinner and post-wedding brunch.

REMEMBER

Your guests will never be in the same place at the same time ever again. If you're looking for another opportunity to ensure you don't miss speaking to those you love, consider hosting a brunch after your wedding.

Picking the guest list

Who should you invite to the post-wedding brunch? This will be something to consider when planning the event and the location. You can invite everyone who was on your guest list. Another option is to only invite the bridal party and family for this event. Or you can invite only those who have traveled to be with you for your wedding.

REMEMBER

If you're inviting family, make sure to invite both sides of the family. If you're inviting close friends, make sure both sides are equally invited. Just as in picking the guest list for your wedding, it's best to play fair and balance the guest list so it's a perfect representation of both of your lives that have just become one.

The guest list will determine the budget. It's hard to know your guests' travel plans. The numbers of those who attend the brunch are typically significantly less than those who attended your wedding. If you have 100 guests, you may have only 50 guests at the post-wedding brunch. Your guests may not be able to attend due to their travel plans, or they may just not attend because attending your reception was all they needed.

If you're wanting a smaller group of people at this event, you can simply inform them of the party details. If you're inviting your entire guest list, you can include this information with your wedding invitation. I would suggest making sure that you also get an RSVP for those guests who are attending the post-wedding event.

TIP

Another option is to put the post-wedding event information on your wedding website. You will need to include the date, time, and location. Typically, the post-wedding event isn't as formal as the wedding but notating the dress code on your wedding website or invitation will help your guests know what to pack for the weekend.

Selecting the location

When deciding where to hold the post-wedding brunch, consider where your guests are staying. If you're hosting a destination wedding at an all-inclusive venue, pick a location for all your guests to come and grab breakfast and say good-bye before they leave. For all other events, consider a location that is close to either the venue where you hosted your reception or the hotel where your guests are staying.

TIP

If you book a hotel room block, reach out to that hotel and see if they have a room that could be rented in the hotel. This will allow your guests to simply wake up, get ready, and not have to leave the hotel to be able to attend. Make this location simple for your guests to get to so that more will attend.

If you don't do a hotel room block, consider a location close to the venue. When your guests book their travel plans for the weekend, most will decide to stay in the general area of your reception venue. Selecting a location close to your venue for the post-wedding brunch will allow more guests to attend.

Depending on the host and the location of your reception, you may also want to consider a small post-event brunch at your parents' home or your home. The post-wedding brunch doesn't have to be a formal or fancy event. Its purpose is to spend a little more quality time with those you love. Pick a location that is easy for your guests to attend without breaking the bank.

REMEMBER

You already provided an amazing wedding and reception for your guests to enjoy. The post-wedding event should be focused on quality time over quality of the event. Pick a location where your guests can come and go during the allotted time-frame. There isn't a set start time but an event duration. This will allow your guests to stop by when they can and leave when they need to. Consider it an open house for your guests to enjoy.

Saying Goodbye to Family and Friends

I don't like goodbyes. Sometimes they make me sad. I typically say, "See you later." I'm not sure what about saying goodbye is difficult for me. You have planned your perfect day. Maybe you planned it for over a year or maybe you planned it in a few weeks or month. Regardless, saying goodbye makes it officially over.

Whether at your reception or a post-wedding brunch, it is important to take time to say goodbye to your guests. In this section, I share some tips on how to say goodbye to your family and friends after your wedding is over.

REMEMBER

Before you leave either event, make sure to thank the hosts. Besides you, they are the most important people in the room. They have planned and funded your event and it is important to thank them for all they did for you to make the event possible. You couldn't have done it without them, so make them a top priority in the list of people you need to say goodbye to.

Allowing time for goodbyes at the reception

Let's first start with your reception. It's appropriate for your guests to start leaving after the cake it cut. Before that, it's considered rude, because you paid for the venue, the food, the flowers, and the rest. Leaving before the cake is cut is rude because you paid for your guests to eat the cake.

TIP

You can expect that once the cake is cut, some of your guests will leave. When planning your reception, add in some time between the cake cutting and the dance floor opening for those who do leave to say goodbye. Make sure to thank them for coming to your wedding. Regardless of how long they stay, they were there and need to be thanked for attending.

At the end of the reception will be your best opportunity to say goodbye to those guests who have stayed the entire night. If you're planning a formal exit, schedule about fifteen minutes before the last song and exit to walk around the room with your spouse and say goodbye to those you love.

REMEMBER

The goodbyes will be quick. This isn't the time to reminisce on your entire life and how they made a difference. That can be done through a personalized thank-you letter. At your reception, it's important to keep the hellos and goodbyes short because there are a lot of guests to say goodbye to. You also want to enjoy your party by spending as much time on the dance floor as possible. Maximize this time by keeping the goodbyes short and sweet.

There will be some guests who don't say goodbye. What do you do in that situation? Every guest should make it a point to say goodbye, but often they don't because you're busy doing something else when they want to leave. If a guest leaves before saying goodbye, make sure to thank them in your thank-you note for attending your wedding. You could also say that you wished you had been able to connect more on the wedding day. While guests understand that you have a lot on your plate on the day of the event, everyone enjoys hearing that you noticed that they missed getting to say goodbye.

REMEMBER

Inevitably, you'll be pulled in multiple directions at your wedding reception. Often, there simply isn't enough time to personally connect with everyone who attended your wedding. This is a natural thing, and I don't want you to worry about it. It happens at every wedding. There is a fine balance between enjoying your reception and spending time with those you love.

Saying goodbye at a post-wedding event

If you're hosting a post-wedding event, there is more time to engage in personal conversations with your loved ones.

Whenever you see guests or get a moment to speak to them, consider it your opportunity to inevitably say goodbye. You don't know for certain that you will get to see them again before the end of the event. Take that time to thank them for coming and share with them how much it meant to you for them to be there. That way, if you don't see them again, you have said what you need to say before they leave.

At a post-wedding brunch, you will have more opportunities to say goodbye then you did at your wedding reception. When saying goodbye to anyone, first thank them for attending. You don't know what it took for someone to be at your event, so it's important to thank them for making your event a priority in their life.

REMEMBER

The guests who attend your wedding are the most important people in your life. Take time to acknowledge that and thank them for taking time out of their life to be a part of your big life moment. It will be over so quickly, so each time you see someone, say something to them.

Chapter **18**

Honeymooning with your BFF

Congratulations, you're married! All the planning and events are over and now you're off to your forever with your BFF. You planned the perfect day, and now you get to head off to the rest of your life. Remember, I always encouraged you to keep perspective through your journey. It was for this moment right now, real life.

Planning the honeymoon is an exciting time. As someone who has been where you are, I can tell you from experience that you may never be able to travel like this again. Your life will change. You may start a new job, you may buy a new house, you may even start a family. It will never be the same scenario as your life right now. This is the time to plan a trip of a lifetime.

In this chapter, we will discuss when you need to plan your honeymoon, when you need to go on your honeymoon, how to pick the perfect location, how to hire a travel agent, going overseas, and packing. We will also talk about life after the honeymoon, and I will share with you some exciting news.

Thinking about Your Time of Travel

When picking the perfect time for your honeymoon, I want you to first consider your life. Do you have a new job and need to wait until you get vacation days? Are you a teacher and have summers off? Are you getting married in the winter and want to wait for warmer weather to travel? The best time to travel is typically between December and April. However, that will depend on your destination.

It's important to consider what is best for you after the wedding. If you're planning a destination wedding, you may consider staying at your wedding location for a few more days. The benefit here is that you're already in the location where you'll honeymoon. You don't have to go anywhere else, and you can just relax and enjoy your time together.

Clients who have done this have also shared a con. Once the guests leave, they are by themselves, and it seems lonely and sometimes boring because they have already been there for a week. However, this may sound amazing to you. A little alone time can be a good thing.

TIP

If you have flexibility, I encourage you to plan your honeymoon to start on the Tuesday after your wedding. This will give you a few days to unpack from the wedding and repack for the honeymoon. It will also give you time to take your marriage license to the clerk's office to get your official marriage license.

Giving yourself a few days to tie up loose ends and make sure everything is in place before you leave will allow you the freedom to truly rest and relax on your honeymoon. Your mind won't be racing with the things that didn't get done. You can spend those few days saying goodbye to your family, reading your cards from your guests, and preparing for the rest and relaxation that is soon to come!

TIP

The most traditional time to travel on your honeymoon is the morning after your wedding. If you plan your honeymoon for the morning after your wedding, make sure to arrange with a family member or friend to pick up your dress or tuxedo. Clients who leave the next morning often get to their honeymoon suite and then they realize they don't know what to do with their attire. Make those plans ahead of time to ensure the safety and protection of those special items.

Selecting the Perfect Location

It's time to pick your perfect place for your honeymoon. We already know that you're good at making choices. You picked your perfect spouse. You picked your perfect venue. You picked your perfect team. You picked your perfect bridal party. Now, one more thing to pick — the perfect location for your getaway.

TIP

When considering a location for your honeymoon, work with your partner to create a short list. Think about anywhere in the world where you have wanted to travel. Think about places that may be special to you both. Are there favorite memories? Are there places on your bucket list? Write down five to ten places where you would like to spend your honeymoon.

After you have determined the best time to travel, take that short list and start researching availability. You'll want to make a list of the locations, flight costs, and accommodations costs. You may be surprised by certain locations offering amazing deals. You may also be surprised at how expensive it is to go to one of your short-list locations.

In doing this initial research, you have a better idea of how much your honeymoon will cost and how much you want to spend. Until you research the costs to travel to your destination, it may only be a dream. That dream can quickly turn into reality after researching the costs associated with the honeymoon.

I created table 18-1 to help you organize your initial search. I included places to list your top ten destinations, time of year, flight or driving cost, hotel costs, food and beverage cost, and the total cost.

TABLE 18-1   **Top 10 Honeymoon Destination Costs**

Destination	Time of Year	Travel Costs	Hotel Costs	Food & Beverage Costs	Total

TIP

When researching the perfect location for your honeymoon, ask your resources. There's a good chance those around you have traveled somewhere they love and will tell you all about their experience. Additionally, read the reviews online. Travel reviews are a great resource for narrowing down your perfect destination search.

WARNING

I didn't do a lot of research before I booked our honeymoon. It was one of the only all-inclusive resorts in the United States and that was where the research stopped. Make sure to take the time to research the destination so that you aren't checking in and then checking out like we did!

THE NOT-SO-PERFECT LOCATION

I wanted to share with you a personal story, not a client's story. My husband and I were supposed to be married before COVID-19 but had to postpone our wedding. Not only did I postpone 90% of our clients' weddings but also my own.

Our original plan was to honeymoon in Jamacia, where we met. I was working a wedding and he was the best man. I can assure you that wasn't on the detailed schedule of events for the night. When the time came to plan our wedding again, we didn't know if we were going to logistically and financially be able to go on our original dream honeymoon.

My industry had completely shut down, which meant I wasn't making money and there were several travel bans still in place. We also have three children so we couldn't risk not being able to get back to the United States from our honeymoon. So I started to research locations in the U.S. where we could drive. Since we met at an all-inclusive resort, we wanted to research a similar experience.

Well, we got an experience for sure. I found an all-inclusive resort in Florida. I showed my husband the website and honestly, I need to hire their marketing team because it looked amazing. If we couldn't go back to Jamaica, this was going to be the best option. So we booked it and were looking forward to a little time away together.

Little did I know that three weeks before our honeymoon, I would have an emergency hysterectomy. This wasn't part of the plan in more ways than you know. Due to the severity of the surgery, I wasn't sure I would even be able to walk down the aisle, let alone go on a vacation with my new husband. I was channeling my inner "perspective" and kept planning for our big day.

The wedding was a success and I made it down the aisle. After getting the kids settled a few days after the wedding, we headed off to our all-inclusive resort in Florida. Upon arrival, we pulled up and we could see immediately that it didn't look like the photos online. It was run down and there weren't friendly faces greeting us when we pulled up. I walked into the lobby hopeful that things would start to look up. The woman at the counter seemed annoyed that we were there. I was trying to check in while my husband was starting to pace in the lobby.

Our room wasn't ready yet, so we left our bags and went to grab a drink at the bar. We got to the bar and again, the staff wasn't pleasant. I could tell we were bothering them. We asked for two mimosas. They served them to us in Dixie cups. We took our Dixie cups and went for a walk around the property waiting for the text that our room was ready. Let's just say the walk to view our paradise honeymoon destination wasn't exactly paradise.

We got the text our room was ready and grabbed our bags and hauled them all the way to our room on the other side of the resort. I asked for a map, which was obviously not the right thing to do because the woman at the front desk was annoyed by that too. The room was . . . well, it wasn't the nice luxurious room on the website. We did have a walk-out room, but we walked right out of the patio of our room to the dumpster. Absolutely no view of anything.

We arrived between lunch and dinnertime and so there was one place we could go to grab a snack before the dinner buffet opened. I ordered a chicken Caesar wrap. I also ordered a side of hummus, which was a tiny cup and two celery sticks. When I ordered my food, the waitress looked at me and said, "Enough, you have had enough, no more." That was the straw that broke the camel's back. We went back to our room and ate our snack, which was not even good, and contemplated having to stay at this place for a week.

I immediately started googling hotels around us. We repacked our semi-unpacked bags and left the resort. The staff at the front desk just said, "Okay, bye." They didn't ask why we were leaving so soon after checking in. We didn't have the ideal honeymoon that we envisioned, but we did spend the rest of the week exploring towns in Florida that we had never been to.

When I returned home, I reached out to the customer service department of the resort and explained our experience. I gave him all the details, a lot more than I have given you. After going back and forth for several months, he offered me a voucher to come back to the resort. There is no way we will ever go back there.

Working with a Travel Agent

I compare working with a travel agent like working with a wedding planner. Can you plan your own honeymoon? Yes. Can you plan your own wedding? Yes. However, booking these services is valuable when it comes to your overall experience, stress, resources, and planning. They are the people with the insider information and that should always benefit you in the end.

TIP

There are several benefits to booking a travel agent for your honeymoon. Following are my top reasons why booking a travel agent can help you create your dream honeymoon.

» **Less stress:** Working with a travel agent can help eliminate the stress on you for planning your honeymoon. Their job is to research and plan the honeymoon based on your top destinations. They have all the contacts you need for a successful honeymoon. Booking a travel agent will give you the peace of mind to be able to fully rest and relax on your honeymoon.

» **Expert advice:** If the thought of booking the perfect honeymoon is overwhelming, a travel agent can give you expert advice on popular destinations. They can also advise you on what to do when you get there. It's one task to figure out the destination, but then what will you do when you get there? They know the popular excursions that will enhance your honeymoon experience.

» **Sweet deals:** A travel agent has exclusive deals that you may not be able to access on your own. Their job is to build relationships to save you money. They have insider information and ways to save you money in the end. They also know the time in which you need to book your honeymoon to get the best deal.

Going Abroad

Traveling abroad at any point in life is a big-deal moment. Most people may never be able to do that in their lifetime. Getting the opportunity to travel abroad for your honeymoon may be a trip of a lifetime. That is why it's important to consider if this is a good option for you.

If you do travel abroad, I highly recommend using a travel agent. A travel agent will know how to book your trip in a safe area and help with any language barriers. Their job is to do all the research for you and help plan a trip overseas. They can advise you on currency changes, languages spoken in that country, and help navigate jet lag.

I will never forget when I traveled to Rome. My internal clock was so off that I slept through bus tours of the city, and it took me a few days to feel normal. This happens naturally when you travel abroad, so a travel agent can help you plan your time accordingly. You'll need a few days to recover from jet lag, and then on the way home you'll also need some time to acclimate back to your regular routine.

If you resource a travel agent or not, I highly recommend that you purchase travel insurance. International shutdowns happen frequently. We saw those numerous times during COVID-19. Make sure that you protect yourself from circumstances that are out of your control. The last thing you want to happen is to lose the money you spent on your honeymoon.

Depending on where you're traveling, make sure you know the culture. What languages are spoken? What is the currency? What side of the road do they drive on? What are the traditions of that country? In some countries, they take a siesta in the middle of the day for a few hours. Everything shuts down during a certain time. Make sure you know as much about the culture as you can before you travel.

If you're traveling to a country that doesn't speak your language, this is the time to purchase a *Dummies* book on that language. Consider it a bonding experience with your fiancé. Learn some of the language so that you can navigate your way through a foreign country as if you lived there.

Another important piece to traveling abroad is to make sure that you have an updated passport. The name on your passport must be the name on your travel reservation. If you plan to change your name but leave immediately following your wedding, you'll travel with your maiden name to your destination. An updated passport is a must when traveling outside of the country.

Make sure that you inform all your financial institutions that you'll be traveling abroad. The last thing you want is to be stuck in a foreign country without access to any of your money. International transactions are a red flag for all financial institutes, and they will put a hold on your account. Inform them before you go internationally the time that you'll be there. That way, you can keep using your bank and credit cards without any hiccups.

Wherever your honeymoon may take you, tell the staff around you that you're on your honeymoon. I can assure you, you'll be taken care of and made to feel special. Everyone loves seeing a couple who is just beginning their life together. They will pamper you and you only get one honeymoon, so take advantage of the time you have together.

Packing for the Trip

If you're anything like me, you put off packing for a trip until the very last minute. To me, it's the worst part about traveling. I have a hard enough time picking out an outfit in the morning, let alone multiple outfits, along with accounting for weather changes and the unpredictable moments. Remember, I'm a planner and packing makes me feel like if I don't remember to pack something, the trip will be a disaster.

However, if you're someone who loves packing for a trip, you can't wait to make your lists, plan your daytime and evening outfits, and include all your favorite accessories, I applaud your enthusiasm! In this section, I share a list of items to consider when packing for your honeymoon. It really is all about where you're going, the time of year, and the weather, but there are some important must-haves you don't want to forget before you close your suitcase:

>> Appropriate clothing for the weather

>> Casual, semiformal, and formal attire

>> Casual and dressy shoes

>> Bathing suits (weather permitting) and coverups

>> Rain jacket and small umbrella (unpredictable weather)

>> Underwear and PJs

>> Sunglasses and/or eyeglasses

>> Light jacket for cold evenings

>> Hat

>> Prescriptions, anti-nausea medicine, and sleep aids

>> Sunscreen, insect repellant, and lip balm

>> First aid kit and pain relievers

>> Backpack to carry your personal items

>> Toiletries

>> Passport and driver's license

>> Bank cards and credit cards

>> Cash

>> Copies of travel documents such as immunization records, travel reservations, travel insurance, and emergency contact information

>> Cell phone, charger, and camera

>> Thank-you notes (Traveling downtime is the perfect time to knock out your thank-you notes.)

Make those packing lists and check them off twice. Additionally, check with your airline on their bag policy. If you check a bag, know the maximum weight limit. And don't pack your bag to the maximum limit; you may want to bring home some things your purchased while on your honeymoon.

TIP

It's best to pack your essential items in your carryon, especially if you're traveling abroad. The last thing you want is to have your bags get lost and you don't have your toothbrush or medication. Keep those essential items with you just in case. Prepare for the worst, and hope for the best.

Life After Wedding Planning

Guess what — there is life after wedding planning. I know right now you may not believe that statement, but this is what it's all about. We have been planning for your first day but the best part of getting married are the days that follow your wedding day. That is when real life begins.

Experiencing the bridal blues

There is something that is very real that happens after you plan your wedding day, have your wedding day, and return from your honeymoon: the bridal blues. It happens to the best of us, and I couldn't write this book without letting you know all about it.

Just think about this — you got engaged. That was an amazing moment in your life. Everyone around was so excited for you. You had all the parties and showers, and it was so special. Everyone was happy and you were over the moon with excitement and anticipating your wedding day.

You planned your wedding day, likely for a long time. Chances are for the past however long you have been planning your wedding, all you have done every day is think about this one day. You have spent hours focusing on every single detail. It's a big-deal moment.

Then you have your wedding day. You invited all your favorite people. You danced the night away and never wanted it to end. You laughed, you cried, and you hugged your people who got to experience it all right with you. And now, you're married!

You and your spouse go on a honeymoon. It's the best trip you've ever been on. You had devoted alone time with the person you love the most. You were pampered and treated like a celebrity. You ate the best food and drank the fanciest wine. You indulged and you have no regrets.

Then, you come home. Cricket, cricket, cricket, silence. You go to pick up your planning book (this one of course) and you quickly realize Sarah's already helped you plan your wedding day. (I already miss you too!) You pick up your phone to reach out to a bridesmaid to make sure she got her dress, already done. You woke up and no one did your hair or makeup. You ate fast food for dinner instead of a five-star meal. Your house is messy rather than someone cleaning your sheets and making your bed every day.

All of a sudden, you feel very sad.

You are normal. You just went through an amazing, big-deal moment in your life. It's okay to feel a little sad. However, what I want to encourage you to do is to think about what's next. Having something to plan for or a goal keeps normal life exciting, and when you don't have anything, it can make you sad.

REMEMBER

You have just planned a big life moment and it was a big deal. Now, think about what's next for you. Stay focused on the future. You can miss the big day for a little bit and then move onto bigger and better things — real life! Also be sure to cherish a little quiet time after all the hustle and bustle of wedding planning. Find beauty in the ordinary moments; those will be the ones you remember forever.

Thinking about what's next

It's officially time to let you go. It's time to live your amazing life with your spouse. There will be moments filled with joy and there will be moments of great pain. That's what makes it beautiful.

This is the part of wedding planning I love the most. The moment I get to watch my clients build their lives. The moment I watch their failures and successes. The moment I watch them start their family. This is why I do what I do. It's now your time to build the life you want together.

Continue to date each other. Continue to invest in your relationship. Continue to seek each other's hearts. You won't always get it right, but you committed to love each other in good times and in bad, in sickness and in health, for as long as you both shall live.

I didn't think divorce was going to be a part of my love story. When I think about it, no one did. To everyone else, we were a power couple. We were unbreakable. Until we broke. Going through a divorce was one of the worst moments in my life. The experience of divorce is not easily shaken off. It's the last thing I want for you, for anyone, in fact.

REMEMBER

It's vital that you make your marriage a priority. First, take care of yourself, so you can take care of those you love. Without self-love, it's impossible to give yourself to others. Next, take care of your relationship. You officially are in the circle. Remember the rings you exchanged; that is the circle. The circle is only for the two of you. Keep that sacred and be intentional so that it can't break.

I am not a family counselor by any means, and I don't have all the answers. What I am is a real person who plans weddings for a living and went through a divorce. It wasn't the story I wanted to write but I am now writing a new story, one that I am very proud of.

What's next? Whatever you make it. Cheers to making it beautifully imperfect.

7

The Part of Tens

IN THIS PART . . .

Ten things to do to ensure a bad wedding day

Picking the best team and squad for your day and avoiding drama

Continuing to date your fiancé and maintaining perspective

Ten things that prove you're normal and not crazy

Chapter **19**

Ten Ways to Ensure a Bad Day

Through the years, I have learned a few things about creating and producing a successful event. I have also learned what not to do when it comes to planning a wedding. In this chapter, I will share with you my top ten ways to ensure a bad day. Do these and it will not be the perfect day that you dreamed it would be. This is one of my favorite parts about the *Dummies* books. Learn from past clients so that you can have the best day ever.

Don't Set a Budget

As I have said before, even the wealthiest clients have budgets. They are often some of my most frugal clients. That's probably why they have money, right? It's important to set a budget with your fiancé. This is a team effort. Just as in married life, you will need to determine a budget that fits for your family.

WARNING

I can assure you that if you don't set a budget, you will overspend, and before you know it you will be stressed and overwhelmed. Do not commit to anything that you can't afford.

When I go into the grocery store without a plan, I spend way more than I have budgeted. It's like I grab whatever I see when I go through the aisles. When I get home, I can't figure out what I'm going to make for dinner. I don't have a plan or budget in mind, and I overspend and end up with little or nothing that I can piece together and turn into a meal. That is very easy to do with wedding planning. If you don't go in with a budget, you will continue to add on things that you don't need. There will be life after wedding planning, and I don't want you to go into marriage stressed about your finances.

Don't Hire a Good Team

I always say that your wedding is only as good as the vendors you put in place on your team. You need to be able to trust that the vendors you hire are doing their job that you're paying them to do. You also need to be able to find the value in their services. Additionally, you need to be able to trust that they have your back if things go south on the wedding day. I love my team. So many unpredictable things can happen on a wedding day, but I know that if any of those happen, my team will do what it takes to make sure the client is happy at the end of the day.

REMEMBER

If you don't trust your vendors, you will micromanage every move they make. If you don't value them, you will second-guess everything they present. If you don't think they'll keep the ship afloat, you'll be anxious and nervous all day. There will come a time when you need to let go and let them do their job. Having a good team in place will give you the ability to do so, allowing you the opportunity to be present on your wedding day.

Skip the Timeline

A timeline of events is vital to eliminating the stress of a wedding day. I always tell my clients it is our "bible" of the day. If it isn't in there, it isn't truth. I understand that things can come up and delay the schedule, but with a plan and timeline in place, you'll be able to make up that time rather than losing track of the entire day.

REMEMBER

A timeline is necessary for all vendors so that they know how long they have to set up and tear down, when they need to be ready to go, and what activities you're planning so that they don't miss anything. Imagine that your photographer has left the reception for a few moments, and you're having your first dance. If they don't know that there is a first dance, there is a chance they may miss it. Or maybe you're planning a special moment at the end of your reception, but the photographer has only been hired for six hours. Having a timeline in place will eliminate the stress that can occur if your vendors are unaware of the plan.

Don't Communicate the Plan

Along with the timeline comes communication. Your timeline and event details — including a list of vendors, bridal party names, schedule of events, floor plans, decor, and guest list — should be consolidated into one document that you will distribute to all your vendors. Make sure they received this document and ask them if they have any questions about the logistics of the day. Additionally, distribute this to your bridal party. They don't need to know all the details, but make sure to communicate with them when they need to be where and what they need to do when they get there. They will have a lot of questions and answering all those questions leading up to your wedding day can be extremely stressful.

TIP

Let's call this an exercise in communication for your marriage. Communication is a vital part of a successful marriage. Communicating the plan to your vendors and bridal party is also a vital part of a successful wedding.

Invite Everyone You Know

When working through your guest list, every person you have ever known does not need to be at your wedding. For every guest you invite, there is a chance they will come, and if they do, you will have to pay for them to be there. If they are someone you could walk up to, hand them cash, and ask them to come to your wedding, invite them. Your friend group will change as you create a life together. The last thing you want is to have a bunch of people at your wedding who don't need to be there and you likely will never speak to them again.

TIP

Pick those people who are the most important to you in your life. You can hang out with everyone else after the wedding is over. A night out for dinner is much more cost-effective than paying for them to be at your wedding.

Don't Pick a Supportive Squad

Your bridal party should consist of people who love and support you as individuals but also as a couple. I can't tell you the number of times clients have walked into my office and complained about someone in their bridal party. Typically, it's because they're making the wedding all about them. Well, it isn't about them, it is about you and your fiancé. Creating a supportive squad will help eliminate stress on your wedding day.

Additionally, make sure they want to be in your wedding. Being a part of a bridal party requires financial responsibilities that some may not be able to manage. Your bridal party will have travel expenses, attire expenses, and parties to attend and potentially contribute to financially. Make sure that this isn't causing a strain on them. They likely won't tell you, but it is an important part when you are selecting your squad.

Get Caught Up in the Drama

Planning a wedding is an emotional event that often brings out some drama. Remember to stay focused on you and your fiancé. There are just certain people in life who thrive on all the drama. Avoid feeding that by not oversharing the details of your day. Trust me, they will have an opinion and it may not be one that you want to hear. It's always fun to know a secret, right? Consider the details of your day as something that is a secret shared between you and your fiancé. You will inform those who need to know certain details when they need to know them. Until then, stay focused on the bigger picture.

Ignore What You Want

I'm not sure why, but often in planning their wedding, a couple's dreams are put on the back burner. If you want pink and purple flowers, then get pink and purple flowers. If you want to serve pizza at your wedding, serve pizza and don't forget to invite me. The opinions of others should remain just that: their opinion. They should never become your dreams.

This is your day and everything you do reflects who you are as a couple. Remember to consider what you want over the opinions of those around you.

Stop Dating Your Fiancé

I want you to think back to before you were engaged. In fact, I want you to think back to your first date. Do you remember the butterflies? For some reason, we're told that should stop. But what if it didn't have to? Yes, life happens, and yes, life is hard, but you're choosing to navigate life with your best friend. I am a person who believes that every day you should wake up, choose to love each other, and continue to pursue the other.

During the planning process, continue to date each other. After all, when all the planning is over, the real adventure and journey begins. Make sure you aren't shaking hands with each other at the wedding because you don't know each other. There is life after wedding planning, and it is important to invest in each other through this process of planning your first day together as a married couple. There will be so many more to come.

Lose All Perspective

I always tell my children that there is a reason why the rearview mirror is so small. If you look out the front window, the view is so much bigger. It's easy to get so caught up in the little things that you forget the big picture: your marriage. That's what we're really planning. Remember through this process to stay focused on the front window. What happens if it rains on your wedding day? You might get wet. There will be rain in life and what will you do then? Will you run for cover, or will you jump in the puddles of life?

REMEMBER

You're planning a wedding and that is a wonderful life moment. But this isn't the only moment you'll have. There will be many more, and if you're intentional about focusing on the bigger picture, you'll be able to see the rainbow, even in the storm.

Chapter **20**

Ten Reasons You're Normal

L et's face it, you're planning a big event, quite possibly the biggest event of your life thus far. I know, no pressure, right? Planning a wedding can bring up so many emotions. But the good news is, you're normal! Although you may feel like you're on the edge of a major breakdown, you will be fine. You will make it and it will be perfect. In this chapter, I'll do my best to prove that you're totally normal. Isn't that good news?

Wedding Dress Frustration

If you're frustrated that every dress you try on ends up sending you into a downward spiral, you're normal. If you're worried about picking the perfect dress that will make your fiancé cry like a baby, you're normal. If you're concerned about tripping as you walk down the aisle and becoming a viral sensation, you're normal. There is so much pressure on picking the perfect dress. All the guests will be watching and wanting to see your dress. You'll be looking for your fiancé's reaction and hoping it's a good one. I know, it's a lot of pressure.

REMEMBER

I want you to know that you will find that perfect dress. Make sure it's one that you're comfortable in for an extended period of time. Additionally, make sure you feel beautiful in it, no matter who else in your life has an opposite opinion. It's only about you, and I can assure you that when you find the right one, you'll know.

Fiancé Frustration

If you and your fiancé go on a date and only talk about the wedding and always end up in a big fight, you're normal. If you're concerned no matter how many times you have discussed not smashing cake in your face, that your fiancé will all of a sudden become a member of the Three Stooges, you're normal. If you're blowing every argument out of the water and crying if you see puppy dogs at the dog park, you're normal. If you're surprised by some of the things that have come up in premarital counseling that you knew nothing about, you're normal.

TIP

Premarital counseling is kind of like spring cleaning. It's a time to clear out all the cobwebs. While I believe it's a vital part of your marriage, sometimes clearing the cobwebs makes you sneeze, and that's okay. Things will come up, and that is good. It's better to discuss those things prior to marriage in a safe environment, where you can do some spring cleaning before getting married. Work together to build the marriage that you want that will last a lifetime.

Having Nightmares

If you're having nightmares that involve a different fiancé at the altar, a vendor who messes everything up, kids who are running crazy and putting their fingers in your cake, the caterer bringing chicken nuggets instead of filet mignon, or your dress never arriving, you're normal. I've lost count of how many times a client has said to me, "The nightmares have begun." I want to reply, "Trust me, I know. I have nightmares too, and for all my clients, not just yours."

Nightmares are normal and although I don't have a solution to them, they are part of the process because you're planning a big event. I sometimes tell clients that you must go through the nightmares to get to the perfect dream. Your perfect dream day will come.

Disappointed with the Bridal Party

If you're disappointed with the best man's choices, you're normal. If you're wanting a better wedding than your maid of honor who decided to plan her wedding at the exact same time, you're normal. If you're frustrated that your bridal party has now become people you don't even like to be around anymore, you're normal. If you're under some sort of fantasy that the flower girl, who is five, is going to act perfect on your wedding day, you're normal. If you're picking your bridesmaids based on who won't look better than you on your wedding day, you're normal. If you have threatened to tackle the best man or maid of honor if they speak the truth and nothing but the truth at your wedding, you're normal.

As I have said in the past, emotional moments in life don't often bring out the best in people. That's why it's so important to pick a good squad who love you and support you. Pick friends who have had your back no matter what. If the drama begins, have an open and honest conversation with them about it, and then move on to the bigger picture. You'll soon be surrounded by so many people who love you and are excited to be a part of your big day.

Totally Obsessed with Checking the Weather

If you're worried about the weather for your outdoor wedding and you're checking the farmer's almanac, asking psychics, and praying a lot that it won't rain on your wedding day, you're normal. Mother Nature is not always our friend. Here's the facts. Do you ever turn on the local news in the morning and watch the weather? Even the trained meteorologists can't figure out what the weather will be. How many times in your life has it rained when the forecast wasn't calling for rain? I live in a valley and so the weather is extremely unpredictable. You can't stress about the weather. It will do no good.

TIP

What you can do is plan for the worst-case scenario and be prepared. If it rains on your wedding day, there is absolutely nothing you can do. Repeat that with me: "If it rains on my wedding day, there is absolutely nothing I can do about that." It's just the facts. However, we can prepare so that even if it does, it will still be perfect.

Practicing Your Facial Expressions

If you're worried about the "ugly cry" and sit up at night staring in the mirror while sniffing an onion just to see what your normal facial reactions are, you're normal.

I will tell you about my biggest regret on my wedding day. My dad tried to say something to me before we walked down the aisle and I made him stop because I didn't want to have the ugly cry. Still to this day when I ask him what he was going to say to me he says, "Oh, nothing." I wish I hadn't been so concerned with how my face looked and just took in the moment.

You may or may not be a crier on your wedding day. Whichever way your emotions lead you, follow them and embrace the fact that no one looks good when they cry.

If You're Totally Freaking Out

Enough said — you're normal. If you're sneaking off in the middle of the night to have a party of one and eating anything and everything in sight, you're normal. It's okay not to be okay. You're planning a big emotional event and it's okay to have a freak-out moment.

REMEMBER

Make sure to surround yourself with people who can help you through those moments. Additionally, make them last only a moment and then move on. It's all going to be okay, and at the end of the day, you will be married!

If You're Drinking Too Much

If you spend the months leading up to your wedding day testing how your body will react to alcohol so that you can see how much you can handle on your wedding day, you're normal.

TIP

Instead of drinking more and more leading up to your wedding day, focus on your mental health and taking care of your body. Go on a walk, practice yoga, read a book. We don't want you throwing your stress into a bottle. Trust me, it will be there when you wake up. Instead, focus on you and give yourself some self-love.

If You're Frustrated with Your Guests

If you're inviting people to your wedding out of family obligation and it's frustrating because you don't want them there, you're normal. If you're thinking about your guests way too much and wondering what they will think about your napkin color choice, you're normal. If you spend sleepless nights wondering if your guests will want hot chicken bites or stuffed mushroom caps, you're normal. If you're prepared to give anyone who wears white on your wedding day the stink eye, you're normal. If you're annoyed that no one is sending in their RSVPs and you have to track them down for an answer, you're normal. If you're upset that guests are posting photos on social media before you have a chance to, you're normal. Boy oh boy, do I have some stories about wedding guests.

Here's the thing: you can't control them; you can only love them and all the things that frustrate you about them. Take a deep breath and know that it doesn't matter what anyone thinks about your wedding day. It's your wedding day, not theirs.

If You Have Practiced the Kiss

If you have given your fiancé specific instructions on how to kiss you and you have practiced, you're normal.

TIP

I am actually a big fan of practicing the big kiss. It needs to be long enough to be captured by the photographer but not too long to gross out your guests. Take time to practice the kiss with your fiancé so you aren't caught off guard for the big moment. It is a special part of your wedding, so practice it and know that you are normal!

Index

About the Author

Sarah Lizabeth Barker is passionate about serving others. Her mission with each client is to listen and give them their wedding dreams that reflect who they are as a couple. While she is the one who plans and moves all the pieces, her clients are the stars. Sarah has spent over two decades building relationships with clients and vendors. It is her purpose: to do good in the wedding and event industry that impacts others' lives.

Sarah is the owner of Sarah Lizabeth Events, a full-service wedding and event planner, florist, and decorator based out of Nashville, Tennessee (www.sarahlizabeth.com). She and her husband also own and operate a wedding and event venue called Pinewood Retreat (www.pinewoodretreat.com). Sarah is the CEO and founder of Give A Wedding, a national mission-based organization that gives to couples in need and gives business to their partners in the wedding industry across the United States (www.giveawedding.com).

Sarah's work has been featured in the HuffPost, BuzzFeed, PopSugar, MSN Lifestyle, Every Last Detail, Wedding Chicks, Desiree Hartsock Bridal, *Southern Weddings,* Nashville Bride Guide, Expertise, Green Wedding Shoes, and Borrowed and Blue. She has also won several industry awards, including best wedding planner and florist in Nashville, and was named an Industry Leader for *Smart Meetings* magazine. Sarah also has a series of stories from her past clients' weddings on YouTube called *Stories with Sarah Lizabeth.* Through those stories she shares the good and bad from the over 600 weddings she has had the honor to produce through the years. You will laugh and you will cry, but most of all you will feel normal.

Sarah's favorite moment on a wedding day is one that very few get to see. When a bride is standing behind the closed doors, waiting to take her first step down the aisle, she can't help but think of all the steps in her life that led to this one. In that moment, there is pure joy.

Dedication

God, thank you for loving me unconditionally and giving me this opportunity to serve others. My prayer is that my work will honor you and your light will shine though me.

Clayton, I've never had a friend like you. Thank you for choosing to love me even on my worst day. You are the calm in my storm. Thank you for being my best friend and partner in life. I wouldn't want to be on this journey with anyone else.

Georgia, Bailey, and Parker, thank you for giving me purpose in this life. I am grateful for the love you show me every day. It is an honor to be your mom. I will always fight for you. Always remember that you have the power to write your own story. I can't wait to watch what you will write throughout your life.

To my family, thank you for always cheering me on and supporting me in whatever adventure is next. I love you all dearly.

To Grandpa Wiley (yes, my maiden name is Wiley, but no relation to my amazing publisher!), thank you for being a part of this book through your artwork. You always supported me to write my own story. I wish you were here to see it being written.

To Momma Jo, I love you beyond this life. Thank you for giving me a voice in this world. I am the woman I am today, because of you.

To my past clients, thank you for writing this story. I truly appreciate the opportunity you gave me to serve you. It was my honor.

Author's Acknowledgments

This is the first edition of *Planning a Wedding For Dummies.* This book wouldn't be possible without those who have entrusted me to give them the best day ever through the years. Each one is special. Each one has a story, and now their stories can be told. I wouldn't be where I am today without each client and family who believed in me. Their perfect day has made me better.

To the Wiley team: Since day one, you believed in me. Thank you for your hard work on this project and for allowing me the freedom to create a wedding resource that is authentic. It has been an honor to work with each of you through our process of creating a book that will help others in the wedding industry. I believe together we have made a difference.

To my amazing artist and illustrator, April Jae: Thank you for gracing these pages with your artwork.

To the photographers who have shared their artwork and told the story of some of my past clients: Thank you for your hard work and dedication to serving others. I appreciate you sharing your gifts for everyone to enjoy.

To my team: I couldn't do what I do without you. Thank you for providing top-notch service to our clients. I am grateful for how you serve our clients selflessly. It is a tough job doing what we do and it is an honor to serve next to you.

To my technical editor, AnnaMarie Rubio with AR Weddings N Events: I am so grateful that our paths crossed through Give A Wedding and that we were able to work on this project together. Thank you for making sure I was speaking truth in this book.

To the readers of this book: Thank you. This is an amazing journey that you are on and it should be celebrated. My hope when you read this book is that you will have the tools and knowledge to plan the perfect day of your dreams. Thank you for spending this time with me and entrusting me to guide you through your process. Remember, your wedding day is only yours to write, and I am certain that your story will have a happy ending.

Publisher's Acknowledgments

Senior Acquisitions Editor: Jennifer Yee

Project Manager and Development Editor:
  Christina N. Guthrie

Managing Editor: Kristie Pyles

Copy Editor: Amy Handy

Technical Editor: AnnaMarie Rubio

Production Editor: Tamilmani Varadharaj

Cover Photos: © Prostock-studio/Shutterstock

Dummies is the global leader in the reference category and one of the most trusted and highly regarded brands in the world. No longer just focused on books, customers now have access to the dummies content they need in the format they want. Together we'll craft a solution that engages your customers, stands out from the competition, and helps you meet your goals.

Advertising & Sponsorships

Connect with an engaged audience on a powerful multimedia site, and position your message alongside expert how-to content. Dummies.com is a one-stop shop for free, online information and know-how curated by a team of experts.

- Targeted ads
- Video
- Email Marketing
- Microsites
- Sweepstakes sponsorship

20 MILLION PAGE VIEWS
EVERY SINGLE MONTH

15 MILLION **UNIQUE**
VISITORS PER MONTH

43%
OF ALL VISITORS
ACCESS THE SITE
VIA THEIR MOBILE DEVICES

700,000 NEWSLETTER SUBSCRIPTIONS
TO THE INBOXES OF
300,000 UNIQUE INDIVIDUALS EVERY WEEK

# of dummies

Custom Publishing

Reach a global audience in any language by creating a solution that will differentiate you from competitors, amplify your message, and encourage customers to make a buying decision.

- Apps
- Books
- eBooks
- Video
- Audio
- Webinars

Brand Licensing & Content

Leverage the strength of the world's most popular reference brand to reach new audiences and channels of distribution.

For more information, visit dummies.com/biz

PERSONAL ENRICHMENT

9781119187790
USA $26.00
CAN $31.99
UK £19.99

9781119179030
USA $21.99
CAN $25.99
UK £16.99

9781119293354
USA $24.99
CAN $29.99
UK £17.99

9781119293347
USA $22.99
CAN $27.99
UK £16.99

9781119310068
USA $22.99
CAN $27.99
UK £16.99

9781119235606
USA $24.99
CAN $29.99
UK £17.99

9781119251163
USA $24.99
CAN $29.99
UK £17.99

9781119235491
USA $26.99
CAN $31.99
UK £19.99

9781119279952
USA $24.99
CAN $29.99
UK £17.99

9781119283133
USA $24.99
CAN $29.99
UK £17.99

9781119287117
USA $24.99
CAN $29.99
UK £16.99

9781119130246
USA $22.99
CAN $27.99
UK £16.99

PROFESSIONAL DEVELOPMENT

9781119311041
USA $24.99
CAN $29.99
UK £17.99

9781119255796
USA $39.99
CAN $47.99
UK £27.99

9781119293439
USA $26.99
CAN $31.99
UK £19.99

9781119281467
USA $26.99
CAN $31.99
UK £19.99

9781119280651
USA $29.99
CAN $35.99
UK £21.99

9781119251132
USA $24.99
CAN $29.99
UK £17.99

9781119310563
USA $34.00
CAN $41.99
UK £24.99

9781119181705
USA $29.99
CAN $35.99
UK £21.99

9781119263593
USA $26.99
CAN $31.99
UK £19.99

9781119257769
USA $29.99
CAN $35.99
UK £21.99

9781119293477
USA $26.99
CAN $31.99
UK £19.99

9781119265313
USA $24.99
CAN $29.99
UK £17.99

9781119239314
USA $29.99
CAN $35.99
UK £21.99

9781119293323
USA $29.99
CAN $35.99
UK £21.99

dummies.com

dummies®
A Wiley Brand